CW01501708

WHO
ME!

WHO ME!

HOW *DOCTOR WHO* CHANGED MY LIFE

DAVID J HOWE

Bedford Square
Publishers

First published in the UK in 2025 by Bedford Square Publishers Ltd,
London, UK

bedfordsquarepublishers.co.uk
@bedfordsquarepublishers

© David J Howe, 2025

A Maxim Jakubowski book

ISBN
978-1-83501-330-4 (Hardback)
978-1-83501-331-1 (Trade paperback)
978-1-83501-332-8 (eBook)

2 4 6 8 10 9 7 5 3 1

Typeset in Joanna MT Std by Palimpsest Book Production Ltd, Falkirk, Stirlingshire
Printed in Great Britain by CPI Group (UK) Ltd, Croydon CR0 4YY

The manufacturer's authorised representative in the EU for product safety
is Easy Access System Europe, Mustamäe tee 50, 10621 Tallinn, Estonia
gpsr.requests@easproject.com

Dedicated to my long-suffering family. To my amazing mum
Sheila and much missed dad Ted and nana Gladys, to brothers
Alan and Robert, and sister Caroline. I love you all! To my
children James and Andrew, and their mum Rosemary...
and of course to James's wife Rachel, and grandkids Ben and
Phoebe. Also to Sam's daughter (and hence my daughter) Linzi.
Something to show your grandchildren's grandchildren!
And to Sam... always.

Contents

Author's Note

While this is a work of fact, because this is about me, and my memory can be notoriously bad sometimes, I have reserved the right in the book to talk about things as I remember them. Where possible I have 'fact checked' myself, but of course other people might have differing memories, or an alternate view of some of the things. On occasion I have also extrapolated from what I remember and whatever information I can glean to better tell the stories. So please don't get upset if my memory differs from yours, or that Google or Wikipedia or some other strange website you found has a different answer. I'm sorry. Just enjoy the book.

My father, Ted, with Alan and David in June 1967.

1

The Pre-Title Sequence

On that evening in August 1961, Ted went off to work as usual. He was a printer, working for the *Daily Express*. Every night he drove the ten miles or so from South London to Fleet Street in London to work on the machines producing the next day's newspaper.[1]

Sheila was, as usual, at home, but because the baby was now a week overdue, her mother, Gladys, was staying with her. Saddled with a large, overdue baby bump was no fun. But Sheila had a plan… the best way to make a baby come was a hot bath, along with a drink of hot milk and castor oil. So that's what she did… and like magic it worked!

It was three in the morning. The door to Gladys' room cracked open and Sheila popped her head in. 'Mum,' she called quietly, 'I think it's time.'

'Right,' said Gladys. 'I'll go and get the midwife!'

But that wasn't so easy in 1961. There was no house-phone, and so, leaving Sheila in the house alone, Gladys ventured out into the

1   And no, I wasn't in the news the next day! I'm sorry but I'm going to pepper this book with footnotes containing asides and interesting information which will hopefully enhance the reading. Don't blame me, blame Terry Pratchett and Douglas Adams!

night to the nearest telephone box, only to find that it was not working, and so she went to another... which was also not working.

Eventually, she found one which was operational and called the midwife to come round, and then returned to Sheila. And so, a few hours later, at 5.30 am on 24 August 1961, little David John Howe entered the world.

Ted returned from work at exactly the same time as I was born, and the first thing he heard as he entered the house was the debut cry of his new son. Ted was a proud dad. 'Everyone says he looks like me,' he said to a neighbour the next day, 'but I think he looks like a 90-year-old monkey!'

It was an inauspicious start for David, Sheila and Ted's first son. Twenty-four-year-old Sheila had not been prescribed the drug thalidomide to help with nausea and morning sickness, as she didn't need it, but it was available. As it happens, this was a very good thing, as thalidomide was shortly after to be found to be the cause of thousands of babies being born with shortened arms and legs and other severe birth defects, and was banned. Thalidomide was licensed in 1958 and withdrawn in 1961, and of the approximately 2,000 babies born with defects, around half died within a few months and 466 survived to at least 2010. Look it up,[2] it's terrifying. And I could so easily have been among their number.

But David was born as complete and as perfect as a 90-year-old-monkey could be... well... nearly perfect. As I am David and I am writing my own story here, I'm happy to report that, yes, I was physically okay... but I was also an inquisitive child... fascinated from a young age by all things horror and magic and science fiction... and driven by a desire to find out how that trick worked, how to do it myself, how those effects on the television worked – even how entertainment machines on the seaside piers worked. This is something which has stayed with me my whole life.

2   en.wikipedia.org/wiki/Thalidomide_scandal

I was born into a loving family. Sheila, my mother, was a schoolteacher of everything to seven- to eleven-year-olds, and Edward – 'Ted' to everyone – worked for the newspapers. I lived in Tolworth, about ten miles south of the centre of London, and close to Surbiton and Kingston. Thus these were my childhood stamping grounds.

Like many, I don't recall much about my very young years, but our family has the benefit that Ted was a great lover of music – he met my mum at Ballroom Dancing School, which is what all the young kids were up to back in the fifties. Unless, I suppose, they were bopping along to Elvis and those other 'devil sounds' coming from America. But I digress. Dad loved music and radio. He was a fan of the Big Band Sound, of Buddy Holly, of Gene Krupa and other drummers, and indeed of the Goons: he had marvellous taste. He had managed to scrape together the money, goodness knows how, to own a reel-to-reel tape recording system, and he recorded shows off the radio. But he also recorded me.

And so, we still have those precious early tapes of little David.

As well as having tape-recording machines, Dad also loved his gadgets, and also had an 8mm cine film camera… and this went everywhere with him. As I say, I've no idea how the family afforded these things. We also had a television set. Black-and-white, of course, but we had one… and this was a rare thing in the sixties.

But back to the tape recordings.[3] The recording is of little David in his cot (I assume it was a cot, as I was two years old) and it was Christmas. I'm talking with Mummy and Daddy about a visit to Santa earlier that day. This was to Bentalls in Kingston, then just a big department store in the town.[4] Of course, Santa paid a visit there just before Christmas.

The year was therefore 1963. And this tape must have been recorded in late November, perhaps, in the lead-up to the Christmas period.

3   This is important.
4   Apparently first established in 1867. It'd been there a long time.

David is explaining what Santa gave him on his visit to the Grotto.

'A skeeky ammer' – a squeaky hammer. That is, a toy one which makes a noise when you hit things with it. Obviously I was keen on hitting things with my new hammer.

There's also a fascinating discussion about Santa and that he has whiskers. And he has ears. And he has eyes! 'All people got eyes,' observed young David in a very thoughtful manner. I was obviously on the ball, processing all this information through my two-year-old brain.

And what did David want for Christmas? 'A music-a-box.' And what colour might this 'music-a-box' be? 'A geeb one.' Yes, that's right... a green one.

But wait. Why is any of this important? Why am I telling you about Christmas 1963? What possible relevance could a late November Saturday have to this story?

Well.

It was 23 November 1963 that the first ever episode of a new BBC television show called *Doctor Who* was transmitted. At 5.16 in the late afternoon. So.

It is therefore *very* possible that this historic recording of David burbling on about hammers and music boxes was made while *Doctor Who* was *actually being transmitted!* If not the first ever episode, then perhaps the first episode of the story that introduced the Daleks to the world (21 December 1963). At the end of which, the Doctor's companion Barbara, having been trapped in some futuristic corridors, confronts one of the creatures for the first time: all we, the audience, see at that point is a sink plunger on the end of a rod coming menacingly towards her.

Just think. If Barbara had had a skeeky ammer, maybe a geeb one, then she could have used it to hit the Dalek!

That'd teach it.

* * *

The weather was mental back in those days, and some might say it still is. There is a documentary on one of the streaming channels about the winter of 1962 into 1963 – which would have been my first proper winter.[5] This is now known as 'The Great Freeze' and was one of the coldest winters on record in the UK.[6] The cold weather started on 12–13 December when it snowed across the country. Snow continued to fall and drifted to more than 20 feet high in many places, and towards the end of December, remote parts of the UK were completely cut off. In January the sea froze for one mile at Hearn Bay in Kent. The icy weather and snow continued until 6 March, which was the first morning without frost in 1963.

I mention all this as we have 8mm cine film of little David helping to shovel snow, probably a few years later – it looks like I might be three or four years old by now... but I certainly have memories of the great winters we had back then. Proper snow which came down in great drifts. So deep you couldn't see the kerbs of the roads. Happy times.

Other happy times were spent watching television... and among the shows that I was enjoying were, of course, the old classics like *Watch with Mother* – the adventures of Andy Pandy and Looby Loo and Teddy were required viewing back then! This show was narrated by Maria Bird, and I was fascinated by Teddy, who was naughty but everyone loved him. Also that Looby Loo only came to life when Andy and Teddy were not around – she was like a pretend friend that the adults just didn't believe in. Only 26 episodes were made, and these were shown on rotation! No wonder I remembered them! And, of course, *The Flower Pot Men*, shown as part of the same series.

This show has a special relevance as the Flower Pot Men were

5   The winter of 1961 into 1962 was, of course, my first winter, but as I had literally just been born, I wouldn't have known much about it.
6   Only the winters of 1683–84 and 1739–40 were colder than 1962–63.

5

voiced by an actor called Peter Hawkins. Hawkins invented a language for them which he called Oddle-Poddle – a mix-up of words and phrases which were almost, but not quite, a recognisable language. I mention this for two reasons. The first is that Mum was a big fan of the comedian and actor Stanley Unwin – someone who probably no one has heard of these days. But Unwin was famous for inventing his own language, Unwinese, which mixed up words and came out sounding like gobbledegook. Mum loved this and had several records of his famous monologues. So, these languages which sounded sort of like English but weren't, fascinated me. The other thing about Peter Hawkins is that he was the voice of the Daleks! What a revelation... the man who brought us the Flower Pot Men was also the voice of the most evil creatures in the universe! Who would have thought it.

Muffin the Mule (a string puppet horse which was talked to and presented by Annette Mills) is another show that I remember from Watch with Mother in the early sixties.

I also have a persistent memory of something I saw which terrified me at the time, and which has stayed with me ever since. There was a giant pumpkin which was chasing some children. It moved slowly, however, and just followed them wherever they went. No matter how fast they ran or where they tried to hide, the pumpkin was always there, slowly catching them up, and we knew it would eventually catch them. Quite what it might then do to them, I have no idea... but the idea of something slowly coming after you, that you could not escape or evade, was terrifying. Of course, this concept is also the plot of a horror film from 2014 called It Follows... but I very much doubt that those cinematic horrors were inspired by this old television series.

As to what that series was, I didn't know for many, many years. I thought it might have been some mis-memory from a series called Escape into Night, a kids' show from 1972 which was also quite terrifying. Based on the 1958 book *Marianne Dreams* by Catherine Storr,[7] the show followed a young girl who came down with some debilitating illness, and so, to escape the confines of her bedroom, starts drawing a house and a boy who lives there... but then she dreams the same things she draws, and the whole thing starts to become something of a nightmare as outside the boy's house are strange, mobile standing stones which have a single eye... and each night they're getting closer and closer. You can perhaps see why I thought this might be the origin of my 'pumpkin' terror. But most of *Escape into Night* still exists to watch today, and that showed me this wasn't my memory.

Nor was it something from *Doctor Who*... though I can completely understand if you thought it might be. In actuality, it seems to be from a show which no longer exists called *Knock Three Times* from a book written in 1917 by Marion St John Webb. This was transmitted from August 1968 and had six episodes. The show starred Jack Wild and Hattie Jacques, and it was made by LWT (London Weekend Television). As it is no longer available to see, I have only my vague memories of watching it... but it obviously made quite an impact!

Another show that I remember watching was *Lost in Space*. Now, this was a sixties film series imported from America. From the same camp as *Voyage to the Bottom of the Sea*, *The Time Tunnel* and *Land of the Giants*, it told the story of the Robinson family, who are blasted off from Earth in a spaceship called the *Jupiter 2*. But, unknown to them, a saboteur (the fiendish and devious Doctor Smith) is also on board, and he causes the ship to go wildly off course... and thus the whole lot of them are indeed lost in space.

What appealed to me, however, was that the show had a sort of 'monster of the week' approach, and I loved monsters! So, it was right up my street. I would have been watching this any time

---

7   Strangely also the name of a character from a 1967 *Doctor Who* story. Storr. Not Catherine.

from its UK debut (which for most of the UK was on 2 October 1965, though in the LWT region, which is what we had, it didn't start until 16 August 1968!) through to when it finished in the UK on 24 January 1969 (though this may have extended into the seventies)... which was also the time that I was watching *Doctor Who*! For me it was all in black and white, as we had a black-and-white television. I do remember one time being out shopping with Mum, and along the Tolworth parade of shops there was a television shop. I don't think such things exist these days, as televisions are all vast flat-screen things that you only see in larger retail stores and parks. But back then, there was a shop which had a selection of televisions in the window... all different sizes[8] but all tuned to one of the two television stations. The idea of playing some tape or DVD or whatever they do in shops these days was long in the future.

These televisions were tuned to the BBC or ITV, and of course they showed whatever happened to be on television at that time – there was no time-shifting by recording stuff: if you missed something on transmission, you missed it for good!

It was an evening as I recall, it was getting dark, and we were trying to get home after school when we passed the shop. One of the televisions was showing *Lost in Space* and it was in colour! Now, this blew my mind. At home, television was all in black and white – that was all there was. But here was my favourite *Lost in Space* in full colour! If you know the series, you'll know that it was quite lurid in its colours – each of the Robinson family and crew had different coloured jerseys and the planets were a riot of reds and pinks and whatever was in the prop store that day; so, seeing this episode leaping out the screen and the shop window at me was quite amazing. I can even remember which episode it was: 'The Galaxy Gift', at the start where the crew are making a play, and a

8   All small.

monster emerges from behind a door! I remember stopping there, in the street, transfixed by the screen. I can't recall what Mum was doing or how she managed to get me to move along. Even though we all take it for granted now, I still recall my first glimpse of television in colour. Wonderful.

I loved the series, and I remember one episode, 'The Space Destructors' from the third season, where there's this machine in a cave[9] which manufactures android duplicates of Doctor Smith. Will Robinson gets caught in the machine and so it starts making duplicates of him as well! It was amazing. The machine started a bit like a bread-maker with dough being plonked on a conveyor and moved along to have glitter added, and be pushed and prodded, and then an android came out the end! I was so taken with this that I created my own machine in the back garden from the slide, cardboard boxes, and various ropes and bits of stuff. Fortunately none of my home-grown androids actually worked, or we would all have been in a lot of trouble!

Another story that stood out for me was 'The Keeper', where Michael Rennie, apparently hot off the set of the 1951 film *The Day the Earth Stood Still*, plays an intergalactic zookeeper who wants the Robinson family for his collection of beasts. A superb performance and a brilliant two-parter for the show. Again, I liked the monsters, and at the end of the first episode Will and Doctor Smith escape from the Keeper's spaceship, but allow all the other monsters and creatures to escape with them! So, we have a procession of alien monstrosities coming out of the ship! Superb imaginative stuff!

* * *

Another big part of my childhood were the holidays... and these come into play later in this book as well. My grandmother (or Nana, as we called her), Gladys, initially lived about a mile away

---

9   In *Lost in Space* the machines and aliens were always in a cave.

from us in Tolworth, and we saw her often. Like my own mum, she was amazing – a force of nature – and like my mum she was also a teacher. Maths, though, rather than 'everything'... this cleverness with maths seems to run in the family. My uncle Brian is also a maths genius... but the gene seems to have skipped me. I can't do maths to save my life! I need that little handheld calculator, or mobile phone, to do that sort of stuff!

Now, sidestepping slightly, it is Nana who I have a very early memory of, giving me a Dalek toy. I was at her house, and in her kitchen. And I remember the Dalek toy flashing and sparking at the top as it moved. Friction powered, and on the kitchen table. It might have had that clever thing they called 'tricky action', where you never quite knew if it was going to happily spin off the table to smash on the floor, or whether it would change direction at the last minute.

The me today knows that this must have been one of the 1965 Marx Dalek toys. There was one which sparked inside the head space and flickered through the red-tinted plastic that lined the head. It was friction drive, but no 'tricky action', and cost 12s 11d (which was quite a lot of money!) I often wonder where that Dalek went! I never found it; I never kept it – which would have been strange for me not to have done. But I don't have it today, and I wish I did!

I mentioned holidays. We often took family holidays to either North Wales or to Cornwall. Cornwall because, in 1967, Nana moved to Newquay to live. And so we had somewhere to stay down there when we holidayed. A couple of years later, in 1969, my uncle Brian (Mum's brother) and his wife Kathleen bought a house in the same street, and this is why we enjoyed many extended family holidays down there. There was Mum and Dad and Nana, me, and my brother Alan (who is three years younger than me), and Brian, Kathleen and their three girls: Susan, Jennifer and Jacqueline (my cousins). There's more *Doctor Who*-related stories and adventures surrounding the holidays, and I will tell those in good time when we get there, but for the moment, I want to talk about the holidays. We would arrange to all rock up in Newquay at the same time and so spent a lot of time running around the town and the beaches. There was a rather nice zoo there, and a large area called Trenance Gardens with a boating pool, kids' playgrounds and so on... lots to do, basically. But what did we kids do? Five went bin-diving for empty Corona bottles left by the tourists.

Why, you may ask, would we do such a thing? Well... back in those days the large fizzy-drink Corona[10] bottles were made of glass, and what's more they had a return of 5d on each bottle. For every bottle we could rescue from the bins, we got 5d to spend on ourselves! So, we checked all the bins on the route from Nana's house to the town, collected all the bottles we could find, and then got 5d for each one!

The other source of income for us five was the amusement arcades in the town. Now, I still love visiting arcades and playing the 2p push machines – it's a relatively cheap way to spend an enjoyable few hours! Back then they were 1d machines and the same basic principles applied, but without the electronic jiggery-pokery which closes the exit chute if you're not actually playing the machine. A wander around the arcades would almost always result in many pennies being 'found' in the exit chutes of the machines. Which, when all collected together with the 5d from each Corona bottle, meant that we could make quite a lot of money on a given day.

And what, I hear you ask, did young David spend the money on? The answer is, unexpectedly, teddy bears! One of the shops in town had a large glass jar on the counter full of small colourful teddies... I think they were 25d each or something, and so when we had enough money, we would go to the shop and annoy the

10   Corona produced fizzy soft drinks in a variety of flavours.

heck out of the shopkeeper by asking to see each one in the jar; we had to choose carefully based on colour and character and position of the eyes and so on. It was a serious business! Then, of course, the bears had to be named. We then carried them with us on our adventures. Most of the bear names have been lost to posterity, but my main bear was called Brownz, and a second was called Toosiepegs (which actually meant 'teeth' or 'toothie-pegs').[11] Jennifer had the awesome Snoduss (a corruption of 'Snowdust' – a white bear), and there were many, many others.

And thus, we spent our summers: diving in bins; collecting money; scavenging for Corona bottles; buying small teddy bears; and adventuring among the caves, beaches and parks in Newquay.

And that sets the scene for this book. It's about me, David J Howe, and my adventures in Doctor Who. You already know that my young childhood was heavily influenced perhaps by items and activities unconventional, and I hope that my adventures and experiences through later life will be equally as entertaining.

But for the moment we're going to stay in the sixties… and find out more[12] about that strange show called Doctor Who and how and why it so captivated the young David, and set him on a more or less unwavering course for the rest of his life!

---

11   Remember my love of the Flower Pot Men and Stanley Unwin?
12   A lot more.

My small Yeti model made from modelling clay and some fur from an old stole; and my Dalek model made from Milliput.

2

The Sixties

It's a Saturday night[13] and the date is 1 July 1967. I am five years old, and snuggled in front of the television. There's most likely beans on toast on a plate on a small table in front of me. I can still remember the smell of beans on toast. The toast lightly buttered. The beans have to be Heinz (of course).

On the flickering black-and-white television in front of me, we're possibly just reaching the end of Juke Box Jury. I'm not sure that at five I had much appreciation of music… or who any of the people on that edition actually were! Mel Tormé, Janette Scott, Chris Denning and Penny Valentine.[14] Not a clue for any of them, though I at least recognise the first name: for what I have no idea, though. However, it is just as likely that we were watching Wimbledon Tennis on BBC 2, as Mum was a big fan of the tennis. And I certainly wouldn't have had any interest in that.

So, beans on toast it was… and either after Juke Box Jury, or when

---

13 . In those days, it was always a Saturday night.
14 Mel Tormé – an American musician, singer, composer, arranger, drummer, actor, and author; Janette Scott – a British actress who was married to Tormé and was Dame Thora Hird's daughter; Chris Denning – a BBC DJ and convicted sex offender(!), his career ended in 1974; Penny Valentine – a British music journalist and rock critic.

the tennis finished at 6.30 pm, we switched over to BBC 1... and I think this is then my earliest memory of watching *Doctor Who*. For at 6.25, the final episode of a story called 'The Evil of the Daleks' was transmitted.

It's interesting looking back at the listing in the *Radio Times* that at the bottom it says 'Dalek stories created by Terry Nation', as he didn't actually write this one. 'The Evil of the Daleks' was written by David Whitaker, a writer who was actually *Doctor Who*'s first ever story editor, and which was, at the time, intended to be the Daleks' last ever appearance in *Doctor Who*.[15]

As I discovered much later, at the time, the Daleks were hugely popular. They had captured the imagination of the British public, and the ratings for the show had climbed and climbed whenever there was a story which featured the Daleks! Terry Nation was the writer who had created them. He wrote their first story back in 1963, and they were an instant hit, making Nation a much sought-after writer. He was also a very busy writer, working for several other shows, and he had the idea that he wanted the Daleks to star in their own show. So, he had written a pitch for that, and was touting it about in America, hoping for funding to bring the Daleks to their own television series. But it was not to be. There were no takers.

However, while he was doing this, he was happy for Whitaker to write this Dalek story for *Doctor Who*, but on condition that it was their last appearance. And Whitaker obliged, delivering a seven-episode epic which brought the Daleks to their own destruction.

I remember two key elements from this episode, one of which has no basis in anything which exists today, and one which does.

The first thing I remember is that when the Doctor and his friends passed under a special 'conversion arch' that the Daleks had

---

15   I suspect that Nation's credit in the *Radio Times* was contractual.

built in their city, they got turned into human Daleks: that is, their minds were reprogrammed with 'The Dalek Factor', which the Doctor had spent the story unwittingly helping the Daleks to discover. When the Doctor and Professor Maxtible go under the arch, they are apparently converted. As a part of this conversion, I remember that the actors did what millions of children did in the playgrounds across the UK when 'playing Daleks'. They raised one hand in a fist up to their forehead while the other was held out like one of the Daleks' appendages (either the gun arm, or the sucker arm: it doesn't matter which).

Another slice of *Doctor Who* history now, and not everything that the BBC made in the *Doctor Who* series still exists today. Many of the stories do, and can be watched over again, but many were wiped by the BBC in the seventies and don't exist at all. There are soundtracks recorded by enterprising fans that still exist for everything, and many of the missing stories do have numerous off-screen photographs which were taken as a service for directors back in the day to provide a record of their work.[16]

So, for 'The Evil of the Daleks', only episode two exists today, but there is a soundtrack and there are off-screen photographs of the first episode.[17] But none of these show the characters with their fisted hand held up to their foreheads as I describe. There is even a BBC animated version of the story, but this again doesn't show this action. While it is possible that it never happened, and that my mind has made it up, it is something that I distinctly remember from the story.

The second memory comes right at the end of the episode.

16 Of course, back in the sixties, there was no way for a director, producer or actor to have a record of their work on television, barring *Radio Times* listings and on-set photographs. There were no videos, DVDs or other ways of having a visual record (unless they went to the trouble of filming their work off their televisions with expensive 8mm film cameras.)

17 These are also called telesnaps, and the service was provided by an enterprising man named John Cura.

The Doctor has fomented rebellion on Skaro and the Daleks are attacking each other, exploding and burning all over the place. The massive Dalek Emperor has been destroyed, and the Dalek city is burning. As the Doctor, Jamie and Victoria make their way back to the TARDIS and safety, they find themselves overlooking the city, and as the Doctor looks down on it, he says, 'The final end!' And as such it was just this for the Daleks. That scene has stayed in my memory all these years. A good end to an exciting and action-packed episode.

My next memory of watching *Doctor Who* is actually the very next story. But it wasn't transmitted the following week, as 'The Evil of the Daleks' brought to an end the fourth season of the show. The fifth season didn't start until 2 September, just under two months later. I was very taken with the end of 'The Evil of the Daleks', and was asking when that show would be back on television again. It helped that when it did come back, the issue of the *Radio Times* had a front cover dedicated to the show.

This time it was a new monster − new to me, anyway − the Cybermen, and that *Radio Times* cover, showing loads of them, was brilliant. There was also an article on page three all about *Doctor Who*, and once again it was being transmitted on Saturday evening, following *Juke Box Jury* and ten minutes of news and weather. I don't think, or at least I don't remember, the *Radio Times* at all, and my memory from this whole four-part story, called 'The Tomb of the Cybermen', is a single sequence from episode four, shown on 23 September 1967.

The story is a great one from this period in the show's history. The Doctor, Jamie and new companion Victoria (rescued at the end of 'The Evil of the Daleks') have arrived on an alien planet, where a group of archaeologists are trying to find the lost tombs of the Cybermen. The Doctor ingratiates himself in with the team, and they find and enter the frozen tombs. But the Cybermen are not as dead and inactive as they appear, and soon they have released their impressive Controller from deep freeze, and he's out to try to ensure the survival of the Cybermen. Battles, chases and all sorts ensue as the humans try to get out of there with their lives.

There's one moment, the one which I vividly remember, and this is where one of the group, a bodyguard to one of the women, grapples with a Cyberman. He pulls at its chest unit, and then foam erupts from within, covering the front of the Cyberman as it twitches and falls to the ground dead, the foam still bubbling from out of it. A very dramatic scene and well done in the show. It's no wonder that I remember it!

'The Tomb of the Cybermen' was for a long time another lost story, wiped by the BBC and thought gone forever. But in 1992, a copy was discovered lurking in some film vaults in Hong Kong! It was returned to the BBC, cleaned up, and released initially on VHS tape. So, we can now see this story again in all its glory, and it truly is a classic.

I was pleased to see that the scene I remembered was intact and there! There's always a slight feeling with these things that what you remembered wasn't quite how it happened. A popular term is 'the memory cheats', and indeed it does and can. But in this case, despite being very young when I first saw it, mine was spot on.

This effect of the Cybermen erupting with foam from within wasn't used in any further Cyberman adventures, which is a pity. It's a good and relatively cheap effect to create, and gives the impression that these things have all this gunk inside them under pressure, just waiting to spill out. For a young boy watching, it also reinforced the alien nature of the creatures. That they weren't made from blood and bone, but from something extraterrestrial and different… it sparked the imagination!

From this point, I have many random memories of watching the show… some stories I don't remember at all, others I have flash memories from. The next memory for sure that I have is about a month and a half later, and it is of not watching a story called 'The Ice Warriors'.

I don't know if I watched the intervening stories or not... there are just no memories there... but with 'The Ice Warriors'...

The story featured the third Ice Age on the Earth, and some scientists working on the ice fields discover something embedded in the ice. They dig it out, and it defrosts, and turns out to be a gigantic lizard-like alien life form originally from Mars, the captain of a Martian spaceship which is still trapped beneath the ice. Of course, Varga (as was the Ice Warrior captain's name) sets out to free his comrades and his ship! These things lumber and speak with a brilliant sibilant hissing voice... and they are genuinely quite terrifying!

So much so, that I was too scared to be in the room when the show was on. My brother Alan, who at the time would have been about three, was fine, and I remember being in the hallway outside the living room, and hearing the soundtrack as these Ice Monsters lumbered and hissed their way through whichever episode it was. Alan was laughing at me, too... he was in the room, completely happy with his reptilian companions.

Sometimes life just isn't fair! But now I think my blossoming and slightly older imagination meant that I recognised more than he did how terrifying the idea of an alien creature of this sort was.

* * *

Before we go too much farther forward, perhaps I should explain a little about this strange show called Doctor Who. There can be a habit in books like this where the writer (me) assumes that the reader (you) knows what I am going on about... and that's probably the case for a lot of readers, as you probably picked this book up because you are familiar with the show and all it entails... but, of course, that's an assumption on my part, and I don't like to assume things, which is why I'm trying to explain things as we go along, so that you, gentle reader, have all the information you need to hopefully understand what I am talking about.

So... Doctor Who.

There are TV shows and there are TV shows. And there is Doctor Who.

There are science fiction TV shows. And there is Doctor Who.

There are horror and fantasy TV shows. And there is Doctor Who.

For, you see, despite attempts to try to pigeon-hole or classify Doctor Who, it remains resolutely unclassifiable.

It started life through discussions within the BBC, back in 1962, for a new kids' drama series that the schedulers wanted to fill a perceived gap in the schedule on Saturday nights. The evening schedule had shows like the cartoon series Deputy Dawg (about a sheriff's canine deputy in a backwoods Southern American town), then the BBC News, then Circus Boy (a family adventure western series set in a Big Top) or Juke Box Jury (a pop music voting show) followed by Garry Halliday (Halliday was a pilot for a commercial airline and flew to his adventures) or Dixon of Dock Green (a homely police drama series). They wanted a new show that was faintly educational, and which could run over several weeks.

A panel of BBC people discussed it all through and decided that a science fiction show would be good, and started looking for books or ideas they could adapt. In the end they went for something completely original, and newly written by the writers they commissioned. It was called Doctor Who.

The idea was that it was about this mysterious old man and his granddaughter, Susan, who travelled in space and time in a fantastic space/timeship called the TARDIS. The ship was supposed to change its form to blend in with wherever they landed: so, in a desert it might look like a rock, or in a forest it might look like a tree. Basically, something which would not draw attention. So, when they arrived in London of 1963 – the show started in a then-contemporary setting – for whatever reason it took the form of a London Police telephone box, but sitting in a junkyard somewhere in London. The ship's chameleon circuits then stopped working, so it was stuck in this shape thereafter.

The show was called *Doctor Who* because this lead character, Susan's grandfather, was deliberately mysterious, and we knew nothing about him except that he was called 'the Doctor'. 'Doctor Who' was not his name… it was a question about him. We didn't know if he was human, alien or what, but the narrative veered towards him, and by association Susan, being aliens of some sort.

While on Earth, Susan went to a local school, and the Doctor tried to locate the various bits and pieces he needed to repair his ship. But one night, two of Susan's teachers, suspicious of this strange pupil who knew far too much about some things and nothing at all about others, decided to follow her home, and discovered that 'home' was the junkyard. They are then 'kidnapped' by the Doctor when he suddenly takes off in his ship, whisking them far back in time to an adventure with a Stone Age tribe who are just discovering fire. From there they head to the planet Skaro, where they encounter the Daleks, hideous machine-creatures, survivors of a neutronic war which wiped out the planet and mutated the survivors so that they had to create machine-shells to survive.

From there the adventures came thick and fast, as the Doctor couldn't completely control the TARDIS. Every week another challenge, more monsters, more planets and more excitement.

To fulfil the brief that it should be educational as well, initially there were occasional adventures in history, where 'lessons' could be learned by the TARDIS crew (and by the viewers), but over time these were phased out as they were simply not as popular as the stories set on alien planets and with the ever-present threat (or expectation) of monsters!

The show found an eager and willing audience for the adventures, and the initial commission of 13 episodes was expanded... and expanded... until the show was running nearly all year round, and Dalek toys were flooding into the shops.

But was it science fiction? In a way, yes. As a show about time travel, it couldn't really help but be... but for a show supposedly about time travel, very few of the stories were actually *about* time travel.

I have always argued that it was far more a horror show, in that the excitement and thrills were what kept kids watching. They love to be scared – we all do – and *Doctor Who* was able to scare in a way which was both thrilling and terrifying, but also safe, as you could always avert your eyes to your mother sipping her tea, or your father eating a slice of toast, and know it was just a television show.

It was in these early years that the phrase 'behind the sofa' came into usage, describing the fact that some viewers preferred to watch *Doctor Who* literally from behind the sofa in the living room. For me, when it got too scary towards the end of the 1960s, I used to watch through the crack in the door. So, I would be in the hallway, peeking at the happenings on screen, but protected by the door to the living room.

Doctor Who was an escape from reality and into a world where the TARDIS was your home, and the doors could literally open to any place in the entirety of time and space. Where there could be aliens, or humans, or battles, or space monsters, or exploding planets, or time paradoxes, or intrigue or comedy or danger or ray guns or cowboys or space museums or... the list is indeed endless.

It was a show that captured the imagination and was always the talk of the school playgrounds on Monday morning. How would the Doctor escape? What were the Daleks planning? Did that bomb explode?

But it also provided a creative spur to the fertile minds which watched it. Could I draw a picture of the Daleks? How would you build a spacecraft out of old washing-up bottles? Could I write a story like that?

Out of this, a generation were inspired in creative endeavours – as, indeed, you will see I was – and many of these people have gone on to work in and shape the creative industries themselves.

All from a humble television programme.

* * *

As we got to the end of 1968 and into 1969 (I was seven years old), my memories of watching the show start to ramp up.

'The Web of Fear' was a tremendously creepy and chilling adventure where the Doctor and his companions Jamie and Victoria were battling robot Yeti with web-guns in the London Underground system.[18] I was terrified by the lumbering Yeti in this one. So terrified, in fact, that later in the seventies I built a little model of one of them. Given that I cannot draw a stick figure that looks like a stick figure, my modelling prowess was equally rubbish, but I somehow managed it. There was this putty-like stuff you could buy which would harden in the air, I think it was called Milliput: a modelling clay of some sort. And I created the body shape for the Yeti from this, and carefully moulded into its chest a cavity for its control sphere.[19] For the sphere itself, I found a large silver ball bearing which worked perfectly. Then I had to add the fur. Mum had an ancient fur stole which had been in the closet for years and years, so I asked if I could have it. I cut this up to create the fur

18 And why not. I have no idea how the writers came up with the idea of the Yeti having guns which fired a spiderweb-like substance which suffocated and killed people, but it was genius. The visuals for that alone were enough to guarantee nightmares. And, of course, we went on the London Underground trains. I remember well, eyeing the tunnel openings with wariness, just in case a Yeti might be lurking in the darkness beyond. I still do!

19 The Yeti were actually robots, controlled by the Great Intelligence through a silver control sphere which was held in their chests. Remove the sphere and the Yeti stopped working.

for the Yeti, and fashioned a small hatch for the sphere from cardboard. For the Yeti's claws and feet, I used small red plastic straws. It all seemed to work well, and indeed I still have my little Yeti to this day!

Like 'The Tomb of the Cybermen', this adventure was mostly missing for many years, but one episode (part one) existed, and four of its remaining five episodes were recovered from some foreign television vault in 2013, in time for the show's 50th anniversary, and I cannot tell you the thrill of sitting down to watch it through for the first time since childhood. Even the lack of episode three didn't seem to matter. It's a stone-cold classic story, superbly written, directed and performed. And, of course, still scary as heck, especially if you are wary of spider webs!

'The Wheel in Space' was another Cyberman adventure (the first since 'The Tomb of the Cybermen') and featured the Cybermen trying to infiltrate and take over a Space Wheel as part of an elaborate plan to attack the Earth. I don't remember much of it, but there's a scene at the end of episode four and into episode five where the Doctor and Jamie are exploring a cargo bay, and a Cyberman comes in behind them, forcing them to rapidly scramble for cover and hide until the creature has gone. That really terrified me. In this story the Cybermen made a strange electronic whirring or whining sound all the time, so when you heard that noise, you knew one was close. Very effective indeed!

Following transmission of 'The Wheel in Space' was a full repeat of 'The Evil of the Daleks'. This was only the second ever *Doctor Who* story to be repeated by the BBC,[20] and while it's possible that my earliest memory of that story comes from this repeat, I

20   The first repeat was actually of the very first episode in 1963, which was shown again the following week before episode two was transmitted, as the week before – 23 November – was the day after President Kennedy was assassinated in America, and the schedules and news were, of course, full of that. The BBC felt that this had perhaps hampered the launch of their new show, and so decided to show the episode again!

don't think this is the case. The repeat led into a new series, this time with a new companion in Zoe, a teenage astrophysicist and librarian from the Space Wheel. Zoe was great, and my eight-year-old self was quite taken with her. She and Jamie were at loggerheads somewhat (Jamie was a Scots lad from 1746 – the Battle of Culloden – who wore a kilt and was all for using his fists to protect the Doctor and his friends) as his knowledge of the modern world was limited. Their first full adventure together was 'The Dominators', which was a somewhat typical story where a couple of bloodthirsty warmongers arrive on a planet inhabited by pacifists, with expected results. The Dominators (as, of course, they were called) had with them some rather neat robots called Quarks. Boxy things with glass spike-tipped heads and two gun arms, mounted at the front, which could slot back into their bodies. I loved the Quarks!

Other memories from this period include the next story, 'The Mind Robber', an adventure set in the Land of Fiction, where all the characters in it speak lines from fiction past or future (depends on your perspective). I recall a great scene here of Zoe going up into a creepy castle. She pushes open the door, which swings with an enormous creak, and then vanishes inside with a piercing scream. When the Doctor and Jamie try to find her, the Doctor realises that it's a riddle – the story is full of riddles and word puzzles – 'When is a door not a door?'... to which the answer is... 'When it's ajar!' And there Zoe is, trapped inside an enormous glass jar! Jamie breaks the paper seal on the top and lifts her out. It's an interesting memory to have, as it's not a monster, or an episode ending, but just a simple piece of slightly humorous action in a story that is full of the whimsical and the strange.

At this point I started to watch most every week... or at least for the next eight weeks, as the next adventure was another Cyberman one, and in my opinion, one of the best ever *Doctor Who* adventures. It was called simply 'The Invasion', and the Cybermen didn't appear until a few episodes in. Instead, we have the Doctor, Jamie and Zoe back on Earth, and trying to get the TARDIS fixed again (it became invisible as they arrived). They try to find Professor Travers from the Yeti stories, but he's not around; instead, they meet with the daughter of his colleague, Professor Watkins, a girl named Isobel, and end up having a battle of wits with an industrialist called Tobias Vaughn, who is somehow behind all sorts of strange shenanigans. Lethbridge-Stewart is back from the previous Yeti story, and is now a Brigadier, running a military outfit called UNIT, who are also investigating Vaughn and his companies. But behind it all are the Cybermen, again trying to invade and take over the Earth.

The scene I remember comes at the end of episode five, and involves a sequence where the team realise that the Cybermen are hiding in the sewers of London, and so Isobel, Jamie and Zoe head off there to investigate as the Doctor is involved elsewhere. They go into the sewers, chased by a London policeman, to try to get some photographs of the Cybermen to prove to the Brigadier that they are real.[21] Meanwhile, Vaughn has tested a machine to try to destroy the Cybermen, as he has a plan to take over once they have invaded. The machine, invented by Professor Watkins, projects emotions, and when they try it on a Cyberman it drives it insane. Raging in confused pain, the Cyberman heads down into the sewers to join its fellows.

So, Zoe, Isobel and Jamie find themselves down in the sewers. The policeman comes down after them and comes face to face with a patrolling group of Cybermen, who kill him… and then, from the other side of the group comes the insane howling of the mad Cyberman. They are trapped between the two groups!

Cue episode ending and end title music!

Phew!

This was the most thrilling and exciting episode ending ever,

---

21 Are you following all this? No one ever said a *Doctor Who* story was simple!

and it made a big impression on me because it took place in a very familiar setting that we could all relate to. One of the things I notice about *Doctor Who* and the stories is that sometimes they reflected the fears and phobias of our daily lives. This took place during the Cold War, and growing up I was aware of the possible threat of nuclear weapons, because my parents' generation still talked about and remembered the Second World War and the residual threat that existed then. But, because the stories were fictional, they were easier to digest, while letting you explore the fear element in a safe way.

Part of the thrill (and the point) of *Doctor Who* was that it had these exciting cliff-hanger endings. The Doctor and his friends would be put in peril, and you then had to wait a whole week to find out what happened and how they got out of it, meanwhile discussing with your own friends in the playground just how they might escape from what seemed to be certain doom. It was all part of the excitement and fun of *Doctor Who*. It made you think, and was always a kind of puzzle to solve.

Strangely, after this story, I have no further memories of watching the show in the sixties. Which is odd, as there were a fair few still to go, including more alien robot things ('The Krotons') and another Ice Warrior story ('The Seeds of Death'), and, of course, the very end of the Patrick Troughton years in 'The War Games'. I'm not surprised that 'The War Games' didn't grab me, as it starts out appearing as though the TARDIS crew have arrived during the First World War, and this would not have interested me at all. I have never been a fan of wartime films or stories, and so this could well have been an instant wander-out-of-the-room moment. I think the problem with those stories for me was that my parents and grand-parents had lived through the war, and tales of those times were often still on their generation's lips. It wasn't such a distant history as it is now. I suspect this is why I had no interest in these stories. It was always the fantastical, the futuristic, the supernatural and the horror which appealed to me far more than any 'real life' drama. I feel the same about Westerns as well. They just don't appeal to me, regardless of how much I can appreciate the cinematography and acting and so on.

What I do find stranger still is that I have very few memories from the sixties which are not in some way related to *Doctor Who*. There was something about that show which attracted and beguiled me in a way that not much else did. One non-*Doctor Who* memory I do have is staying up late to watch the real-life Moon landings on 16 July 1969. The wonder of that evening was amazing. Actual men walking on the actual Moon. Again, it's that futuristic/space-related element which appealed to me.

I couldn't tell you the names of my friends at school, or what the teachers' names were, for example, but I certainly knew all about the Doctor and his friends Jamie and Zoe, and at least some memories of their adventures in time and space, which is incredible when you think that the episodes were only shown once and were not accessible to be repeated as they are now. They had an impact on my formative years, and as time went on, I remembered more personal events when they were associated with various episodes.

There was one other item which I recall, and again it's related to this show. Back in 1964, Armada Books released a paperback edition of a *Doctor Who* hardback book. I had no idea about these, but somewhere as the sixties progressed, a copy of *Doctor Who in an Exciting Adventure with the Daleks*[22] came into my possession. Possibly from a school jumble sale. It had an evocative cover with a mysterious figure, his face strangely unformed,[23] standing outside the blue Police Box shape of the TARDIS.

22 Yes, it was genuinely called that.
23 I like to think this was because they were deliberately not wanting to suggest any specific Doctor… which is odd as, at the time, there had only been one Doctor on television. Maybe they had a time machine…

I read it a few times, I think, enjoying that this was an adventure that I did not recall, something new to me. For all I knew, it had never been on television at all (although the book suggested that it had), but the black-and-white line drawings inside evoked images in my mind as the Doctor, together with his friends Ian and Barbara and his granddaughter Susan, travelled to the planet Skaro and met the Daleks!

The book actually starts completely at odds with the television series. There is no junkyard and mysterious student; there are no schoolteachers following her 'home', and no adventure on Stone Age Earth. Instead, we're told the story from the point of view of Ian, who, when driving home one foggy night across Barnes Common, comes across a car wreck, and an injured Barbara who is concerned about Susan. From there, we meet the strange old man with his everlasting matches,[24] enter the TARDIS, and are taken to Skaro where the Daleks live. It was magical stuff, and easily on a par with other books I was reading, which I seem to remember as being some of Enid Blyton's 'Adventure' series of novels,[25] the Narnia books by C S Lewis, and a book about gnomes by someone mysteriously called BB.[26]

My original copy of *Doctor Who in an Exciting Adventure with the Daleks* has long since vanished. Probably worn away with multiple readings, but it's a book I have a great fondness for. I have since replaced it with further copies. But what's important about this book, along with other children's fiction of the era, was how they aided my passion for fiction and my love for fantasy and science fiction and encouraged me to read for pleasure. These books were exciting and fun. Unlike some of the materials we

24 These were also never in the television series.
25 I much preferred these 'Adventure' books to either the Famous Five or the Secret Seven books.
26 The book I recall was probably the 1955 novel *The Forest of Boland Light Railway*. 'BB' was the pseudonym of Denys Watkins-Pitchford, a prolific author who penned around 60 books between 1922 and 1990.

were given in school to read, which could be a turn-off for the pastime.

So, as we entered the seventies, and these memories intensify, my path towards *Doctor Who* geekdom was growing, even though I didn't know what that meant at the time!

The cover for the influential book *The Making of Doctor Who*, published in 1972.

3

The Early Seventies

The sixties end, and 1970 dawns. I'm eight years old… but I suspect what might have been of more interest to me was that the *Radio Times* was announcing a new Doctor in the form of Jon Pertwee!

Now, at that point, of course, I had no more idea of who Jon Pertwee was than probably most people, but my dad was a fan of *The Goon Show* and *The Navy Lark* on the radio, so I suspect that he might have had an inkling… but as for remembering the show… I can't. I've no memories of Pertwee's first story, 'Spearhead from Space', although it would have been right up my street. With an alien intelligence coming to Earth in strangely shaped plastic meteorites, and dastardly goings on at a plastics factory, complete with shop window dummies coming alive and terrorising Ealing Broadway. Perfect Saturday night viewing!

The story I do have a memory of was the third in Pertwee's first season, a curious politically themed affair called 'The Ambassadors of Death'.

I mentioned earlier that the family often spent a lot of our holidays down in Newquay in Cornwall – well, 1970 was no different, and I know from the *Doctor Who* connection that we were holidaying around April 1970. This seems an odd month to go on holiday, to me – perhaps it was a late half term, it wasn't Easter as that fell at the end of March that year.

On this particular Saturday, I know that us kids had taken ourselves off down to Trenance Gardens in Newquay and had spent the day at the zoo, or just messing about by the lakes and the boats… just wandering and being kids! I realised, however, that *Doctor Who* was on at 5.15 pm, and so we had to get back in time. My memory, therefore, is of racing back from Trenance; a distance of perhaps a mile.

Back in 1970, this part of Newquay looked very different. Where there are now houses around Tretherras Road and Towan Blystra Road, there were just fields and scrubland, and so our route back to our house was across all that and up the playing fields to the backs of the houses at the top of Glamis Road. A much easier route than following the roads. And so, I remember racing through the spring fields of grass and flowers, hoping that we got home in time to see the episode.

I'm pleased to report that I did. I'm not certain which episode it was, though, as my main memory from this story is of an episode ending… I'm assuming it's the *end* of the episode that I remember from this day, as that has more impact. So, it was the conclusion of episode four, where the Doctor bursts into a room where one of the alien Ambassadors, dressed in a human spacesuit, has just killed a ministerial type, and has destroyed some top secret documents held in a safe. The Doctor throws open the door, and the Ambassador is blocked from sight behind it. The Doctor sees the dead man and goes over to him, to see if he's all right, not seeing the Ambassador approaching him from behind, his deadly irradiated hand outstretched to touch and kill the Doctor next…

A great ending indeed, and it's fascinating that my main memory of that holiday in Newquay is actually of the ending of a *Doctor Who* episode!

* * *

I have a vague feeling that I did see all of this first season of Jon Pertwee's Doctor, if only because my desire not to miss that episode was so strong, it makes no sense for that to be there if I'd not been watching the show! I have a sense that I saw the preceding story, uniquely called on the title card 'Doctor Who and the Silurians',[27] as I have nagging half-memories of the reptilian creatures from it. And the story after, 'Inferno', I also think I watched, as again I remember the regressed scientists, wolf-man-like, attacking everyone as the Earth burned. It was a great season of adventures. Looking back at it, it's perhaps aimed a little higher than the Patrick Troughton season which preceded it. Most of the stories are seven episodes long, which is a lot to take in and sustain, and the themes of the show had changed from being adventures in space and time to adventures set on Earth, as in terms of the show's own continuity, the Doctor had been exiled to Earth at the end of 'The War Games' and his form changed to that of Jon Pertwee. So, the Doctor was stuck. His TARDIS didn't work anymore, and so any threats had to either come to Earth (as with the meteorites bringing the alien intelligence, or the Ambassadors actually turning out to be peaceful alien creatures, misled and used by corrupt politicians for their own ends), or they were here already (as with the Silurians being ancient inhabitants of Earth who were in hibernation, woken to find they were no longer the dominant life form; or the scientist Stahlman in 'Inferno', who was so obsessed with drilling deep into the Earth's crust that he didn't care what damage it did. When a strange green goo is released which starts turning everyone into monsters... well, we did tell you to be careful!) So, the stories were more about ecological horrors, and corrupt and bad men rather than nasty monsters. Which is an interesting thing about *Doctor Who*, that it often showed humanity to be far worse than any alien beastie. A lesson in life, perhaps?

27 Normally the *Doctor Who* episodes omit the 'Doctor Who and the' part from the title. This one didn't.

The next year, 1971, Doctor Who was back again with another set of adventures, and this is where my memory really kicks in about the show. Unlike in my younger years, I remember watching all of them, and loving them.

From more killer plastic shop dummies, and even a killer inflatable plastic chair in 'Terror of the Autons', through a mind parasite ('The Mind of Evil'), the brilliantly realised and terrifying Axons ('The Claws of Axos'), an adventure set on an alien world but which was actually some china clay pits in Cornwall ('Colony in Space'),[28] and finally a great gothic horror story about a horned demon coming to terrorise a small English village ('The Daemons')...[29] there wasn't a duff story here!

Interestingly, here it's 'The Daemons' which I remember most, because I missed a couple of episodes of it towards the end. So, this was June 1971. Another strange time to take a holiday, but I know that I missed the episodes because we were on holiday in North Wales.

Spring Bank Holiday was Monday, 31 May in 1971, so it's most likely that the family holidayed at this time because of it. We went to Butlins in Pwllheli (as we almost always did), which is now a Haven Holiday Park, but back then it was one of the big Butlins camps. Mum and Dad enjoyed the North Wales scenery and so liked driving all over the place and using the camp as a base. For us kids, it was okay as there were amusement arcades to go and haunt, and usually some sort of films or entertainment or something in the evenings.

28 And you can be sure that I nagged to go visit the china clay pits, the mounds of white soil which could, and still can, be seen from the A391. They are at the evocatively named Old Baal Clay Pit (Baal is an ancient name given to several false gods or idols, as well as a Canaanite-Phoenician god of fertility and rain. Baal is also associated with Beelzebub, demons, and the devil) and it's today next to the St Austell Enterprise Park in Carglaze. I don't think we ever visited.

29 The village is Aldbourne in Wiltshire, and I have visited there many times. It's something of a Doctor Who legend, and a place of pilgrimage for many fans!

So, dutifully at about six o'clock on the Saturday, I headed for a small hut where there was a television, only to discover that *Doctor Who* was not being shown! I remember being somewhat panicked, as I wasn't certain what time it was on, but I was sure it was around six... But there was nothing I could do. The chalets at the camp did not have television, and we didn't have a portable television to bring with us. There were also the proverbial 'bigger boys' in there, watching whatever they were watching, and me, being a nine-year-old skinny weakling that the chap who had sand kicked in his face kicked sand in the face of, I wasn't going to ask if they would change the channel.

So, I skulked away into the night, cross that I had to miss episodes of *Doctor Who*! I suppose this is when I really knew how important the show was in my life and what it meant to me. It wasn't just entertainment: I was learning a lot about life, loyalty and friendships from the show.

The other main thing about 1971 was that it was the year all our money changed.

Up to that point, the UK had, in hindsight, a completely crazy system of money that was all worked out in pounds, shillings and pence. There were 12 pence in a shilling, and 20 shillings (or 240 pence) in a pound. The penny used to be subdivided into farthings (until the end of 1960), and there was a half-penny coin too (until 31 July 1969).

So it was that on Monday, 15 February 1971, I was on my way to school. Clutched in my hand I had a coin. Maybe an old sixpenny piece. And on my way to school there was a sweetshop. I headed in, and saw that everything was marked in both the old and new prices. You could now get four chews for a new penny (Fruit Salad were my favourite, but Black Jacks were okay), but everything seemed to have become a little more expensive, as the shop had rounded the amounts up.

One old penny (1d) was now worth 0.4167 of a new penny.

But the price of the Black Jack had leaped from 0.20835p to 0.25p... and everything else along with it. I may have only been nine years old at the time, but even I could see that this decimal-isation had increased the prices of everything.

I bought a few sweets, and received as my change shiny new coins. Maybe one new penny and one new half-penny. It was amazing to actually spend money and be given new change for the first time!

* * *

The next year was when my appreciation of Doctor Who started to change... slowly at first... but then like a tsunami of interest.

The third year of Jon Pertwee being the Doctor: 1972. And arguably another cracking season of stories which just threw everything into the mix.

We kicked off, at the tail end of 1971, with a repeat of 'The Daemons'.[30] But I have no memory of that, and suspect I never saw it! Awful. I missed a couple of the episodes and also missed the repeat! But then, first week of January, the Doctor returned, with another cover on the Radio Times proudly proclaiming that the Daleks were back too!

As mentioned earlier, while Terry Nation had wanted to stop the Daleks from appearing on Doctor Who as he was trying to sell the idea of their own show... well, this didn't work, and so for the third year of Pertwee's tenure as the Doctor, the production team of producer Barry Letts and script editor Terrance Dicks wanted to bring the Daleks back. So, they reached out to Nation and he agreed: his attempts to further exploit his creation elsewhere had failed, and so he was happy for them to appear in the show once more. And again, he didn't write the story, it was by Louis Marks and was called 'Day of the Daleks'.

30 Doctor Who repeats at Christmas became commonplace at this time.

Somewhere along the way I had discovered Lego. That amazingly versatile brick-building system from which you could construct anything from castles to dragons to sailing ships, and which would cripple you if you stood on it. And what did I build from Lego? Why, only the disintegrator blasters that the monstrous Ogrons were using in the show.

I remember thinking they were so cool. You could kill people and they just vanished! So, there were no bodies to clear up, no mess... awesome to a ten-year-old. The problem with trying to build a gun out of Lego, though, was that by definition it was blocky, not sleek and smooth like the ones on television. And, of course, it didn't light up. However, by that time there were some transparent bricks available, and so I did the best I could to build a very wobbly, and falling apart all the time, representation of a disintegrator gun.

The Ogrons were a vaguely ape-like guard dog creature which the Daleks were using, and I suspect that the subtleties of the story were lost on me. It's actually a story which uses time travel to the full – the plot is built around it – and the paradoxes that can occur if you're not careful. But it also had Daleks and Ogrons and battles with UNIT troops in the gardens of a country house... what's not to love?

The next story was, and is, one of my favourites.

When I'm asked what it was that 'got me into' *Doctor Who*, I usually answer that it was the monsters. I'm a sucker for a good monster. It's the same thing that I loved *Lost in Space* for, even if some of the creatures on that show were a little too rubbery for their own good. Also, I liked the seriousness of *Doctor Who*. Unlike *Lost in Space*, where Doctor Smith and the Robot camped and clowned it up all the time,[31] adding levity and silliness to the situations they found themselves in, on *Doctor Who* they never did this. Whatever

---

31   'Oh, the pain, the pain!' and 'You bubble-headed booby!' and, of course, 'Danger! Danger Will Robinson!' etc.

the threat or the story, the characters in it always took it all very seriously. There was, as a result, a sense of real threat which came through when watching.

The following story was called 'The Curse of Peladon', and from the outset we are taken, quite literally, to an unknown alien world. The Doctor suddenly gets the TARDIS to work again, and he and his companion Jo Grant find themselves on the mountain slopes of some thunder-and-lightning-wracked planet. And perched on top of the mountain is an imposing citadel.

Meanwhile, in the citadel, we find that delegates are assembling for some conference, and they are all great alien monsters. We first meet Alpha Centauri, who is a human-sized six-armed bug thing, with a single giant eye which takes up all of its head. It also speaks in a disarmingly squeaky voice. An impressive and complex design for the show, and one which has not really been beaten.

Then there's Arcturus, and at first sight this appears to be some sort of robot: a boxy base with a clear dome on top, and ridged tubes going up the sides. But closer inspection reveals a wizened and shrunken alien head inside the dome, and green fluids being pumped around it. A masterpiece of design. This creature had an impressive electronic warbling voice.

Last, but not least, we discover that the Ice Warriors are here too... two of them. A large lumbering hissing creature like the ones in 'The Ice Warriors', and another, smaller, sleeker one who is in charge.

If I had watched, or could remember, 'The Seeds of Death' from 1969, then I might have recognised this variant as one that had appeared in that story. But I didn't.

Monsters galore! And a great story of intrigue and death, as someone in the room is a traitor and doesn't want this conference to succeed. But which is it?

I was very taken with this story. Loved it. But there was one episode which I was going to miss, as it clashed with another show on the other channel which my dad wanted to watch. This was Gerry and Sylvia Anderson's UFO.

I don't know why my dad suddenly wanted to watch this... I have vague memories of seeing bits of it way back in the past, but it wasn't for me. Perhaps I found it too scary, or the themes and ideas it was playing with were way above me at the time. Looking at UFO now, with adult eyes and perspective, I realise how dark the stories were, and how the messages within them were perhaps contrary to the ones in Doctor Who, which invariably had the 'good side' always winning over the 'bad'. Not so in UFO, where characters you were invested in died: as when Straker's wife does, leaving you with a knowledge of the character's inner pain. These were subjects that perhaps my young mind wasn't ready for, hence my preference for Doctor Who and the monsters that were always defeated in the end.

I do remember thinking it didn't have nearly enough aliens and UFOs in it for a show called UFO! And I also remember I liked the Moonbase scenes best, and also all the hardware. Like many others, I got the Dinky metal models of the SHADO Interceptor with its single large rocket on the front,[32] and the green SHADO 2 Mobile truck (with a small rocket in the hatch on the top). I still have them to this day!

Whatever the reason for it, that night Dad wanted to watch this episode, but because he was a kind dad, he offered to record Doctor Who on audio for me, so that I could listen to it afterwards.

Now, we only had one television... and that was in the living room... so how could my dad record it for me?

I mentioned earlier that Dad was a great lover of music and radio comedy, and to this end he had obtained a couple of reel-to-reel tape recorders, and an amplifier and tuner, as well as a record

---

32 I always thought this was hugely impractical, as you only had one shot to fire at anything. If you missed, you were done for. Luckily, on UFO, they were very good shots.

player: everything he needed to be able to record off the radio, and then to edit the bits he wanted to keep onto other tapes for future appreciation.

Dad was also a tinkerer, and loved to keep all sorts of random items because they might come in handy one day. We had an old shed in the garden which was full of old kitchen furniture, and in the drawers and on the shelves were glass jars full of screws and nuts and washers and bolts of all sizes. There were old discarded bicycle parts, bits of toys which had broken but which might be useful. Pieces of wood of all shapes and sizes. Metal pieces, rods and threads, and nails and fasteners... just all sorts of things. There were also the tools to work with: a multitude of screwdrivers, hammers, wrenches, saws of every persuasion, a vice to hold things firm, glues and oils and tapes. An electric drill complete with drill bits for wood, metal, concrete... basically anything and everything ended up in that shed!

Now, among the salvage that Dad had was an old television set. No idea where he got it from. Maybe a neighbour was throwing it out? Maybe he 'found' it somewhere... it could even have been one that the family had had and moved on from. I've no idea.

But Dad took that television apart, isolated the tuning elements from it, and then wired them into his radio tuner in the house. Add an aerial, and lo and behold, you could tune it to a TV station and record the sound from it! Complete genius!

Thus, I was able to listen to and record *Doctor Who*, while Dad was watching *UFO* in the other room. Obviously, I had no idea what the visuals were, but just being able to listen to it was such a thrill!

I think after this little experiment with the tuner, Dad either took pity on me, or decided that he didn't like *UFO* after all, and I have no memory of us using this setup to record *Doctor Who* again. Indeed, when I started to record *Doctor Who* off air for myself in a couple of years' time, we didn't use this arrangement and I had to resort to the tried and tested method of a small portable tape machine and a microphone by the television. Oh, and telling/reminding everyone to keep quiet during the show.

However, this experience may have prodded Dad into action, as the very next story, we got a new colour television in the middle of it!

I talked in the first chapter about my amazement at seeing colour televisions in the shop on Tolworth Broadway, and that, because we only had a black-and-white television, it was a revelation to see *Lost in Space* in full colour. Well, to actually be getting a colour television was so exciting!

Mum tells me that long before this, in the early sixties sometime, she saw a sign in said television shop in Tolworth offering 'colour television'. She went in to see what it was all about, and the salesman explained that it was basically a 12-inch sheet of clear plastic that you erected in front of your television screen. The top part of the sheet was tinted blue, the middle part was tinted pink, and the lower part was tinted green. And you watched the television through this sheet.

The colours on the plastic made you think you were watching something in colour, when in fact, of course, you were doing nothing of the sort. Reportedly the filters only worked for certain outdoor settings and reflected only one type of skin tone, so weren't great. My mum was unimpressed anyway and never bothered with it.

The excitement in the house was high on the day the new television was supposed to arrive. And, of course, it was a Saturday. *Doctor Who* day.

Because I vividly remember which episode it was that I first saw in colour, I know this was Saturday, 18 March 1972. And the episode in question was part four of 'The Sea Devils'.

Another great story. The Doctor's arch-nemesis the Master had been captured by UNIT at the end of 'The Daemons', and taken to a secure prison on the Isle of Wight. In 'The Sea Devils', the Master has taken over the prison guards and commander with hypnotism, and is secretly working with a group of undersea creatures to help them take over the world! This was a typical *Doctor Who* adventure in many ways, and, in fact, these creatures were aquatic versions of the monsters we saw in 'Doctor Who and the Silurians' a couple of years earlier.

Episode three ended with the Master using a summoning device to call the creatures from the sea and out onto the beach. So, episode four kicks off with the same scene... the Doctor and Jo are running along the beach from the prison guards; the Master is up on the cliff top with his summoning device, and he activates it. A few moments later, one of these Sea Devil creatures emerges from the waves and starts to approach the beach... a beautiful colour close-up bringing its alien features into view! Wow! What a way to experience colour television for the first time.

But it was close. The television man didn't arrive until late in the afternoon, and the episode started at 5.50! I remember him faffing about, unpacking the television, setting it up, getting the aerial sorted, then trying to tune all the channels – there was nothing like auto-tune or anything in those days, it all had to be done by hand. Slowly getting there.

My memory tells me that we got BBC1 sorted just as the show started, and I think my cries and pleas were enough to either get him to stop until *Doctor Who* was over, or that the whole thing had been completed just in the nick of time.

So, I was able to watch the rest of 'The Sea Devils' in colour, and, of course, the following two stories as well, 'The Mutants' (set on an alien planet where the people are naturally turning into insect-like monsters, a problem accelerated by a land-hungry Marshal in a space station which is circling the planet in space), and 'The Time Monster' (a tale where the Master is back, this time trying to gain power over time through an ancient crystal held in ancient Atlantis).

The other thing that happened in 1972 was the publication of a book which was to become one of the most significant books ever published about *Doctor Who*.

This was *The Making of Doctor Who*, written by Malcolm Hulke and Terrance Dicks, and published by Piccolo books on 20 April 1972.

Now, I very much doubt that I got this on publication day or anything close to it... but I certainly had a copy by the time that season of stories had ended. While I can't recall the circumstances of buying the book, it's most likely from another holiday down to Newquay, where there was a W H Smith's bookshop in the town that I liked to check out for anything which might appeal to me. Even at the age of 11, I was interested in books and reading, and I've always enjoyed browsing in bookshops. So, it may well have been there that I saw it, and then persuaded my parents to pay the 25p that it cost to have it.

To say that I read it cover to cover would be an understatement. I *devoured* this book.

The premise is simple: we have sections looking at the main characters, details of all the adventures to date, along with a helpful listing of the stories, documents allegedly from the Doctor's trial, UNIT memos from the Brigadier, a smashing black-and-white photo section – and we then take the story 'The Sea Devils' as an example, which Hulke wrote for the show, and we're taken through it from script to screen, before we sign off with a piece by the Reverend John D Beckwith AKC (Chaplain to the Bishop of Edmonton) somewhat strangely asking what religion has to do with *Doctor Who*.

The reason why this book was so significant was simply that it was the first time ever that the history of *Doctor Who* had been documented. Up until this title, the only information anyone outside of the BBC had was the numerous listings in the different editions of the *Radio Times*, and, of course, their memories. There was nothing else.

Remember in 1972 there were no VHS tapes, no DVDs, no streaming, no internet... there was simply no way to find out this information. And yet here was a book which contained at least some of the history and background information about the show.

I was intrigued and tantalised. I could see that, far from there being only the handful of stories that I personally remembered, there were actually loads more, and stretching way back before I could remember. I still have my copy of this book, and, interestingly, I added in pen to the listing of stories that it contained:

NNN - - THE MUTANTS

The book only went up to and stopped at 'The Sea Devils' in its scope, and indeed was published between episodes two and three of 'The Mutants', the story that followed 'The Sea Devils'. What amuses me is that I didn't know who the writer(s) or director(s) of the story were, I just put minus signs there, and that I put 'the Mutants' down as the 'enemy' in the story. It just shows that I had little idea of the subtexts or lower level plots of the adventures at the time.

'The Mutants' is about colonisation, and the enemy is actually the Marshal in his space station, wanting to wipe out the insectoid mutants and to chemically change the planet so it could be inhabited by humans. I missed all this and instead plumped for the obvious 'monster' as being the 'enemy'. An understandable mistake, perhaps.

The list of stories in the book, and indeed the book itself, does not include past story titles anywhere. Instead, it uses the BBC's internal designation letters for them, which started with A, then B, C and so on, and when we got to Z, it restarted with AA, BB and so on...[33] I must have simply guessed that 'The Mutants' was NNN as that was the next available letter... there is no way I could have known that!

33 This is a simplification, as some letters were missed along the way, but you get the general idea.

My battered copy of the book is signed by some of the people involved with *Doctor Who* that I have met over the years: Terrance Dicks (writer/script editor), Malcolm Hulke (writer),[34] Tom Baker (the Doctor!), Louise Jameson (Leela), Mat Irvine (visual effects designer),[35] Innes Lloyd (producer) and Dennis Spooner (writer/script editor).[36] Not a bad selection! We shall meet some of these people again as we move forward!

The detail about 'The Sea Devils' is especially pertinent, as I loved reading the real-life information as to how a story was made. How the story breakdown became a script, how it was then filmed on location and in studio, what everyone did! Especially as this was the story that introduced me to *Doctor Who* in colour!

That fascination for how the show is made has stayed with me my whole life, and in many respects is what has driven me to do as much as I have related to the show. I love seeing how things are made, how props, costumes and monsters are created, designed, built and performed. Being on a film or television set is heaven to me. And being able to meet, discuss and write about all the various and different aspects of how a television production gets to transmission is endlessly fascinating, and is why so many shows and films produce 'making of' extras now, because behind-the-scenes footage is interesting to most people.

And, for me, this interest all started here with this book. That tiny spark into a young mind, which resulted in an explosion of curiosity and creativity which would last a lifetime, and possibly shape my future as a non-fiction writer and historian of the show.

* * *

34 Terrance Dicks and Malcolm Hulke signed my book when I first met them during 1977.

35 I obtained these three signatures at the very first *Doctor Who* convention in August 1977.

36 I've no idea where I met Innes, but I met and interviewed Dennis several times.

The tenth anniversary of the show came in 1973, not that I knew or realised that at the time. The stories were a good batch, with various new (and returning) monsters to add to the series' pantheon. We had Omega, an insane Time Lord who had created their power source, but they abandoned him and now he was back for revenge using a number of rather neat orange blob guard things called Gell-Guards; then we had the Drashigs,[37] omnivorous snake-like creatures; there was a war in space in the future between the noble reptile-creatures, the Draconians, and Earth, but the war has been promulgated by the Master using the Ogrons again... and where there are Ogrons, there are of course Daleks; so we visit a planet where they are massing for war, including some invisible ones, and the Doctor has to try to save everyone! Finally, we're back on Earth and some trouble in Wales as giant maggots are roaming the countryside, and a mad computer is hell-bent on taking over! All in a season's work for the Doctor.

At the end of the season, Jo Grant left, and I was sad to see her go as I had liked her as a companion, and the dynamic between Katy Manning and Jon Pertwee had worked so well. Jon used to describe his Doctor as the 'protector' with a cloak that he could wrap around his companion to keep her safe. A little like a mother duck, keeping her ducklings safe beneath her wings. This is a good analogy, and works in relation to his Doctor and Jo. Dynamic and strong, wise and also compassionate.

But before and during all this, there was something happening in Central London at the Science Museum that I was very keen that Mum and Dad take me to.

I think I had visited the London museums before. I suspect my parents were trying to keep me educated as widely as they could by exposing me to various elements of culture. We always used to go to Wimbledon Theatre to see the annual pantomime there, which

37   An anagram of 'dishrags', apparently.

I really enjoyed. And Mum also used to drag me kicking and screaming to see ballet on stage, which I found incomprehensible. Though it does mean that I know what the music for 'The Dance of the Sugar Plum Fairy' by Tchaikovsky from *The Nutcracker* sounds like, so it was educational even if I didn't think so at the time! Mum and Dad also had many LP records, and one of my favourites was Holst's *The Planets* and also Grieg's 'In the Hall of the Mountain King' from *Peer Gynt*, both of which conjured up images of aliens, spaceships, monsters, trolls and demons... stirring stuff. Perhaps this is why I grew up most often preferring instrumental music to songs with actual singing on.

Anyway, I digress. From 7 December 1972 until 10 June 1973, the BBC's special effects department was running an exhibition at the Science Museum... and there were Daleks there! So of course, I had to go!

I remember queuing to go in with Mum, and standing there just wondering what might be inside. Monsters from the show... Daleks... spiders... what manner of terrifying things was I letting myself in for. I remember I could hear Dalek voices as we got closer. It was terribly exciting, but in a scary way... in a way that you had to bottle up your courage and overcome it, as the only other option was not to go in, and then, of course, you would never know what you had missed.

So I *had* to go in... I *had* to!

Inside were a series of areas in which various BBC effects, sets and props were displayed and explained, to show how they had made the magic happen. There was a full size 'Old Mill' set from something or other, which showed (I think) how they could fake everything, from spider webs to rats and dust, bags of milled flour and bags of wheat, and creaking and thunderstorms and whatever, and that when on TV you wouldn't be able to tell that it was a set. It was quite scary, I recall, but fascinating.

There was also a small display showing how they had achieved

49

an effect for *Doctor Who*! And to my puzzlement, I had no idea which story it was from. Of course, I remembered most of them from the last few years, but this one eluded me.

It's only with hindsight that I can see why. It was from 'The Daemons' and showed how a tunnel through a heat barrier had been created with a piece of plastic, some Christmas tinsel and some Vaseline! Of course – I had missed seeing a couple of episodes of that story and so had not seen the effect in action! No wonder I was puzzled.

Through the TARDIS exterior and into a further area, and we finally had the TARDIS console and a display of *Doctor Who* monsters, including the Daleks. There was Alpha Centauri and an Axon, a Sea Devil, a Draconian, an Ogron and a couple of Daleks! There might have been a Cyberman as well. Amazing to see these costumes in real life, even if they were behind barriers and glass in little settings of their own. I could have stayed in that area all day!

I came out of there in awe. What an experience to actually see some of the creations from *Doctor Who* up close. In the gift shop,[38] Mum got me a small metal 'TARDIS Commander' badge which I still own. It's one of the earliest items from the show which I kept.

And this is important, as I am, as well as a writer, a collector, and I started collecting *Doctor Who* items simply by stopping throwing things away and keeping them safe instead. The earliest items I have are a small plastic silver Dalek with a ball bearing in the base,[39] the copy of *The Making of Doctor Who*, and this Science Museum exhibition badge. My little plastic Dalek was damaged by my younger brother Alan at some point, and to try to mend it before I found out, he used a plastic glue that you might make plastic model kits of airplanes with. The glue, however, melted the plastic

---

38 There's always a gift shop.

39 These were originally released in 1965 by Louis Marx and were called Dalek Rolykins, so called because the ball bearing allowed them to 'roll' over a flat surface.

of the toy, so my little sixties Dalek is now more of a slumped and fused lump of plastic. It's still recognisable as a Dalek, though. Over the coming years more and more would start to be added to my collection, as my desire to find out more about the show grew ever greater.

The cover for the *Radio Times Doctor Who* 10th Anniversary Special, published in December 1973 which contained the plans to build your own Dalek.

4

Building a Dalek!

The next revelation came just before Christmas 1973.

Along with the Christmas edition of the *Radio Times*, there was a second magazine available in the newsagents, and this was simply called *Doctor Who*.

Published officially on 11 December 1973,[40] this special magazine had the dynamic Doctor, Jon Pertwee, on the front, running across an alien rocky landscape and looking back over his shoulder. Turning to the back cover revealed that he was being chased by a Sea Devil, a Cyberman and a Dalek!

There was a corner flash on the cover which read: 'The 10th year of BBC1's great adventure series. Inside: the stars, full background, how to build your own Dalek and a chilling new Dalek story by Terry Nation.' The excitement levels were through the roof.

This was a *Radio Times* special magazine, issued to celebrate ten years of *Doctor Who*. Inside was information about the show, its stars and even, for the very first time ever, a complete listing of every story, with story titles and little photographs! Amazing stuff.

As with the previous year's *The Making of Doctor Who*, which provided

---

40   But probably, and most likely, available in the shops a couple of weeks before this.

a taster of the riches that the show had delivered, this added to the available information, and even gave a small insight into what those stories had featured. I still had little idea as to what the stories had been actually like, but seeing pictures of early Cybermen, of a robot from 'The Celestial Toyroom',[41] or the White Robots from 'The Mind Robber' was incredible.

A word on the story titles that they used in the magazine. As mentioned, at this time there was no available list of all the story titles, and at the BBC, they also didn't have anything much to go on. Also, back in the Hartnell days, each *episode* had a title, and there was no overall story title on screen. This has caused years and years of discussion and dissent among fans as to just what the overall story titles might have been. There has been some consensus over the years, but there are still variants flying around depending on how you choose to decide. Anyway, for this special magazine, whoever compiled the list did so by simply taking the title of the first episode from each story... and only a few of them actually matched the overall story titles,[42] but this is far later knowledge. At this point in time, for all anyone knew, these were the story titles.

What the magazine did was open the eyes of the readers to what had gone before. Ironically, even as the *Radio Times* was celebrating the rich history of the show, the BBC was actually wiping it from their archives! But that's a whole other story.[43]

Alongside the listings were little interviews with people who

---

41   Not the actual story title. Keep reading!

42   Those that do are 'Planet of Giants', 'The Web Planet', 'The Space Museum' and 'Mission to the Unknown'. The very first story is here called 'An Unearthly Child', which some have taken as being the actual story title as well as the title of the first episode. My research over the years, however, has informed me that this story was actually called '100,000 BC', but others are free to differ and to use whatever titles they want.

43   The story of how the BBC 'lost' their episodes of *Doctor Who* and then spent years trying to find them again is told in an excellent book called *Wiped!* by Richard Molesworth.

had been on the show, but then the magazine brought things right up to date with a large photo of someone we didn't know. Elisabeth Sladen was her name, and she was the new companion who would be appearing in the new season of stories which started on the 15 December! So, I certainly hadn't seen her yet. Moreover, there was a list of the stories which comprised the new season. And my young eyes were taken at the descriptions! Dinosaurs! Daleks! Another Peladon story! And finally, something which had me more wary: 'Planet of the Spiders'. I didn't like spiders at all, so I was concerned this adventure might be too much for me.

This sort of advance information can be fairly commonplace these days, with the internet watching everything that's happening, and the BBC's PR machine set up to release information as and when it seems appropriate. But back then, literally the first you knew about a story was when the *Radio Times* was published for its first episode. So, this was major stuff and added to the interest – building the hype – for the next episode!

Moving forward through the magazine, next came a piece on Terry Nation, the creator of the Daleks, followed by a short story which told of their fictional creation. An interesting piece and one which has since been contradicted on television. But nevertheless, this was the man who created the Daleks bringing us a story of how it all started. Fascinating to read and for me, this was the first I had heard about the origins of the Daleks![44] Something I didn't realise I wanted to know until I read the story! Superb!

Finally in the magazine there was a section called simply 'How to Build a Dalek', and this fired my imagination to the maximum!

---

44   There had also been an origin story in the Dalek comic strips in *TV Century 21* between 1965 and 1967, but I never saw those comics at the time. That also conflicted with the story in the *Radio Times* special, as well as with the 'Genesis of the Daleks' TV story. The Daleks have more origins than I've had hot dinners!

There was a broken-down image of a Dalek, a photograph of some schoolkids in London who had 'tested' the designs, along with the Dalek they created, and then a list of all the materials you would need, and a suggestion that it might cost you £15! And the rest!! There is no way, even in 1974, that you could build this Dalek for just £15!

There then followed pages of diagrams and measurements, so it seemed that you really could literally build your own Dalek.

Given that the instructions called for making moulds from clay and then using plaster of Paris and fibreglass to create the dome, not to mention that the exterminator arm needed access to welding equipment, I seriously doubt whether any enthusiastic young builder would have the ability to do such things! I know I certainly didn't. Even the tools needed to work sheets of clear Perspex, or even to find 24 polystyrene balls, was out of reach.

So, I decided to do what possibly most kids did, and that was, over the summer holidays, to give it a go and to see how I could get around all the bits I didn't or couldn't get hold of. As mentioned, it helped that my dad had a shed full of bits and pieces and, more importantly, tools!

As it happened, the summer of 1974 was a reasonably good one. The days were long and warm, and there was no (or minimal) rain. I remember leaving the part-made Dalek outside in the garden overnight, and it being fine the next day. Of course, this was two years prior to the legendary summer of 1976, when it was so hot and long that we ended up with water rationing and hose pipe bans. But that was the future. The present was getting a Dalek built.

I did this with the help of a childhood friend named David Butterworth. David lived a bit away from me but went to the same school, and as you do, we became friends and hung out together. He was interested in, and introduced me to, the fantastic music of John Barry, so he had excellent taste, and was also interested in modelmaking and filmmaking, and indeed Dalek building!

To make the Dalek, we had to first find the materials, and as mentioned, the thought of moulds and fibreglass and whatever was ridiculous. So, we started with what we could do, and that was the woodwork elements of the base and shoulders.

To make the frame, we found a couple of large, discarded sections of plywood in a skip down by the local river. One large piece was actually in the river, and we hauled it out. I think they had been used for a hoarding or some such, so we hefted them out of the skip and brought them home. That gave us the pieces for the top and bottom of the base, and the top and bottom of the middle section, and also the struts which held them together.

More harvested plywood allowed us to make the panels all around the base. These things were all glued and nailed together to make them firm, and the results were not all that bad!

For the cladding of the chest section the instructions suggested a sheet of plywood, but we could not find one thin enough to bend around. So, we managed to snag some sheets of aluminium which could be cut to the right shape and used them instead. This gave us the basic shapes for the base and middle sections. The neck was again created from sheets of ply, and a mesh used around it all. It was starting to look pretty good.

Casters were added on the bottom to allow it to roll around, and then all the fiddly bits of decoration around the chest unit. Some hollow tubes for the plunger and gun arm, and some make-do metal rod things for the gun, as, strangely, we didn't have any welding equipment to hand.

The two areas of concern were the head, and the balls for the base. There was a warehouse shop place called Transatlantic Plastics[45] in Surbiton, but trips there didn't turn up anything usable. I managed to find two wooden balls for the arms from a shipbuilder on the Thames at Kingston. But they were expensive! And there was no

45 A shop I used to look at sideways, just in case there were animated shop dummies or killer chairs lurking behind its doors.

way I could afford 24 more of them to make the domes for the base, even if I had the means to cut them all in half! Just not possible.

So, I was stuck on the base. Then one day, my dad said that at his work – he was still a printer in London for the *Daily Express* – they delivered the 'raw' newsprint paper for printing onto on these enormous reels. They were then loaded into the printers. Well, these huge reels had a plastic cap on each end of the central core (I assume this was a thick cardboard tube of some sort), and the caps might work as makeshift 'balls' on the Dalek.

So, he brought one home to see if it might work. It was pretty much the right size and shape, except that it was not domed. It was flattened. But yes, this could work.

My dad procured 48 of these caps from his work and brought them home for me.

I decided to try to give each of them a dome by using *papier mâché*, so with Mum's help we made buckets of this gloopy flour and water and paper mixture, and I slopped it and shaped it into sort-of domes for the little plastic caps. And again, it sort of worked. Forty-eight domes later, and I had something that I could stick to the base.

This still gave us the problem of the head of the Dalek. What on earth could be done about that?

Well, one of my relatives – it might have been Mum, or an auntie, or even the next-door neighbour – had an old ball vacuum cleaner. Long before the days of Dyson, there was an almost circular cleaner on four wheels, which split in the middle to remove the bag, and which had the hose attached to the top half. Research today tells me that it was most likely called a Hoover Constellation, which was available around 1974, and if you look that up, don't you just 'see' the dome of a Dalek there?

We somehow managed to get hold of an old and broken one of these. Removed the top part, cut a slot for the eyestalk, and jury rigged it onto another circle of that old faithful plywood to create the swivelling head for the Dalek.

The instructions from the magazine were long forgotten by this time. We were in unknown territory, just looking and thinking how to make it work, and whether it more or less looked like a Dalek.

The magazine showed a complex arrangement of plywood and screws and slots and ball bearings to make the head turn around, but we just made it up ourselves and got the thing working.

The 'eye' part of the eyestalk was another issue... again suppos- edly made from another of those blasted wooden balls that were mostly unobtainable, but hugely expensive when they could be found. But a solution presented itself when my dad had the need to replace the flush system from our toilet. I realised that the plastic ball-cock float on the flush system looked a bit like a Dalek eye... and so that's what it became.

When we had fully assembled our Dalek, it looked pretty good, and with a coat of paint, it looked even better. Because silver paint was again hard and expensive to get hold of, and it showed every little imperfection in the build, I decided I wanted my Dalek predominantly black. So black it was. However, the domed head was red already, and I reasoned that there was no real point in painting it, so initially that stayed red, and I found an orange/red paint in the garage[46] which I used to paint the balls and the slats around the chest area. I thought it looked magnificent. At some point I painted the dome the same colour as the slats and balls, as I thought it would look better if it all matched.

The seat inside was covered with an old piece of carpet underlay, and the top and bottom sections were held together with bolts.

I think our respective parents were impressed as well. The Dalek made various visits to each of our homes, with us pushing it along the pavements and roads between.

46 I remember that the paint took forever to dry. I have no idea why. Maybe it was getting too old to use!

The first casualties of this were the casters, which were small ones made for lightweight furniture on smooth floors. We needed much bigger and chunkier casters if we were going to use this thing on pavements and roads, so somehow I managed to find four large metal wheels – I have a feeling they might have come off a shopping trolley or something – and screwed them to the base instead. This also meant that we needed a deeper 'base' for the Dalek to cover them up. Even something like that posed challenges, as with no money, trying to think what might be a good material, how then to cut and shape it, and how to attach it were tricky problems to overcome. But we managed it!

Achievement unlocked.

While all this was going on during 1974, I was also starting to get into 8mm films. I mentioned that my dad had an 8mm cine film camera from even before I was born, and he took reels and reels of cine film of all sorts of things. Weddings, my christening, events, holidays… the films still exist, and they are a treasure trove of family memories. We even have film from 1967 of the oil from the Torrey Canyon supertanker washed up on the beaches of Newquay. The oil was thick and brown (not black) and covered the sand and rocks and sea life. It really was an ecological disaster![47]

So, we have films of my Dalek patrolling the streets of Tolworth, and our driveways and back gardens… you can see how unstable and rocky the pavements and paths were.

From the films of the Dalek just wandering aimlessly about, we progressed to actual stories, where a character we came up with called 'the Android' (basically myself or David in a papier mâché mask and marigold gloves) who appeared to try to defeat the Dalek. We even had rudimentary special effects, where a ray and a force field could appear by simply filming through a sheet of clear plastic

47 The Torrey Canyon struck Pollard's Rock, on the extreme western end of the Seven Stones between the Cornish mainland and the Isles of Scilly, on 18 March 1967.

which had those elements drawn on... obviously seeing the way that the effect from 'The Daemons' had been achieved had stayed with me, and I remembered that you could do this.

At some point, I also realised that you could make a 'ray' from the Dalek gun by simply scratching the actual film in the right place, on every frame you wanted it... and this gave a lovely crackling effect when shown. Almost as though the Dalek was really shooting lightning from its gun. The trick was studying each frame of the film and then carefully scratching in just the right place each time. Somewhat painstaking but quite inventive.

* * *

For a Doctor Who fan, the 1974 season was when it all changed. Again. The season which was heralded by the Radio Times special, and which was transmitted through June of 1974, was the last for Jon Pertwee as the Doctor.

There was nothing in that special magazine about this, of course, and so when the end of 'Planet of the Spiders' arrived,[48] it was something of a shock. Jon Pertwee arrived back at UNIT HQ in the TARDIS after going missing for ages, and collapsed on the floor. Lovely Sarah Jane (who we had all grown to love over the course of the season) knelt over him, as he told her not to cry. He then closed his eyes and through the magic of television, and in front of the eyes of Sarah and the Brigadier, transformed into the likeness of Tom Baker.

I feel this was incredibly significant. While the Doctor had changed appearance twice before, the first time had been in 1966 – some eight years previous. And I certainly didn't remember that.

---

48   I was fine with the spiders in it. They were very large but, even to my childhood view, not real. I had clearly grasped the difference and knew that what we saw in Doctor Who was an effect, a fake, made up. Even the giant spider at the end didn't bother me. I wouldn't like to find one on my bedroom wall, though!

The second time was at the end of 'The War Games', but here you didn't actually see him change. And this is the key thing. I may well have watched that (though, as I say, I don't remember seeing it) but even if I had, they just talked about what was happening. You didn't *see* it. So here we have the first proper *bona-fide* transformation. In full colour. It was amazing, as well as slightly concerning, and I was wondering what the new Doctor was going to be like. Would I enjoy watching the show? Of course, I needn't have worried... but at the time all these thoughts rush through your mind, as they still do whenever there is a new Doctor. It's amusing to look back and see people complaining in the *Radio Times* letters pages, or in old newspaper reviews as to how a new Doctor has been accepted or, most often, not. The change of Doctor is something that has *always* seen diverse reactions from the viewing public... and the same thing continues to this day. Humans, as a race, just don't seem to like change.

* * *

At the end of 1974, on 28 December, the new series of *Doctor Who* started. I remember the first episode of the first story, 'Robot', for two reasons. The first was that it was a new story with a new Doctor, but the *Radio Times* did not give this event a front cover. They had done covers for each of the Pertwee seasons (even if the one for the 1974 season was a cover where he was with Michael Parkinson and some other people). And they had done the *Radio Times* special... but no cover for the new Doctor. This was probably simply because the start date fell within the *Radio Times* double issue for Christmas and New Year. Just a case of bad timing. That Christmas edition of the *Radio Times* actually featured actor Michael Crawford as Frank Spencer on the cover, as the comedy show *Some Mothers Do 'Ave 'Em* was incredibly popular at the time and there was a new Christmas special showing on Christmas Day.

The second reason that I remember the episode is because my

grandfather Bobby died that day. I recall that I was left in the house with my brother Alan, while Mum and Dad had to go and help my nan as he had passed. It's a very sad reason to remember an episode of *Doctor Who*, but then life is not always full of happy things. This was a very difficult time for me, as I didn't really know my grandfather that well and he wasn't in our lives very much. Even so, I did experience an odd sense of loss at the passing a close family member for the first time. We were faced with death. This wasn't fiction or a character in a TV show, it was real life. I got through the emotions this stirred up by taking my mind off it and thinking about my favourite show instead that day. This was certainly one of the things *Doctor Who* has given me over the years: a sense of distraction and escape for unhappy moments.

This first season of *Doctor Who* with Tom Baker was fantastic. Not only did we have the return of the Sontarans, who had first appeared the previous year, but also the Daleks were back. And this time we met their creator, Davros, an inspired creation: half-man, half-Dalek. This completely contradicted the story that had been in the *Radio Times* special. But never mind!

The second story, 'The Ark in Space', was the last *Doctor Who* story to give me nightmares. The fact that I can still remember them must mean they were a doozie. The story was about a parasitic insect-creature called a Wirrn, which laid its eggs in the power supply for a space station, and when the grubs hatched, they headed to the humans (who were on the space station in suspended anima-tion) to use them as food. However, once touched by a Wirrn grub, you basically got taken over and slowly transformed into the alien Wirrn adult. This was *Alien* years before *Alien*. I often wonder if director Ridley Scott, an ex-BBC designer himself, or Dan O'Bannon and Ronald Shusett, the writers of *Alien*, ever saw this story, and whether it rooted itself into their psyches as a result.

My nightmares were all about being turned into one of these creatures, and losing your humanity – which, to be fair, was really what the story was all about. My dreams morphed into being shut into an Ice Warrior suit and being turned into one of those creatures too… very strange and very scary.

At this point, I was getting more and more into the show. Exponentially, almost.

In my collection, I still have the cuttings from the *Radio Times* for 'The Monster of Peladon' and 'Planet of the Spiders' at the end of Jon Pertwee's years, so I had started to clip them from the issues and keep them. Furthermore, I started to actually record the audio from episodes of *Doctor Who* as they were transmitted from around 'The Sontaran Experiment'. The idea didn't occur to me sooner, which is why I didn't start from 'Robot'. I think I wasn't sure if I'd like the new Doctor, since I was so used to Pertwee at that point.

What this does mean, though, is that I have on tape the announcer at the end of the 'Genesis of the Daleks' story saying that the next story was called 'Revenge of the Cybermen'. As mentioned, back then you had no idea what the stories in a season were, and the first you knew was when the *Radio Times* came out, so this comparatively early information that the Cybermen were back was amazing. I don't think I could have wanted that week to go past faster.

Because I was recording the episodes, I realised that I could copy some of the Dalek voices from 'Genesis of the Daleks', and dub them to cassette to use in my homemade Dalek. So, this is what I did. By this time, I had my own little cassette recorder. Well, I say 'little', not by today's standards. Probably the size of a thick hardback book, this had those lever switches which you pressed with a satisfying click, and the tape was held above. So, the process of dubbing things over was to plug some handy BNC leads[49] into the output from Dad's amplifier, and then into the AUX IN sockets on the recorder and then recording. Worked like a charm.

Once the season of *Doctor Who* was over, there was then the long

---

49   Red for Left channel, White for Right channel! Or vice versa, of course. It didn't matter!

wait to the next season, but there were other things to keep me busy.

During 1975, I was again on holiday down in Newquay, and again there was a day where I wandered into the W H Smith's there, idly scanning the book racks for anything which might be of interest. And my eyes fell upon the words *Doctor Who*. There on the shelf. Right in front of me.

I looked more closely, and yes, it was a *Doctor Who* book. The title was *Doctor Who and the Curse of Peladon*, and there on the cover was an amazing piece of art which showed the Doctor in the familiar form of Jon Pertwee, my favourite one-eyed alien Alpha Centauri, towering at the top was the furry Aggedor beast which was part of the story, and an Ice Warrior.

Oh. My. Goodness.

The book had just been published, so I grabbed it off the shelf and raced to buy it; 30p changed hands, and that was my reading for the holiday sorted out.

I spoke about this story before, one of my favourites from the 1972 season, but now I could relive it all over again. This was superb!

I realised quickly that there were others in the series, as they were listed in the book I had bought... so the next day it was back to W H Smith's to see what else they had.

They didn't have any of the others, but knowing that they were out there was enough and soon I had all that had been published to that date. Perhaps this was the real start of my collecting of all things *Doctor Who*, because it was important to me that I obtained every one of these books!

I fell in love with the covers. Those amazing covers with art by someone who seemed to be called Achilleos, their name written in tiny letters on the artwork. The colours, the compositions, and the monsters all called to me. I was in heaven.

In the back of the books there was a page which talked about

'The Target Book Club', so of course I sent off and joined. This was a revelation. I actually received post through the mail, and the envelopes contained lists of forthcoming books, colour promotional sheets, and the occasional advance *Doctor Who* book cover. Everything that I was interested in.

The Target Book Club was run by someone called Sandy Lessiter, but I never managed to find out if this was a real person or just a name that the publisher used to make it seem more personal. Whichever, it worked, and these Book Club updates were a source of great enjoyment to me.

I remember that the book after *Doctor Who and the Curse of Peladon* was *Doctor Who and the Cybermen*. And I was so excited by this – a Cyberman adventure that I didn't remember and knew next to nothing about. But the one after that, the cover changed. This was for *Doctor Who and the Giant Robot*. I remember we were down in Cornwall again, and I saw the book in W H Smith's and was so disappointed that the cover had different art to the other ones. But I bought it anyway. And the next. And the next. In fact, I kept buying them whenever I saw them.

Another thing that was interesting me at this time was making films of my own, because I was inspired by those I saw.

I had seen some films on television, including some of Ray Harryhausen's amazing stop-motion work, and this made me want to figure out how he did it. My dad explained how the camera worked: that it took a sequence of single pictures, and that when you put them all together, it appeared to the viewer as continuous action and movement.

By this time, Dad had got a Super-8mm camera. Basically, the same as 8mm but a slightly larger frame size and so the images were better quality. Having made a fair few films with my Dalek, and also realising that you could scratch the film to create a ray effect, I further realised that 'animation' was made by taking a single frame of film at a time, and if you changed the position of whatever was in the frame each time, it would appear to move by itself when you played the film at proper speed.

I started experimenting with making little animated films myself. The camera had a 'one frame at a time' setting, and I used some of my toys and models: there were two plastic, very basic humanoid figures; one of the Zeroid toys[50] that I loved; and I made a little Dalek out of Milliput and painted it black and red like my full-sized one and used that. Another sequence used the backdrops and the cardboard TARDIS that were given away with Weetabix breakfast cereals.[51] There was a little Milliput Cyberman, no doubt inspired by their return in 'Revenge of the Cybermen', and my little Dalek Rolykin. Looking back at them today, they're a bit fuzzy but not bad at all!

Another thing that happened this year was the kick-starting of my love of horror films. Not really the subject of this book, but I'll mention it because it is relevant to who I am.

Published on 27 April 1973, Denis Gifford's *A Pictorial History of Horror Movies* was a seminal work. So many critics and fans of horror have this amazing book on their bookshelves. I must have seen it and grabbed it, maybe a Christmas or birthday present, and I paged through it so many times, wondering at the amazing stills, and reading the short descriptions of the films. As a result of this interest, I later joined the Gothique Film Society, and attended several meetings up in London, enjoying seeing films at them as well, films which were otherwise unavailable to see anywhere. Again, I remind readers that this was pre-VHS or any other way that a film could be seen.[52]

50 The Zeroids were a range of robot toys made by the Ideal Toy Company from 1967. There were initially three of them available: Zerak (the blue one, and the one I had); Zobor (bronze); and Zintar (silver).
51 These backdrops and the TARDIS, as well as a selection of different card figures inside the boxes, were available on Weetabix boxes during a promotion from April–June 1975.
52 The only other way was to buy 8mm/Super 8mm film trailers and cut down versions of films that could be shown at home.

Luckily, television was on hand to save the day, and from Saturday, 2 August 1975, BBC2 started showing what would become their legendary horror double-bills. This initial season kicked off with *The Cabinet of Dr Caligari* and *Quatermass 2*, and then continued each week with films old and new, from *This Island Earth* to *Barbarella*, and taking in several that I had never heard of as well. It was amazing stuff.

The late-night season of horror double-bills was so popular that BBC2 repeated the format each year through to 1981, and then missed a year before 1983 was the last. Finally, we were able to watch these amazing old films that we had only read about in books.

The films led to other merchandise, and I got hold of all the Aurora Monster Model kits, which I dutifully built. They came in square boxes with glow-in-the-dark parts, but they looked better painted without them, so I tended not to use those elements. I remember building and painting them and being so pleased with my kits of Dracula, Frankenstein,[53] the Wolf Man, the Mummy and the Forgotten Prisoner of Castel Mare.[54]

With all this activity kicking off, my love of *Doctor Who* continued unabated, but, really, 1976 would be when things really started to change for me, as I discovered organised fandom – and the rest, as they say, is history.

There was one more important happening in 1975, and this was the birth of my brother Robert. When Mum told me that I was going to have another brother, my response was 'Don't want one!' as I stormed off in a teenage tantrum. But there was nothing I

---

53 Or rather his Monster!

54 Of course, I had no idea from which film the Forgotten Prisoner originated – it was a ragged skeleton chained to a dungeon wall – and years later I discovered that it was not from any film, but was based on a story from an American horror comic magazine. Whatever its origin, it was a cool model that they released in the range. I don't know why it's 'Castel' rather than 'Castle', though.

could do, and in October he arrived in the world. Not knowing whether he would be a boy or a girl, we'd christened him 'Davros' before he was born after the creator of the Daleks. But he turned out to be a great brother and not at all a megalomaniac half-Dalek.

Terrance Dicks speaking at an event I organised on March 28 1978.

5

A First Brush with Fandom

It's all the fault of the postman.

As 1975 became 1976, my passion for all things *Doctor Who* continued unabated. This was joined with a passion for horror, and as I had taken a local paper round in order to earn a little pocket money, I had some funds to spend on copies of Dez Skinn's awesome magazine *House of Hammer*, and before that *Monster Mag*.[55] The local newsagents also sometimes had in strange American magazines which I had previously never heard of, like *Famous Monsters of Filmland* and *The Monster Times*, and so I picked up a few random issues of those as well.

But the main turning point for me came as I started to become aware that most days my parents got some mail through the letterbox, and there was never anything for me!

Most probably the mail that arrived was either bills or junk mail, but my mum and dad were getting letters and I never got anything!

The closest I got was the irregular mailings from the Target Book Club, and I had a French penfriend, Laurence,[56] while at secondary

55   *Monster Mag* was brilliant. Basically a single folded sheet of paper with large movie-still posters on one side, and articles and horror photographs on the other. A superb idea!
56   Pronounced the French way – she was a girl.

71

school: one of those things in French lessons where I guess a school in France swapped details with a school in the UK and they got the students to write to each other. Anyway, I would get occasional letters from this girl, and I would write back, and one summer I even took a trip out to Nevers, where she lived, to stay with her and her family for a week. It should have been great, but right before I arrived she got a boyfriend who had a motorbike, and I barely saw her. Instead, I was forced to stay with the family and to try to get by on my appalling pidgin French. My French teacher at school was called Mr Verrier,[57] and he was astonished that I was actually going to France, as I spent most of the French lessons sitting in the corridor outside as I messed about too much. Yes, I was going through those terrible teen years!

My main take away from this trip to France was that all you ever had to say or reply to anything was ça va! It seemed to be a generic expression that meant, 'I'm fine', or 'indeed', or 'yes', or 'it's okay', or anything really. It could also be a question, or an answer, so it really was a multi-use expression. So, I spent the week saying 'ça va' in response to everything, and getting by through pointing at stuff if I wanted it… or just sitting and watching and absorbing. The night of my arrival, I was told, was an annual cheese festival where people threw cheese at each other and saw how much they could eat. I didn't believe a word of it myself. I thought they were having me on. Or I was just not understanding what they were telling me!

But I digress.

Inspiration hit me like a bolt from the blue. In order to get something through the post, you had to write letters out, or order things first.

And so, I started to write letters.

A couple of my better animated films I sent in to Blue Peter.[58] I got

---

57   I have no idea why I remember this!

58   Blue Peter is, and was, a very popular kids' magazine show which was on the BBC at about 4.40 pm on two weekday nights a week. It covered everything from hobbies to adventuring to pets, and the presenters were

a lovely letter back from Crispin Evans from the show, saying they were very impressed but they weren't going to feature them. He sent me a prized *Blue Peter* badge and a signed photo of the presenting team.

And, of course, I wrote to the *Doctor Who* production office asking something about what was coming up next season, and got back a small sheaf of papers with information about *Doctor Who*, how to knit the Doctor's scarf... all sorts of stuff like that. And one of the sheets contained the address for something called the *Doctor Who* Appreciation Society.

At around the same time, one of those horror magazines that I was getting, a great publication called *World of Horror*, contained an advert for a *Doctor Who* fan magazine called TARDIS...[59] but I never ordered it at that time.[60]

And also, at around the same time, one of the national newspapers had run a piece which detailed all the Doctor's companions – by now I was looking through the newspapers, eager to see if there was any *Doctor Who* coverage in them, and clipping the pieces out if there were.

In a later day's edition, they printed a letter from someone called J Jeremy Bentham, who was correcting their list of companions and explaining that they had missed some. The letter also included an address for the *Doctor Who* Appreciation Society.

It was almost as though the world in 1976 was tilting and prodding me towards this Society.

heroes! Of course, they changed presenters every so often, so different people know different teams, but *my* presenters were Lesley Judd (though I also remember Valerie Singleton, who left in 1972), John Noakes and Peter Purves. And this was long before I even knew that Peter had also appeared in *Doctor Who* as one of the companions! I've since met Peter and he's an amazing man, full of stories and good humour. It's always a thrill to get a birthday message from him on the social medias.

59 When it first started, *TARDIS* magazine was not affiliated with the *Doctor Who* Appreciation Society, that association came later on.

60 *World of Horror* also used to contain a colour feature each issue on some aspect of *Doctor Who*! Another reason to get every issue.

I sent off my application to join the Society along with my postal order[61] for 60p, or however much it was, then settled back and waited.

Thus it was that, in December 1976, I received my first membership pack, a copy of the Society's newsletter, called *Celestial Toyroom* (or CT for short),[62] and some other bumph.

My fate was sealed!

*   *   *

That year, 1977, was a great year to be a *Doctor Who* fan. We had an amazing series of stories on television over the end of 1976 to the start of 1977. The BBC in their wisdom had decided to shift *Doctor Who* from being a show which started just after Christmas each year, to instead be an autumn show starting around September. This pattern commenced in 1975, and continued for a fair few years.

My love of the show was continuing, and during the 1976/77 season, as well as recording every episode on reel-to-reel audio tape, and then dubbing it to cassette tape so I could listen to them back in my bedroom, I also started taking photographs off the television.

This was far more complicated than it sounds! I had a Minolta camera (I think I had been given it as a birthday present or something) and it was SLR. Which stands for single-lens reflex camera, a type of camera that uses a mirror and prism system to allow the photographer to see what the lens is capturing, which was handy when you were peering through the viewfinder to line it all up to take photos off the television.

However, the camera had a shutter which moved horizontally across the image, and at that time a television picture was made up

---

61 In those days you never sent actual money through the post. Instead, there was a thing called a postal order. Basically, you went to the post office, gave them the cash, they gave you a receipt, you sent the receipt, and then the receiver could take it into their post office and change it back into cash! Brilliant!

62 This was issue five, November/December 1976.

of a small dot which moved very, very fast across the screen to create lines, and the lines created the image we saw. So, if your shutter speed was faster than the dot, you didn't get a picture at all, you just got part of a picture depending on how far the dot had proceeded.[63]

To get a decent photograph, you needed to use a slower shutter speed. But then this meant that any movement in the image on the television screen came out as a blur... so you had to just try to take the photographs off live television at exactly the right moment.

Added to this was the complication that, of course, you could not see the results immediately. You had to finish a roll of film, and then send it off in the post for it to be developed (or take it down to a local chemists). And this took a week or so, which meant you didn't know about the camera speed element until the first roll of film came back and nothing came out on the prints. So, you had to figure out what the problem was and try again the next week! All this, of course, without the help of the internet or Wikipedia... all I had was a knowledgeable dad!

The first story I ended up with anything usable from was 'The Robots of Death' (Jan/Feb 1977)... and from that point onwards I was crouched in front of the television every Saturday evening, taking photographs of any nice images I saw on the screen. I still have all the photos I took, and some are really not bad at all. You wouldn't know they were taken off the television they are so sharp. There was a knack to it, and you had to learn through trial and error how to do it.

At the start of 1977, we had another addition to the family as my sister Caroline was born. It's always amused me that she was

---

63   British television used to be on a 405 line system back in the sixties, but over the course of 1968 and 1969 they changed to use 625 lines, which gave a better quality image. It's more complex than this, though, as in order to prevent flickering, there were two passes at creating the complete image, each pass creating alternate lines...

born the day before part four of a story called 'The Face of Evil'...
I wonder if my parents planned that![64]

As 1977 progressed, and now a member of the *Doctor Who*
Appreciation Society, I made contact with J Jeremy Bentham who ran
the Society's reference department, and he had available what he called
'Synopses' of all the past stories, and 'Story Information Sheets' or
STINFOs, detailed story breakdowns of some of them. So, I started
to buy these. The Synopses were basically the information that the
Radio Times had printed, along with a few facts and figures and a couple
of black-and-white photographs, all photocopied onto a couple of
sheets of paper. But these were fascinating. To someone who only had
the *Radio Times* cuttings from the very end of Jon Pertwee's era on the
show, they were a great insight into who had been in the stories, the
titles, transmission dates and times, and so on.

Of more interest to me were the STINFOs, as these contained
the actual detail of what the stories were. The first one I sent off
for was from the Patrick Troughton story 'The Invasion', the one
with the Cybermen in the sewers that I still remembered watching.
I waited with anticipation until that came to me through the post,
and I was able to read, in a fair amount of detail, what had happened
in that eight-part story. It was amazing. I, of course, identified the
sequence I remembered, but there was so much more besides.

It wasn't long before I was sending off for more of these releases,
to find out more and more about both the stories I faintly remembered, and the ones which I had no clue at all about.

I think I must have made contact with the President of the DWAS
at that time as well, a gentleman by the name of Jan Vincent-Rudzki,
who was kind enough to answer questions and so on... and also
they were planning a fan gathering later in the year... and that
was of great interest to me as well.

So, at some point in 1977, I got a call on the phone.

64 I jest, of course. She is totally fabulous and I will fight anyone who says
    otherwise!

Now, this never happened to me. Only Mum or Dad got calls on the phone. I was 15 or 16 years old by now, and just doing my O Levels[65] and planning to move to another school to do my A levels. And my social life was pretty much all taken up with *Doctor Who* and horror film stuff.

But I got a call, and it was a chap called Paul Simpson, and he said he was also a fan of *Doctor Who*, that he had got my number[66] and decided to call me. So, we had a chat and we met, and Paul was smashing. He was a little younger than me but loved the same things that I liked, and we got on well.

This friendship is still going strong today! Paul moved into literary areas and ended up being a key copy editor on the BBC's official ranges of *Doctor Who* books, as well as an advisor on other ranges.

Paul was a great influence on me, and he was far more gregarious than I was. I'm pretty sure that one day he called me up and said he was going to see one of the *Doctor Who* writers, and would I like to come along?

Of course I would!

So, Paul and I set out one day – I'm assuming it must have been a Saturday, or else during the school holidays, and we took the train up to London, and then another train to Hampstead, where we got off and headed off to find a certain address. There was an imposing and large Hampstead house, and we knocked on the door.

This was the first time I met Terrance Dicks.

Terrance was a legend even then. He had been a television writer for years and years, and had worked on everything from *Crossroads* to *The Avengers*, before he joined the BBC as an assistant story editor on *Doctor Who* in 1968, trailing to take over the role in 1970, and working on writing, uncredited, several of the late sixties episodes, before finishing off the Troughton years by co-writing 'The War Games'.

---

65   I didn't do very well at them. I'm not a great academic.
66   I asked Paul while writing this book how we first met, and he recalls he got my number from Jan Vincent-Rudzki, and he just called me up!

In the seventies, he had been script editor of the show for the whole of Jon Pertwee's tenure, and then he wrote stories for Tom Baker, including his debut, 'Robot'. He had kicked off the Target Books range of novelisations that I had been collecting, and was still involved in writing them.

At the time we visited him, he was working on something for the show. Of course, he couldn't tell us much about it, but he was the friendliest man. Especially to two teenagers who went to see him out of the blue![67]

I remember he had a large room in the middle floors of the house, and this was given over to his library. And what a library! He had books of all persuasions on shelves and in piles on the floor. I think he said they were awaiting filing. He had copies, too, of all his own books, including all the Doctor Who books he had been writing for the Target range, and even some foreign editions of said books, which I had never heard of. Terrance had started writing other books for Target as well – the process of doing the Doctor Who titles had opened a new career for him, and he was becoming a prolific and much-admired children's author, with books like a series on the Mounties, and, later, T R Bear – a sort of Paddingtonesque series of books for young readers – not to mention other science fiction novels and all sorts of stuff.

Seeing my eyes open wide at the sight of the foreign Doctor Who novels, which were called Doktor Kim and Douter Who and others, he actually asked me if I would like one of them. I couldn't speak for a moment, but managed to say that, yes, I would, very much. So he picked up a copy of Dr Who: Kampf um die Erde[68] and signed it to me.

Well, I was in heaven.

When I got home, I started to try to find out more about these

---

67 Paul had already visited Terrance previously, and recalls that it was in fact Terrance who put him on to Jan Vincent-Rudzki in the first place.

68 A German edition of Doctor Who and the Dalek Invasion of Earth (literally, Doctor Who: Battle for Earth) published in 1977 by Schneider-Buch.

foreign editions of the *Doctor Who* Target books,[69] and over the years have managed to find copies of all that are known about. Thus adding to my collection.

Paul and I spent a great afternoon with Terrance, having some tea and chatting. At one point, Terrance asked if we were going to see his friend Mac, and we replied, no we weren't. I think we were both slightly puzzled as to who 'Mac' was. But Terrance explained that this was Malcolm Hulke, another writer who Terrance had worked with on *Doctor Who*. And, as it happened, Malcolm lived the next street along from Terrance.

I think we'd run out of time on that occasion, but there were a great many other visits that we both made to see Terrance, both together and on our own, and it was probably the next time we headed up that Paul had made arrangements to go and see Mac as well.

Malcolm Hulke was, like Terrance, a lovely chap. One of a generation of writers who were both humble but happy to talk about everything that they had done.

When we visited Mac, I remember the door to the house opened onto a hallway, and up one side of the hallway was a set of stairs. Probably a standard arrangement for those large Hampstead houses. At the top of the stairs was a large cupboard. And on the door of the cupboard was a poster of Marvel Comics' *The Incredible Hulk*. And Mac (or someone) had added the letter 'E' to the end of 'HULK' on this poster. It always amused me.

The cupboard, it turned out, contained copies of all Mac's scripts for television and whatever else, as well as copies of some of his books. And this again included his *Doctor Who* titles. I mentioned that I had a copy of *The Making of Doctor Who* that I had bought back in 1972, and which was somewhat used and battered. Well, I had brought that with me to see Terrance and Mac, and so got them to both sign it. In the cupboard, Mac had a dozen or so mint and

69   Not easy to do, pre-internet!

pristine copies of that very book. I was quite jealous and sometimes wondered what happened to them. A nice, read, battered and much-loved book is a great thing... but to have a mint copy! Now that's the collector in me speaking!

I liked Mac immediately. He was disarmingly nice and friendly, and whenever we came to visit, he would always have gone out of his way to make sure he had some cake or posh biscuits to go with a cup of tea. He referred to Paul and me as his 'Doctor Who boys'.

These visits with Terrance and Mac continued for some time... Paul and I enjoyed going to see them, and as time went by, Terrance would let slip little things about what he was doing and what he was writing. We never told anyone else what we were told, though, as that would have been breaking a confidence.

One time, Mac told me that he was organising a writers' weekend down in Bognor Regis in September 1978, and knowing that I had an interest in writing, wondered if I would like to come down and help with the event. I was a little apprehensive, but checked with my mum and dad and they were fine about it. So, I travelled down to Bognor to find the hotel everyone was at, and had the best time at this writers' weekend. It was certainly the start of something bigger for me.

Among those attending were: Lord Ted Willis (creator of several TV series including *Dixon of Dock Green*, *Virgin of the Secret Service*, *The Adventures of Black Beauty*, *Sergeant Cork* and *Mrs Thursday*) was one of the co-organisers; John Hawkesworth (writer and producer of five series of *Upstairs Downstairs*, and *Sherlock Holmes* at Granada); Richard Imison (script editor for BBC Radio Drama from 1963 to 1991); John D Vincent (a historian); and Fay Weldon (a massively successful author, essayist and playwright). Quite the line-up!

I recall handing out cups of tea to a roomful of people, and clearing the cups away at the end! I was making myself useful! I do have some regrets that I didn't get to talk more to some of those iconic writers, but that was a lesson to learn in some ways: I had to get more confidence in order to be able to approach people, which I did later on.

On another of my visits to Mac, we were talking about his *Doctor Who* scripts, and I was recording the interview this time. I had brought along a small recorder, and, as with Terrance, was recording the interviews so I could use them in my own fanzine... this was the tail end of 1977, I think. I'm upset that I cannot find the recording with Mac, and I wish I still had it. I have an early tape with Terrance, and recordings of many of the other *Doctor Who* people I interviewed over the years, but I'm sad I don't have the one of Mac.

Anyway, we were talking about his first script for *Doctor Who*, an adventure called 'The Faceless Ones' that he wrote with another writer friend called David Ellis. At one point he stood up and said, 'Hold on,' and headed over to the cabinet at the top of the stairs. He rummaged for a little, and then came back with the actual rehearsal script for the story.

I think this was the first time that I had seen a genuine *Doctor Who* script, and I was amazed. It was foolscap in size,[70] and the loose pages were pinned together with a split-pin in the top left corner. I discovered later that this was how all the *Doctor Who* scripts were produced by the production office to give out to the various people who needed them. I recall these were on a creamy white paper.

We looked through that a little. Episode two was missing, but I didn't care, and he asked me if I would like to borrow it! Again, I was astonished, and of course said 'yes'. So, I left his house with, to me, the holy grail in my bag with the tape recorder.

When I got home, I looked through this amazing artefact, astonished that it even still existed. I wanted to copy it so badly, but in

70 Foolscap, or folio, was an old standard format in the UK before we changed to A4. It was 8 × 13 in (203 × 330 mm). There is a somewhat mind-blowing Wiki page about A4 and paper sizes if you care to look: en. wikipedia.org/wiki/Paper_size.

1977, photocopiers were very much only just coming into existence, and those that did exist were very expensive. Each sheet was 6p for a copy. So 'The Faceless Ones' was six 25-minute episodes, and each episode in script form was about 30 to 40 pages long. So that's around £150 to photocopy the whole thing. I certainly didn't have anything approaching that much money.

To the rescue came Auntie Dorothy! An amazing woman, elder sister of my Nana – the sort of lady that historians should write books about. Indefatigable, kind, generous, just amazing. Anyway, she was round at our house or something and saw my distress, asking what the problem was. I explained that I had this script, and I would really like a copy of it, but it was too much money to do that. So, she asked if I would like her to copy it for me.

She was a typist and worked somewhere that typed up copy from other documents, and she would be happy to do me an exact copy of the script. She took the original away, and a few weeks later delivered it back with another copy that she had typed out for me in her spare time!

I was ecstatic. And will always remember my Auntie Doll[71] who did that for me when she didn't have to!

I liked Mac a lot, and him trusting some kid with one of his scripts speaks volumes about him. As well as wanting to try to give me an opportunity of some sort with his writer friends in a creative environment. These were much more innocent times than now. I feel very privileged to have been able to go to both Terrance's and Mac's homes, and be so welcomed. This couldn't happen in today's world, as writers have to be far more careful of their own

---

71 There's another story about Auntie Doll. When my sister, Caroline, and my youngest brother, Robert, were very young, they were quite taken with the story of the Three Billy Goats Gruff, who trip trap trip trapped over the bridge. And what was it that lived under the bridge? The Ugly Troll! But they used the same name for Auntie Doll... Who's coming over for dinner? Ugly Troll! So, this became a very funny name check for Auntie Doll which has persisted in the family through the years!

reputations and letting someone in, even with the best of intentions, can open you up to all sorts of problems.

Mac died from cancer on 6 July 1979, aged just 54, and it was a great shock to me when I found out. He was the first person that I had known well who had died, and I didn't know how to process it. I never knew he had cancer, I never knew he was even ill. He just didn't talk about those things. I still think his sudden passing was a terrible loss to the writing world and to *Doctor Who*. Today all people seem to be interested in was that he was apparently a Communist and on a 'watch list' with the UK Government, but back then there was no inkling of his political beliefs on show. He was quietly spoken, kind and generous to his '*Doctor Who* Boys', with not a hint of anything else. All I knew was that he had written some of the best *Doctor Who* stories, as well as co-authoring my favourite book about the show at that time, *The Making of Doctor Who*.

At that time (I know this jumps forward a little) I was far more involved in the *Doctor Who* Appreciation Society, and had got to know the people who organised it well. When Jan (the president) heard that Mac had died, he reached out to me, and asked if I fancied going out to the pictures with him and his friend Steven Payne. I agreed, as I was moping a bit. We went to see the film *Saturday Night Fever*, and it was okay... until we got to the scene where Bobby (played by Barry Miller) decides to commit suicide on the bridge. This brought the whole death thing back into sharp focus for me, and I'm not ashamed to say that I cried in the cinema. It's funny, in a way, how silly things like a scene in a film can bring real-life events flooding back to you. But it was also, I think, something of a closure for me... only having experienced death in my life before with my grandfather, who had been distant and someone I barely knew, I hadn't been affected as hard as I was by Mac's death. And seeing that it was something that others had to face and deal with helped.

I've always been grateful to Jan and Steve for that little kindness in trying to take me out of my brooding about it.

83

THE SURBITON

DOCTOR WHO

36p

No 1

SOCIETY FANZINE

PHOTOSPOT

The first issue of my first fanzine.

6

Early Fanzines and Interviews

During 1977, as well as Paul, I made contact with a few other *Doctor Who* fans in my local area. We had a little society of our own going. There was me, of course, and Paul, and also Gavin French – who was also interested in making films and even got into the newspapers in 1980 with the making of a *Doctor Who* script called 'The Thosian Strategy' – and a chap called Owen Tudor, all of whom lived within a short car or bike ride away. Julian Vince, an excellent cartoonist and model maker, lived in Raynes Park, which was a little farther away, and there was Vaughn Hancock,[72] whose parents lived at and were the caretakers of a place called Surbiton Lagoon, in Berrylands.

The Lagoon was a very popular destination in the early seventies summer months for us kids. It was basically an open-air swimming pool complex, with changing rooms, a restaurant, fountains, diving boards, a slide... the lot! The local populace would head there when it was hot to sunbathe, swim, play in the pools, have lunch... just a great communal outdoor place. It first opened in May 1934, and provided facilities for everyone from then until it closed in 1980.

---

72 My mum remembers that Vaughn could talk backwards. Literally speaking the words as if they were written backwards. It was a rare talent!

The fact that Vaughn lived at the Lagoon gave me an idea that maybe we could do a small get-together in the restaurant building there. Around 1977, I had started having small gatherings at my house, where we would watch my 8mm films and generally talk about anything and everything. Mum would make us all some tea and then everyone would go home... a nice way to spend the summer months when *Doctor Who* wasn't on the telly.

At around this time, everything starts to meld together in my mind into one great big *Doctor Who*-related experience. There are so many things that we did that it's hard to work out one from another.

Another person who came along to our gatherings was Steve Cambden. Steve was a great model maker, and had built these incredible recreations of K9 and some *Doctor Who* monsters out of cardboard. A few years later, Steve actually got to work on *Doctor Who* as Assistant K9 Operator! A job that most of us could only dream of! So, the idea for a larger event was certainly percolating in my mind.

In the end, we did have several larger meetings at the Lagoon, probably in 1978/79. Terrance Dicks came to the first one as a special guest, and we had displays of Julian's and Steve Cambden's amazing models, talks, a slideshow with soundtrack... it was great fun!

The idea of doing my own fanzine was also percolating.

The DWAS newsletter, CT, often had mentions of fanzines that were available, little typed adverts asking you to send a postal order for 10p or whatever and a stamped, self-addressed envelope to such and such address, and then by return you received back the 'zine. Often as not very poorly photocopied, or occasionally literally written in ballpoint pen by hand.

Fanzines were not a new phenomenon, they had been around for years and years in the wider science fiction arena, and, of course, there were also fanzines in support of football clubs, or even the punk rock scene, which also started around 1977 with the Sex Pistols coming on the scene and making a nonsense of it all.

I was often disappointed with these fanzines when I received them, and thought there had to be a better way of doing them. The main problem was the reproduction. Photocopying didn't exist in 1976, and in 1977 it was only just starting to happen. But I felt sure I could do better.

The way that many fanzines (including *TARDIS* and *CT*) were produced was using a Gestetner or Roneo duplicator. Many schools and colleges had these, and indeed, the BBC used the same machines for the production of their scripts. You typed (or crudely drew!) onto paper stencils, and then put the stencil onto a drum where ink was forced through it onto the paper. By turning the drum, you could duplicate the stencil onto as many sheets as you wanted. You could do double-sided (just put the paper in again the other way up) and then collate all the sheets manually, add staples wherever you wanted, and you had a fanzine!

What this meant was that you couldn't reproduce photographs or press cuttings or anything which couldn't be cut onto one of these stencil sheets. Even headings and lettering had to be done by hand using plastic stencils, and typing onto the sheet also worked.

Down the road from where I lived was a printing shop of some sort – I never quite understood what it was that they did – but in their office they had an early photocopier. It did foolscap sheets on a shiny, almost heat reactive paper, and it could only do single-sided. But the quality was okay. Photographs could be copied and you could still see what the photo was meant to be of! Which was an enormous win and a step up from the old Gestetner method.

Gavin French and Owen Tudor each had their own Gestetner machine in their respective garages, and they decided to also do fanzines (I have no idea who got there first!). Owen's was called *Beka* (a Kaled word which means Armageddon),[73] and Gavin's was called *Colony in Space* (named, as most *Doctor Who* fanzines were, after

73 Owen is legendary for perhaps being the first person to discuss that the Doctor could be played by a woman within the hallowed pages of *Beka*!

a *Doctor Who* story, or some item or monster from the show). But as they were produced on the Gestetner, there were no photographs!

With the first official DWAS *Doctor Who* convention coming up in August 1977, I decided this would be the best time to launch my own fanzine.

So, I gathered content. I wanted to have some news about the forthcoming Target books, as I was getting that from the publishers via the Target Book Club anyway. I loved the monsters, so I decided to do a page on the Cybermen, with an image traced from a photograph of one of the creatures, and a piece on their first story, 'The Tenth Planet'. We also included part one of an interview with Terrance, which Paul had conducted and written up, and finally a wordsearch, and another piece about monsters, this time with a photograph of a Menoptra (a butterfly creature from the story 'The Web Planet'). This came to six sheets of foolscap paper, and so at 6p per sheet the first issue cost 36p to buy. I called it *The Surbiton Doctor Who Society Fanzine*, and on the front I put one of my first off-screen photographs from 'The Robots of Death'.

I launched the issue at the *Doctor Who* convention in August 1977, and it did well! So, September saw me release a second issue. I realised that the foolscap size was all very well, but at only six pages, it didn't seem great value for money. However, if I cut each foolscap sheet in half, I would have 12 pages... so that is what I did. I laid out the pages two to a sheet, and then cut them down. Again manually stapling the pages together to create a physically smaller fanzine, but which had twice the number of pages! After the first issue, I got it reproduced at Surbiton Library, where they had a photocopier. The main problem with it was that, as it was at the public library, it was often used, and no one ever seemed to bother to replace the toner when it ran out, thus the copies it produced were very variable in quality!

I continued producing it in this manner, month on month, until issue eight, released in May 1978, when I finally managed to get double-sided photocopying sorted at a proper copy shop, and thus of a better and more consistent quality. My friends seemed convinced that I used the copy shop, and did so many issues of my fanzine, because I fancied the slightly older girl named Tina who worked there... but I have no memory of her whatsoever! Maybe I did fancy her, but she's lost to me in the mists of time.

By this time, too, I had been advertising my 'zine in the DWAS newsletter, and was getting more and more orders in. From issue four, released in November/December 1977, I changed the name of the fanzine to Oracle, a name from Doctor Who, but one which, at the time, was from a story that had not been transmitted. Jeremy Bentham, he of the DWAS Reference Department, had suggested it to me, and the cover picture was another off-screen picture, but from 'The Face of Evil' and provided by Steven Payne.

And so, my little fanzine continued, and flourished. With orders coming in from the DWAS, and contributions from artists like Stephen Poole, we had a letters page, a story called 'The Well that Ate the World' which had apparently been submitted to the Doctor Who production office but never used, lots of Target news, and, of course, features on the various monsters.

I went to 16 pages, and with issue 11 (August 1978) started using a coloured card cover. I had funny cartoons from Julian Vince, more interview chats with Terrance, excellent fiction from Owen Tudor, and news reports and articles on all sorts of things.

In October 1978, the 'zine went to a folded A5 size as it was cheaper to produce and get the cover card for, and also the price went down to 30p for 12 pages! These were 12 A4 pages that the photocopying process could now reduce down to A5! A miracle! From Vol 2 Number 3 (December 1978) we went to 16 pages, and I was reproducing the script I had borrowed from Mac for 'The Faceless Ones' episode five. I interviewed incoming Doctor Who script editor Douglas Adams in Vol 2 Number 4 (January 1979)... the 'zine was really going from strength to strength, and moreover I was managing to keep it to a monthly schedule.

While I was doing my A levels, another friend, Chris Dunk, stepped in and edited it for me (from January 1979 to August 1979) and then I was back from the September 1979 issue onwards. In October 1979, I started the third, and what was to be the final volume of the fanzine. Events elsewhere were starting to overtake me, and it was becoming apparent that I would have to forego producing the 'zine.

However, producing it had taught me so much! From the early days when it was literally created by typing onto bits of paper, cutting pictures out from wherever I could find them and then sticking them all down on sheets of foolscap, up until I procured a proper electric typewriter, and technology had progressed such that there were proper copy shops springing up everywhere. Coloured papers and card could be used, photographs and book covers reproduced in much better quality, and when the ability to 'shrink' the pages came onto the photocopiers I could lay out pages at A4 size, and then photocopy-reduce them to A5 for the fanzine.

For the final issue, at the end of 1981, I really wanted a full colour cover. Some of the other fanzines that people had been producing for sale through the DWAS had colour covers, and I wanted one! However, the costs for such a thing were very high indeed. There were some early colour photocopiers around, but the copy shops didn't have them, and proper colour litho printing was way out of the budget. So, I improvised. I got a lovely colourful photograph of Louise Jameson as Leela from *Doctor Who*, and got prints made at a photographic shop. Then, printing the fanzine with a stiff shiny red cover, I literally glued the photograph onto the front of every issue. It worked a treat, and I had my full colour cover for the final issue!

* * *

Doing *Oracle* was an eye-opener to the worlds of organisation, of keeping mailing lists, sorting envelopes and postage, printing labels, and getting the fanzine sent out to people all over the UK. It also honed skills in writing and editing, in selecting items for the 'zine, commissioning artwork, and, of course, dealing with people in a way that didn't alienate everyone along the way. Compromise!

The other main thing it opened up was an outlet for my own interest in how *Doctor Who* was made. I was able to legitimately go and speak to people and interview them and get all the information first hand. But then, of course, I had to write it all up, edit it, type the interviews up, and finally lay them out with photographs so it looked nice.

Let me talk about some items of note from this period.

On Saturday, 26 May 1979, the Surbiton Eye Hospital held a local summer fete, as indeed did most schools and hospitals in those days. Myself, Owen, Julian, Gavin and some others were roped in to help with the day. I've no idea what we did, as we were totally transfixed by the fact that the fete had managed, somehow, to get hold of two actual BBC Daleks for the event! These were two of the Daleks which had last been seen in the story 'Day of the Daleks' back in 1972, and they were remarkable. We were swarming over them like flies, checking them out, even getting in them to drive them around during the fete. It was amazing and we were all like kids in a candy store! I had the Dalek that I had built there as well, and to be honest, I went to a large number of local events with that!

I remember another event at a pub in Berrylands, but the pub was at the top of a steep hill which led down to Berrylands railway station, and my Dalek was a complete hazard as it was near impossible to stop it rolling down the hill! In the end, at that event, I had to abandon the idea of being in it, as some kids at the event kept kicking it as well, and pushing it. I so wished I had an actual exterminator in it, or even a fire extinguisher linked to the gun. But I didn't.[74]

74   If ever the Daleks do invade the Earth, never mind stairs, they will soon be seen off by hordes of children kicking at them and trying to push them over.

At the Eye Hospital fete, when it was all over and everyone had gone home, we stayed on and basically used the two Daleks to take photographs. We had Davros races. I had my Super-8mm film camera with me, and we made a short film using the Daleks (said film has vanished into the ether now!). All in all, we had a whale of a time with these two genuine Daleks.

An interview with new *Doctor Who* script editor and writing legend Douglas Adams came about, I think, because we had met another fan named Kevin Davies at the DWAS convention. Kevin was from North London, and he was as enthusiastic about *Doctor Who* as we were. However, Kevin was also, like me, very interested in filmmaking and animation, and so we had a sort of a bond. Kevin has gone on to direct numerous items for DVD and broadcast release, and is a very talented director.

At that time, and still today, he was a great fan of Douglas Adams's cult radio series *The Hitchhiker's Guide to the Galaxy*,[75] and had met Douglas through that interest. Later, Kevin worked on animation and a few other elements of the BBC television series of the same name,[76] and is actually credited on each episode with various daft titles like 'Mouse Wrangler' and so on.

So, Kevin put us in touch for an interview, and at the time Douglas had literally just started working on *Doctor Who* as the new script editor. This was at the tail end of the 1978 season: he was starting properly in the job with the 1979 season.

I went with Owen Tudor in November 1978 to see him at the BBC, which was a thrill in itself, and we sat on the floor in one of the observation galleries above the studio where they were currently recording the last story of the 1978 series, 'The Armageddon Factor'.

The BBC studios at Television Centre in White City, London, were an impressive place. Vast miles of corridors which were designed

75   Transmitted weekly from 8 March 1978.
76   Transmitted from 5 January to 9 February 1981.

to get you as lost as possible, and then the large television studios where they made all the programmes. Looking down on the studio floor was an observation gallery, which was reached through an upper floor of the complex. There was a large soundproofed glass window through which you could see the tops of the lighting gantries and the lights, and then below them, the sets and studio floor. Of course, you couldn't see everything, as often the sets were hidden by their own walls, and it totally depended on which part of the studio they were recording in on a given day.

The gallery sometimes had some chairs in it, so visitors could sit down to watch what was happening, and it had a small television in it as well, which usually showed the feed from whichever camera was 'active' at a given point. Sometimes it showed the feed from a single camera whether it was 'active' or not – and that was less interesting. The television also had sound, so you could hear what was going on in the studio as well.

On this occasion, the television was on, and the sound too, but there were no chairs, so Owen, Douglas and I sat on the floor. There then followed a very happy hour or so while we interviewed Douglas, recorded it all on a tape recorder, while they went through some rehearsals on the studio floor down below. I remember endless scenes of one character wandering around calling 'Astra! Astra!'

Of course, we had no idea what the story was about, why this chap was calling out, or who or what 'Astra' might be.

Douglas chain-smoked through the entire interview. He lined up all his finished cigarette butts along the window ledge to the studio. But we got a lot of information, and again Owen took this all away and wrote it all up. We used some of the interview in *Oracle*, and a larger part in Owen's own fanzine, *Beka*.

This was the first time that I visited the actual studios to see *Doctor Who* being made!

Another memorable visit came in March 1979.

I think it was through a friend of Mum and Dad's, or perhaps a friend of Owen's, that they happened to discover that their father, or an uncle or someone, worked at Ealing Studios, and that they were going to be making some Doctor Who there. From my point of view, I was called up by someone called Jack Walker[77] on Sunday, 11 March, and asked if Owen and I would like to go up there one day and spend the day watching it all happen.

When I picked my jaw up off the ground, of course I agreed. What an amazing opportunity. This was, it turned out, the first day's filming for the season, and the story was 'The Creature from the Pit', which was actually transmitted third in line.

So, I was up early, and myself and Owen were picked up by this chap who worked there on his way in, and we found ourselves at Ealing Studios. Studio 3B to be precise, on 21 March 1979. They had meant to start on 20 March, but there had been industrial action due to a wrongful dismissal, and that day had to be postponed.

The stage had been transformed into a dense jungle. There were bushes, trees, leaves and plants everywhere. It was incredible. There was a huge backdrop of misty mountains and sky to give the impression of depth, and the branches were hung from the ceiling and in plant pots – none of which would be seen on screen. All that was missing was the sound of crickets or strange bird cries.

There was a large and deep tank in one area, used for 'the pit' of the title, and into which stuntman Terry Walsh would fall in place of Tom Baker. There were even a couple of desiccated skeletons hanging around the pit! Another area had part of a large, cracked egg-like shape – in fact a spaceship for the proverbial creature which was in the pit! And elsewhere was the TARDIS, standing tall and blue in among all the greenery.

Visual effects were being provided by designer Mat Irvine, who I had met at the first DWAS convention in 1977. He was friendly, but working, of course, and so couldn't really give us any time.

77   Unfortunately, I have no memory as to who 'Jack Walker' is!

For our part, we tried to stay out of the way and just absorb everything that was happening. I had been told that photography was banned, so I hadn't even brought my camera. I so wish today that I had ignored this dictum, and brought it to grab a few behind-the-scenes shots. But I was good and did as I had been told.

Mat was wrangling some large balls of green stuff, the wolfweeds in the story, and also a large green mattress-like creation, which was a part of the creature.

Filming seemed to go well. Christopher Barry was directing, and later we became good friends, and I often visited him in Oxfordshire with his wife Venice. They made an excellent chutney! But at this time Chris was, like Mat, hard at work on the first day of a complex shoot, and I don't think I really saw him all day!

The day included the filming of various sacrifices to the creature, and people being thrown down into the pit. Terry Walsh doubled for everyone! Lalla Ward only got to say one line: 'Doctor!' all day, and K9 was only brought out right at the end. There was dry ice pumped everywhere to give the 'forest' an atmosphere, and with the heat from the studio lights, and the people, and the tramping back and forth, it became more and more like a tropical jungle as the day progressed.

Poor Mat's wolfweeds refused to be operated by the radio-control systems, and no amount of tinkering could seem to get them working!

As a day watching the production of a *Doctor Who* story in the studio along with everyone else who was making it, this was an incredible experience. I guess that, as we weren't 'official' visitors in the sense that the visit had been arranged by the Production Office, we weren't introduced to Tom Baker or Lalla Ward, and while we saw Douglas Adams at a distance,[78] and producer Graham Williams, we never talked to them either.

---

78   Douglas was a very tall man, so hard to miss. Even in a jungle!

Most of the time was spent skulking around the back of the forest, and hoping desperately that we weren't in shot, causing a shadow or some greenery to move when it wasn't supposed to, and keeping as quiet as we could!

Once again, Owen did the writing honours on a piece which appeared in a special issue of *Oracle*, which came out on 18 August 1979. This was A4-sized and printed (apart from the cover and an internal page of photographs from a *Doctor Who* stage play, which were both photocopied) on Owen's trusty duplicator.

Another memorable interview was when we asked to speak with a BBC visual effects designer called Peter Logan. Logan had just finished working on the first story of the 1979 series, called 'Destiny of the Daleks', which as the title suggests was a Dalek adventure. Owen and I headed down to the BBC's Visual Effects Department in Acton on Wednesday, 27 June 1979, where we met Peter, interviewed him all about the story for *Oracle*, and spent the afternoon just wandering around the workshop and taking photographs!

Peter was a mine of information, and as I had a fascination for 'how it was done' I think he was pleased to explain to me how they had done the landing and take-off of the Movellan ship for that story. It was a complex effect as the saucer-like ship was shaped like a diamond, and when it landed, the base revolved to burrow into the ground, leaving just the top part exposed on the surface. From all this, and also using storyboards and design sketches, we were able to assemble a 'script to screen' for *Oracle*, again written up by Owen, which appeared in the October 1979 issue, just after the story was transmitted.

We also saw the original *Liberator* spaceship from *Blake's 7* in the effects workshop, along with many Daleks and Dalek parts which were all in the process of being refurbished or stored or whatever. It was an amazing visit! There was even the original Davros mask from 'Genesis of the Daleks' in 1975 sitting on a desk – they were trying to keep it and revive it for Davros in this story, even though this time he was being played by a different actor.[79]

On Saturday, 2 September 1979, there was another fete, this time at Molesey Hospital, and they had managed to get a special guest along to open the fete for them. This was none other than actress Mary Tamm, who hadn't actually appeared in *Doctor Who* yet, but was due to make her debut that very evening in the first episode of 'The Ribos Operation'.

Mary was there with her husband, Marcus Ringrose, and after she had done her duties, Owen and I asked if we might interview her. She graciously agreed, and so we spent an hour or so sitting with her in a corridor of the hospital asking her questions. This was somewhat tricky, as, of course, neither of us had the slightest clue what the stories were about or what her character was, but we got a good and insightful chat with her which Owen then wrote up for *Oracle*.

We also had a stall at that fete, and I have some photos. I can see Owen, and Chris Dunk and Steve Cambden and Julian… all the usual friends.

Another interview from this period, and one which was very significant for me, was with the artist Christos Achilleos.

I was talking about the *Doctor Who* paperbacks that I was collecting, and my love for those early covers. This led me to joining the Target Book Club, and getting advance information and covers for the books. I managed to build up a nice collection of these cover proofs, but even today I have a few very early ones missing.

I had first visited W H Allen's offices with Paul on one of our early visits to see Terrance, so I had a connection there, and I capitalised on this and made sure I returned every so often. One time in 1977, I headed up to their address in London. Once there, I was always in heaven. Books — and *Doctor Who* books — everywhere,

---

79   Michael Wisher had played him in 'Genesis of the Daleks', and David Gooderson took the role for 'Destiny of the Daleks'.

and people, editors, publicists… all sorts of people making the magic happen. Experiences like visiting a publisher's office just lift the lid on the mystique that these companies tend to have when you're young.

So, I was there, in the offices, and they gave me a pile of forthcoming cover proofs for the books. I was looking through these when one of the ladies came over with a book and gave it to me, saying, 'Would you like one of these as well? They just came in.'

It was a copy of the forthcoming novelisation for 'The Talons of Weng-Chiang'.[80] Wow. To actually have in my hands a copy of a book that no one else had yet. That wasn't yet published and in the shops. How incredible was that! I was so grateful to them, and they seemed to like me, so I tended to go back every so often to see them, to pick up advance copies of covers and books and whatever they had that they would let me take!

I remember another time I was there and I knew they had all their cover proofs in a filing cabinet, so I asked if I might have a look as I was missing a few, and if they had lots of anything, might I have one of the spare copies. They agreed, and so I raided their filing cabinet for anything that I didn't have at that point. There wasn't quite everything I needed there – hence the gaps in my collection – but it did a good job of more or less bringing me up to date.

I had realised by this time that you could find people fairly easily by simply looking in the telephone book! I remember asking Terrance about this, as Paul had originally found him in the London telephone books, copies of which were available in most libraries, but the houses in and around London used to get copies as well. Terrance explained that the reason he kept his details visible in there, rather than going ex-directory, was simply that someone might want to contact him to offer him a job. Which is, of course, very true! Terrance was nothing if not practical!

80   Actually published on 15 November 1977.

So, when I was planning my final edition of *Oracle* during 1981,[81] I wondered if I could find this Achilleos person. I realise now that of course I could have simply asked the people at the publishers for his details, but for some reason that never occurred to me. So instead, I headed for the London phone books, and there was an Achilleos listed. How many Achilleoses can there be, I reasoned, so I phoned the number and spoke to Chris for the first time.

A child of Greek immigrants, Christos Achilleos had come to the UK early and found his feet as an artist. He was working for an agency, and doing work for W H Allen for the *Doctor Who* books, as well as many other pieces of art.

We hit it off immediately and I arranged to go up and see him at his home and studio in North London. We had a wonderful day (2 May 1981) talking about his work and his art. He showed me several of the original pieces he had: paintings of a loaf of bread sliced to look like money, and numerous fantasy pieces of dragons and girls. But also many of his *Doctor Who* pieces of art, and at that time he still had all the original art.

I was very taken with the *Doctor Who* art. The vibrancy of the colours, and the design and composition, as well as the accuracy of the images. As I was by this time working, I had some disposable money, and so I asked Chris if he might be willing to sell me any of his pieces. Chris had been treated quite badly by the BBC and by the publishers in the past: using his work without permission, credit or payment, and a couple of pieces of original art had 'gone missing' as well... so he was wary. But I think he liked me, and so agreed to sell me some of the originals.

I was in heaven, and figured out what I could afford and what I wanted. We made the deal, and I later went up to see him again and took the pieces away with me. I still own most of the paintings that I bought at that time. A couple I sold on to collector friends

---

81   It was published in December 1981.

who were after some examples of Chris's work, but the majority are still with me, and still very much loved. I have loaned some to exhibitions over the years to try to share my love and appreciation of Chris's work with others.

I took photographs of some of the original art to use to illustrate the interview (there was no scanning or any other way to get copies) and wrote the piece up for the fanzine.

Chris and I stayed in touch and were friends for many years. The last time I had a chat with him was when I was writing a piece[82] about some of his other early covers: for Kung-Fu[83] and Western[84] books, which also had the same sort of vibe to them as the Doctor Who covers, and which also featured the lead character in black and white against a coloured backdrop painting.

In 1983, I was doing a special publication for the DWAS about the 20th anniversary Doctor Who story 'The Five Doctors'. I wanted to do this as a behind-the-scenes 'making-of', following my love of the background information about the show. When I approached the production office about it, John Nathan-Turner, the producer at the time, declined to give me any access or help at all. Despite this being done for the official fan club, and despite that he met regularly with others from the Society at the time (but not with me). I suspected I was being sabotaged!

So, I had to basically go it alone! And always one for a challenge, I did just that. I spoke to Terrance, who was writing the story, and the visual effects guy, John Brace, and the composer, Peter Howell, among others. Jan helped with interviews too, some of which we had to do after transmission as, due to Nathan-Turner's dictum, they wouldn't speak to us beforehand, and we also were able to include a review, and photographs from off-screen and from people

---

82 The article can be found here: howeswho.blogspot.com/2021/12/design-classics.html

83 A series called King Kung-Fu by Marshall Macao.

84 A series spinning off Sergio Leone's film A Fistful of Dollars.

who were on location watching parts of it being made and snapping away all the time with their cameras... it came together as a pretty good celebration and look at the development of the story, despite the lack of any official help.

For the cover, there was really only one thing that I wanted. I wanted Chris Achilleos to create a new painting! So, I approached Chris and asked... explained the want... and in order to make sure we had enough money to pay Chris for such an undertaking, I also decided that for the cover I would print the colour cover with no titles on it, and then add the title to the front with a foil overlay. This meant we could print more copies of the cover, and then use some of the unfolded covers as posters, which Chris could sign and number as a limited edition. This made the commissioning of the original art achievable, and so Chris did that for me. I helped him with photographs of the things he wanted to include, and he came up with an incredible painting, very large, which featured all five Doctors, plus monsters, for the cover of the magazine.

I'm still very proud of that publication, one of the best I did for the DWAS. And the poster, too, went well, and we didn't lose any money on the overall item. Which was always a worry when dealing with fanzines and DWAS publications back in the day.

Chris died suddenly in 2021. I have on my phone to this day the last voice message he sent me – asking me to ring him back about something – and the day I heard he had died from a heart attack[85] was sad indeed. I knew that I would never again answer the phone to his distinctive Greek-tinged English, and his wry and subtle sense of humour. Chris was an incredible talent, and humble too. A truly excellent fellow. I miss him.

85   6 December 2021.

The cover for the booklet given to attendees of the very first *Doctor Who*
convention in August 1977. The art is by Stuart Glazebrook.

7

DWAS Days

I mentioned that I had to stop my own fanzine. Well, this was in part because, at the end of 1979, I had started working at Lloyds Bank in London as a computer programmer... but also because of events unfolding with the DWAS, the official fan club.

From 1977 onwards, I was an eager customer of pretty much everything the DWAS published. The quality was great, the art was superb, and for a *Doctor Who*-obsessed youngster, it was amazing. I especially loved the items that Jeremy Bentham was doing for the Reference Department, and as time went on, I started to offer to help compile some of these things as well. Jeremy was always open to people helping, and so I started writing some of the detailed synopses myself, with the aid of the off-air recordings that I had made myself.

There came a time when Jeremy asked if I would tackle something older, but of course I had no recording of that. But Jeremy did!

It transpired that I was quite late to the fold in starting to record the stories onto audio, and some people had been doing it since pretty much the very start. I was astonished, and so I started to collect all these old audios from wherever I could find them.

In those days, audios – and later videos – were like gold dust.

There was a black-market trade in them amongst fans, and unless you were in the right 'circles' with the right 'contacts' you just couldn't get hold of anything! Unfortunately, despite all my *Doctor Who* friends, I was never in the right 'circles', and so I tended to get things only when others found out I didn't already have them and took pity on me.

So, I started to help Jeremy with these Reference Department publications... and I got to know Jan Vincent-Rudzki, the President of DWAS, Steven Payne who ran the Photographic Department, Keith Barnfather who had edited CT in the early days and who had organised the first convention in 1977... all these people became friends through our shared love of *Doctor Who*.

What came along, and was to some extent the thing that upset the applecart, was *Doctor Who Weekly*.

Created by Dez Skinn for Marvel Comics in 1979, *Doctor Who Weekly* was a weekly (later monthly) publication which presented a comic strip, with a few associated features on the show, interviews, story details and photographs. All wrapped in some nice colour covers.

Because it was obvious to Skinn that he needed some expert help, he reached out to the DWAS (probably put in touch by the *Doctor Who* production office) and Jeremy was there, willing and able. Jeremy started consulting on the magazine and bringing in various friends to write the bits and pieces for each issue.

What happened was that in one issue, Jeremy mistakenly used a photograph which Jan had previously given to Jeremy on the understanding that it would go no further. Jeremy had forgotten this, and it was published. Jan was understandably upset, and so as a result, Jeremy left the Society.

From my point of view at the time, I knew none of this, and Jeremy got in touch with me one day and asked if I'd like to take over the running of the Reference Department. Of course I was up for it! So, around the start of 1980, aged 18, I was now part of the DWAS organising committee!

Shortly thereafter, Jan and Steve decided that they no longer wanted to be involved, and Keith had handed over the convention-organising duties to someone else, so he wasn't involved... so there was something of a crisis at the top!

I still lived with my parents at this time[86] and they had a large dining room, so at some point I, along with some other friends who were involved in DWAS stuff as helpers, all got together in a sort of 'summit' meeting and agreed how the DWAS was going to carry on. None of us wanted it to just stop because Jan and Steve were stepping down, and we all knew that it was a valuable thing and we didn't want to throw it all away.

At that point a new committee was formed, and we all went away with our roles and plans and aspirations!

Obviously, running the Reference Department was going to take time, and I just couldn't carry on running my own fanzine as well, so something had to give.

I really enjoyed doing stuff for the DWAS. I decided to revamp and continue with the two main releases, producing loose-leaf card story sheets for each new story as it was transmitted, and also came up with a new publication which I called *Plotlines*, to contain detailed synopses of older stories, but each season of *Doctor Who* collected together. I did the first release on the seventh season (Jon Pertwee's first) from 1970 as one A4-sized magazine, but the work to bring it all together was immense. So, subsequently, I opted for a

---

86   I had met my first wife, Rosemary, through the *Doctor Who* meetings that
     we organised. I think our first 'date' might have been a visit to the BBC
     Radiophonic Workshop in Maida Vale, where we met sound experts Dick
     Mills and Peter Howell, and were shown how the music and sound effects
     were done. This trip was organised by another of the DWAS committee,
     Mark Sinclair, who ran the Drama Department and who was making fan
     films and other dramas.

loose-leaf format so that individual stories could be released when they were ready, rather than waiting for everything in a given season to be ready.

I pulled on the talents of a lot of the better fanzine editors and writers to help me, and also expanded a little with special publications like the aforementioned *The Making of the Five Doctors*, and publications for the conventions and yearbooks, posters, a special A5 fanzine for when Tom Baker left as the Doctor, and loads more besides.

My whole philosophy for the publications was to add value and to try to provide a service. To this end, I ran them in the same way as I had run my fanzine *Oracle*. All the finance was held in a separate bank account, and I never took money from anywhere else. Everything had to be self-funding. So, I would take orders for a special publication, or the synopses, or whatever, then use that money to pay for the printing (and the labels, envelopes and postage). This way I could never run out of money, and, assuming there was a little bit of cash left over each time (which there was, as I was careful and circumspect), then that could be put towards colour printing on a special, or on something we wanted to give away as a promotion.

David Saunders, the coordinator on the DWAS committee, didn't seem to like the fact that I was profitable and independent in what the Reference Department did. He wanted all the DWAS money to be in one place, and that I would have to come and pitch what I wanted to do and ask for the money to do it from him – he wanted to control what I was doing. And I didn't like this at all. Especially as the production of CT was draining the money that the DWAS had (which came from memberships), and I could see that the Reference Department and my efforts would be propping that up, rather than the editor of CT managing their costs so it fitted within what was available. I felt that Saunders was looking in the wrong place for the problem (or maybe he saw a simple solution)!

I ran the Reference Department, hopefully successfully, for many years, eventually stepping down towards the end of the eighties. An unsettling blow for me was a suggestion from Saunders, who had been blocking and picking at me all along, that I shouldn't receive any credit for what I did for the Society. Publications should just be credited as 'DWAS Publications' without my name attached. I found this ridiculous. I was the one putting all the effort and time (and indeed money, as I never took anything for expenses for petrol or trains to travel to DWAS meetings, or for the raw materials to create the publications: pens, paper, typewriter ribbons, white correction fluid, cow gum, and all the other tools of the trade) so why shouldn't I be credited for my efforts?

In the end, I think the rest of the DWAS organising committee also became fed up with this person's over-politicking of the fan club, and what had started as a fun hobby was becoming a chore. Meetings were overlong, with Saunders constantly wanting to go back over old decisions because he didn't agree with them. Ultimately, he walked away during one meeting in 1985 and resigned… we simply appointed someone else to do what he had been doing and carried on. The moral of this story being: no one is irreplaceable.

Once they had gone, we had a new team in place for a while, and things were fun once more. But all good things have to come to an end, and I was eventually starting to get restless and wanted to do something for myself once more, after nearly a decade of working for the DWAS.

It was time for a change.

* * *

Apart from the issues of dealing with people who were constantly trying to score points off you and to get others around them who agreed with them (thus meaning that in any vote they would always win!), my time helping the DWAS was a lot of fun. I met a lot of lovely people, many of whom are still friends to this day.

The DWAS was also hugely influential and important in the establishment of organised *Doctor Who* fandom in the UK. Before the DWAS there really was not very much: just a handful of fanzines and mentions in other science fiction and general television fanzines. The main 'thrust' of more organised *Doctor Who* fandom came from a William Hartnell (Doctor Who) Fan Club in the sixties, which morphed into a more general *Doctor Who* club when Troughton took over the role. And then a different *Doctor Who* Fan Club in the seventies, when Jon Pertwee was playing the Doctor. In each case, the *Doctor Who* Production Office at the BBC saw a benefit in there being a semi-official club – they could point some of the letter writers and queries there for information and thus save themselves some work! So, Jan and Steve having the idea to start a *Doctor Who* Society, first at the college they attended, Westfield College in London, and then to change that to be a national society and to join up with the remnants of the Pertwee-era Club was inspired.

One particularly good idea was to hold the first ever *Doctor Who* convention in London, and the man behind this venture was Keith Barnfather.

I first met Keith in the lead-up to the convention. He lived in Clapham Junction in London, and the venue was the Broomwood Road Church Hall, just down from where he lived. I remember going to a meeting at someone's house – it might have been Keith's or it might have been Jan's – to discuss the event, and I just sat there and was quiet the whole time. In early 1977, I was 15, and everyone else was a bit older than me, so I was just interested in what was going on.

In the end the event was amazing. Compared with what we have today, the massive ComicCons and events all over the world, it was very small-scale indeed: there were 200 people came along. The church hall was set up with seating facing the stage, and on the stage there was a Dalek and a TARDIS (both supplied by Mark Sinclair), plus posters on the walls of the Doctors. There was a lovely photographic display of pictures from the whole history of Doctor Who, many of which I had never seen before, and also a display of props from the show, which effects designer Mat Irvine had brought along. The guests included Jon Pertwee, Tom Baker, Louise Jameson, and producer Graham Williams. It was an astonishing event. More astonishing that all these people were not paid to be there. They gladly gave of their own time and effort to be with us all on that day, and they were just amazing.

I remember queuing for autographs, and when I got to Louise she looked at me, and she had the most amazing beautiful blue eyes. I think I fell in love there and then! I remember telling Mum all about it later, and all I could remember was Louise's blue eyes!

I helped run a table selling DWAS publications and fanzines on the day – including my own modest effort – and then after it was all over, I helped to take down the posters and generally put the hall back the way it had been beforehand.

After this, the DWAS organised a big event every year, and eventually it was given the moniker PanoptiCon, after the great meeting chamber of the Time Lords as seen in the story 'The Deadly Assassin' – as I mentioned, fans love to name things with references from the show!

I was more involved after the first one, helping to organise the dealers' room which was full of people selling fanzines, and generally helping to set up and take down the displays.

At the second convention in 1978, we had a large display of Doctor Who props and costumes which had come from the BBC. Someone had obviously reached out to them to see what we could use, and among the items were some incredible things from the sixties, including a Quark costume from 'The Dominators', and the Servo Robot from 'The Wheel in Space'. It was amazing to see that these things even still existed! There were more current displays also, but these two were the ones which stuck in my memory.

As the years ticked by, so these events all blend together in my memory and it's really hard to separate them out. I started to interview people on stage at the events as I seemed to be good at it, and of course had a lot of reference material to research stories and questions and so on. Mainly, though, I was selling DWAS publications and just being an on-hand gofer at them, helping wherever needed.

It was through the conventions that I first met many of the people involved with the show, both through interviewing them, and through seeing them in the green room. There are way too many to mention, but this access meant that I became something of a familiar face to many of them... and thus, in later years, they didn't treat me as 'just some fan' but as someone they recognised and knew was okay. Which was nice.

One big memory for me, though, was an event held down in Brighton in 1985. Organised by Paul Zeus, he had invited the usual slew of star guests, but among them was Patrick Troughton.

Now, Troughton was notoriously shy at attending events. He had done quite a few in America, and loved them, clowning about with Jon Pertwee and the other guests, but in the UK he preferred not to attend the events.

The only one he had done so far had been the big Longleat event in 1983, celebrating 20 years of the show, and even for that, reportedly, Jon Pertwee and John Nathan-Turner, the producer, had to convince him to come along.

Anyway, Troughton had somehow agreed to attend this DWAS event in Brighton, and I remember dashing about running errands, finding stuff out for people. And I was heading down a corridor towards the hotel reception, when coming towards me I saw a man in a coat and carrying a case... it was Patrick Troughton! He seemed confused, so I asked him if everything was okay. He smiled and said, yes, but he was trying to find Mr Zeus, the organiser of the event! Of course, I knew where Paul was, so I escorted Troughton to him, and left him with Paul to get ready for his stage appearance! What an honour, an actual meeting with the second Doctor himself, certainly my favourite!

On stage, Troughton had changed into his Doctor outfit which he had brought with him, and interviewer Gordon Roxburgh did his best to get a serious interview with Troughton, but he was having none of it! He was in character as the Doctor, and so Gordon had to make do with what he could get. But it was funny and brilliant all at the same time. And the applause at the start and the end was deafening.

I had seen Troughton at a distance at the Longleat event, and after this I never saw him again. Which is a great shame. I guess some actors are indeed shy, and prefer to hide behind their popular characters rather than to be themselves on stage. I think Troughton would have enjoyed himself had he attended more of the UK events, but as it happened, this event in Brighton was the only UK fan event he ever went to. All the others were in America, something that made us UK fans more than a little bitter.

* * *

I had met Paul Zeus through the DWAS. He was organising the annual PanoptiCon event and other smaller gatherings, and he was a lovely man. He was tall but wore these great big stacked heel boots. Nimon boots, we used to call them.[87] I discovered that he lived quite close to me, and so we arranged to get together for a regular evening once a month or so.

---

87 'The Horns of Nimon' was a fairly recent story based on the myth of the Minotaur. It featured the Nimon, tall and imposing bull-like monsters with human bodies but bull heads with power-horns on their heads. They wore enormous platform boots... hence the reference.

He was caretaker of a large school or college off Worple Road and down towards Wimbledon,[88] and he had a flat in the premises where he lived. So, I would arrive at the place and Paul would let me in and we'd walk deserted and dark and creepy corridors to his flat, where we would have beer and wine and pizzas and talk the toot, and also enjoy watching pirate VHS tapes!

VHS was something of a revelation! All through the sixties and seventies, you could not watch back *Doctor Who* at all. You couldn't see any television programme again, unless the channel happened to repeat the show. And films. Forget it. It was either at the cinema, or if one of the channels happened to be showing them.

But towards the end of the seventies, the first commercial home video recorders started to become available.[89] In our house, because my dad loved his technology, and liked to keep ahead of the curve, we got a VHS video recorder in 1979, around the start of August.

The reason I know this is that the BBC was repeating two *Doctor Who* stories over July and August that year. July was 'The Pirate Planet' and August was 'The Androids of Tara'... and I know I recorded the latter of those. Plus, of course, the new season started in September with 'Destiny of the Daleks', so that, and everything which followed, was recorded as well.

Having actual *Doctor Who* recorded on VHS was amazing, and meant that the stories could be re-watched, either for pleasure, to check certain details, or to take specific off-screen photographs should they be needed for the fanzines and DWAS publications.

Paul Zeus had a VHS machine as well, and when we got together, he always had a film or two which had been obtained from 'somewhere or other' that we could watch. The one I remember was a very dodgy copy of *Alien*, and this copy had the usual dark and

---

88 This might have been what is now Hall School, or perhaps the Ursuline High School, both off The Downs. I'm not sure which.

89 The UK received its first VHS-based VCR, the Victor HR-3300EK, in 1978.

murky picture of a pirate copy, so bad in some places that you really didn't have a clue what was happening!

I'm not sure if it was this film or another, but these copies were recorded by enterprising types in the cinema. They would smuggle in their VHS camera (which had the little red 'record' light taped over so anyone watching for this in the dark wouldn't see it), and then literally record the film off the screen as it was shown. So sometimes the picture would jiggle a little as the camera was moved about. Sometimes the film didn't quite fill the picture, or one side or the bottom was cut off. And sometimes, someone in a row in front would get up to go to the toilet in the middle of the film, and you'd literally see their silhouette on the video moving across the screen as they did this. Or they'd be smoking, and you'd see the cloud of smoke rise up over the picture. Crazy!

But I enjoyed our get-togethers, and our chats. Happy times.

One year, and I'm not sure which it was, Paul held a New Year's Eve party, and I went along. All the DWAS pals were there, plus some of Paul's other friends, and we had a great time! My main memory of that party was that Keith Barnfather was there, and I'd not seen Keith for a couple of years at that point, so this was probably something like 1980 or 1981. We started chatting, and it was as though we had never been apart! Sometimes that happens, you just click with a person without quite knowing how or why. So, we spent the whole evening talking away and renewing our friendship... and it has lasted to this day! Keith is someone we see quite often. He always drops in when he's passing, and we have a natter and a good meal and a hearty breakfast and then he's off on his way again.

I lost touch with Paul over the years. He moved to Ireland, I believe, and eventually Facebook allowed some limited contact, but then he suddenly passed away early in 2021. A shame. He was a really nice chap. Very thoughtful, but clever and personable.

I got married to Rosemary in 1984, and we moved to a new

house a few miles from my parents'. Settling in there, my *Doctor Who* collection was relegated to the attic room, which was low and cramped, but it was fine as at that point I didn't have too much stuff.

Luckily, Rosemary was interested in *Doctor Who* as well – I had met her, after all, at one of my gatherings at my parents' house and she had come all the way from Croydon! – and so she would come to events and help out as well.

As well as working for Channel 4 at the time, Keith Barnfather was starting up his own company, Reeltime Pictures, and among the fannish things they were doing was a new range of VHS videos, each containing an interview with a person from *Doctor Who*. The amazing thing is that this range has grown to over 200 releases, and covers just about everyone from the Classic Series[90] of *Doctor Who*. It's an incredible archive of personalities, stories and background to all these people, many of whom are now no longer with us. Keith has kept them alive by re-releasing them on DVD, and now they are all available online to buy and stream.[91]

Having made my re-acquaintance with Keith at Paul's New Year party, I was keen to get involved with what Keith was doing (as if getting married, running the DWAS Reference Department and working full-time at Lloyds wasn't enough!).

So, I asked if I might direct one of his interview tapes, and in 1986 the opportunity came to do just that.

The subject was to be Ian Marter, an actor who had appeared in *Doctor Who* as companion Harry Sullivan at the start of the Tom Baker years, but who had in more recent years turned to writing, and had novelised a few of the stories for the Target range. I think Keith knew what a fan I was of the Target books, and felt I would be good to look after this release.

---

90   'Classic Series' is a generic term now used to denote *Doctor Who* stories from 1963 (the start) to 1996 (which is when the Paul McGann American TV movie was released).

91   They can all be found at www.timetraveltv.com.

I started thinking of how I wanted to do this tape, how I wanted the interview to be presented, and how we could make it interesting and a bit different.

Several of the previous tapes had just been 'talking heads', in other words it was a static interview, with the star in one seat; Nicholas Briggs,[92] the presenter, in another; and they just talked. Some had a little more interest in the location, with the actor and presenter walking around chatting, and those I found more interesting.

I decided I wanted to use an actual *Doctor Who* location for the tape... but which one? Ian had been in several stories, but many of the locations were a little too hard to find in the days of no internet and limited idea as to where they actually were.

I plumped for the locations for one of the stories called 'Terror of the Zygons', which opened the 1975 season. This has long been one of my favourite *Doctor Who* adventures, and an example of when everything seemed to go right. The monsters, the Zygons, were giant orange foetus-like creatures with octopus suckers all over their arms and bodies, and they spoke in sibilant hisses.[93] The story was set in Scotland (but not made there) and brought in an undersea 'Loch Ness Monster' which the Zygons were using to destroy oil rigs. The Zygons could also change their appearance to look like humans they had kidnapped. All in all, it's a rollicking four-parter and recommended watching if you fancy some superb seventies *Doctor Who* with Tom Baker!

I had set myself the challenge of finding where it had actually been made! There were newspaper reports around from the time of the filming taking place at Climping Beach in West Sussex, near Worthing on the south coast of England, so I reasoned that the

---

92 Nick has gone on to act and do much voice work for *Doctor Who*, and also currently runs the multiple award-winning audio production company Big Finish.

93 Just like the Ice Warriors which so terrified me as a child!

production team wouldn't venture too far from there to find the village they used. I scoured paper Ordnance Survey maps and tried to find roads that looked a bit like the shots and configurations seen in the show.

By this time, I had managed to acquire several VHS of older *Doctor Who* stories, as they were being shown regularly in Australia. Some fans had pen pals who lived out there, and tape swapping was rife! The Australian fans would record the Jon Pertwee and early Tom Baker adventures, and send them over to the UK in exchange for the latest Tom Baker or Peter Davison adventures. Luckily, Australia used the same VHS and television formats as we did.[94] The power of fandom. Amazing! So, I had a tape of 'Terror of the Zygons' to refer to, in order to see how the show had been shot and where the cameras were placed and so on.

However, my searching of maps was not throwing anything up. In the end, one weekend, Rosemary and I (and perhaps Keith) took a road trip down south and drove around all the little villages and roads, trying to find this dratted village! It was impossible!

In the end, and I think in desperation, Keith reached out to John Nathan-Turner, and asked him if there was any way he could find out where 'Terror of the Zygons' had been made. Thankfully, John was able to come back with the village name: Charlton! And so, we had our location!

We did a recce there and it was pretty much still exactly as it had been for the show, so I noted where we could place our camera to mimic the BBC shots, and also found a deserted woodland area between Climping and Charlton where we could also record.

Thus, in September 1986, the cast and crew travelled down to

---

94   Which was PAL (Phase Alternate Line). The Americans used a different system called NTSC, which some commentators said stood for Never Twice the Same Colour (actually, National Television System Committee), which summed up what an NTSC tape looked like if you tried to play it on a PAL system – it was unwatchable!

Climping to shoot some scenes and part one of the interview in the morning. Then on to Eartham Woods for a second shoot over lunchtime, and finally to Charlton in the afternoon for the final sequences, and the final part of the interview. It was amazing fun, and I tried as far as I could to match some of the camera positions used by director Douglas Camfield for the *Doctor Who* story. We had a ladder with us as I wanted to get some high shots in the woods as Ian was 'stalked' by a Zygon, and to 'sell' the idea I asked Julian Vince to make me a Zygon hand and arm and a control panel, so we could have the effect of the Zygon 'seeing' Ian as it watched him in the woods via its control panel and screen.

The overall production came out really well. I was very pleased with it. The interview flowed and was interesting, and Ian Marter was just such a nice man to talk to and to work with. Nothing was too much trouble for him. At one point on the beach, someone had an idea that maybe he should emerge from the sea at the start, and Ian was all for stripping down to his trunks and doing just that! But it was September, and cold, and we didn't think that would be a good idea.

We had such a good time making the production that it came as a great shock, around six weeks later, to discover that Ian had died suddenly on his 42nd birthday on 28 October 1986.

This was another salutatory message that life is transitory, and you have no idea how long you have got. Of course, Ian never got to see his finished interview and tape as well, but I hope it stands as a great tribute to the man and his career.

Because I had such a good time making this one, I was very keen to direct another, and in October 1987, Keith again gave me the opportunity.

This time the subject was to be actress Mary Tamm, who had played Romana on the show, and I'm not sure if Keith realised that I had already met her!

Again, I wanted to do an actual location shoot, but when you look at the season of *Doctor Who* that Mary was in, there really isn't anywhere you can go. I thought about the Rollright Stones from 'The Stones of Blood', but they look so much better on screen, in real life they are very disappointing. We couldn't get permission to use Leeds Castle from 'The Androids of Tara', and 'The Power of Kroll' was all wetlands and marshes, so very impractical and difficult. 'The Pirate Planet' was made in South Wales, so that was too far to travel, and the other two stories were studio-bound!

In the end, Keith suggested using Eynsford Castle in Kent, which, while having no relevance to *Doctor Who*, was a visually interesting location, and fairly easy to travel to.

Having sorted the location out, we did a recce so I could see what it was all about, and I decided I wanted to have an *Alice in Wonderland* theme to the interview. I felt that Mary just lent herself to that role, and with the 'three act interview' I again wanted to do, it also fitted with some of the characters from *Alice*: most notably the Caterpillar and the Mad Hatter.

At one point I wanted to try to get an otherworldly look to a sequence, so decided that a shot of Mary walking over the bridge towards the castle ruins would be recorded backwards, and then played in reverse in the actual production. So that's what we did. But Mary was so good at walking backwards and performing in reverse, that when we reversed the footage, you could hardly tell that this was what we had done. I know it's there, though!

Mary was again delightful to work with and a real trooper. At the end of the day, I wanted her to get dressed up in an Alice costume (I had hired all these costumes from a local fancy dress shop for the day!) and to skip around the location while we set off smoke bombs all around her. Again, trying to get a fantasy feel and flavour into the production. She did it without a complaint! Amazing lady.

Keith said to me during the shoot that Mary thought I was a real director, so I doubt she remembered our somewhat awkward interview at the fete some years earlier, though I probably mentioned it to her!

As for me, I thoroughly enjoyed making the two interview productions. I loved all the planning and working it all out, and then the directing and getting the shots I wanted, and finally the editing of it all together and adding music. Just a satisfying thing to do.

THE

FEB 1987

No: 1

FRAME

The cover for the first issue of my second fanzine *The Frame* published in February 1987.

8

Another Fanzine and Live *Who*

As the 1980s trundled to a close, I had spent a very busy decade working, writing, researching, publishing and generally having a whale of a time indulging my passion for the show.

I was still working full-time for Lloyds Bank, having been trained as a computer programmer in the PL1 language,[95] and had moved slightly up to a Team Leader, and also some testing – you tended to do a bit of everything as the various teams and projects at Lloyds shifted about. This was a very exciting time at the bank as well, and the very first project I was assigned to in 1980, after my initial training, was working on a system called BIT, or Branch IT. This was the very start of the computerisation and automation of the branches and the bank's systems.

When I first started at the bank in 1979, they were still using punch cards to create the programs, and these would be read into the mainframe in a stack and 'compiled' to create the executables to run the programs. So being a programmer meant first getting

---

95 There was a choice of PL1 (which stood for the imaginatively named Programming Language 1), COBOL (Common Business Oriented Language), or Assembler (basically machine code). I was put on PL1, and for that I was grateful!

a 'Specification' for a program from an Analyst: what it had to do, how it should behave if things went wrong, and so on. Then you had to design the program using flow-charting to map all the various options and what the program would do, and then you had to code it by writing the code, line by line, onto coding sheets by hand. Then the coding sheets would go off to the typists to create a stack of punched cards. You then ran those through the computer, which would pick out any obvious errors, typing mistakes and so on. You then went to the punch room and created new cards to replace the ones which were wrong. Back through the computer and repeat until your program compiled. And then you could test it with data you created, and again punched onto cards... it was a long-winded and complicated process!

As the years progressed, so technology got better and better. When I started there were no desktop computers and no mobile phones. Everything was done by hand! But slowly desktop computers started to appear. At first, they were on a bank of four desks in the area we worked in and could be used to do things on, and then everyone had them on their desks. But it was a slow process.

While all this was going on, my two sons, James (April 1988) and Andrew (January 1994), were born, so this added to workloads and available time at home.

As the 1980s drew to a close, I was getting the urge, the itch, to do something myself again that was connected with the show. Another fanzine seemed to be the answer, so I started to think about what I wanted to do and achieve.

By this time, technology had moved on a lot, and many fanzines were moving to early litho printing, which meant that the photographs were reproduced really well, and the text and layouts were crisp and attractive.

My interests in Doctor Who being mainly in the behind-the-scenes and visual/photographic/artwork aspects meant that I wanted this for the 'zine. Luckily, on the DWAS committee at the time was a chap who I had suggested to run the art department. I had seen his work somewhere else, or he had written in, and I thought he was great! This was Mark Stammers, and he and I got on well. So, I asked Mark if he would like to collaborate on a new fanzine, and whether he might be interested in doing the layout and design for it, as he had a real flair for that. He agreed, as this was something he was interested in as well.

I also heard on the fan grapevine that another chap, Stephen James Walker, who I knew well,[96] was also thinking about doing a fanzine. Steve had been writing detailed synopses and also editing a fan partwork being published by Jeremy Bentham, called *An Adventure in Space and Time*, which looked at every *Doctor Who* story, in order, and in as much detail as was known at that time. So, I figured that if I was starting a new *Doctor Who* fanzine, I didn't want immediate competition from someone else who was superb at reference and research and everything I was good at! I reached out to Steve and asked if he too would be willing to help with my fanzine. To my pleasure he agreed, and the three of us started to map out what we wanted our new 'zine to be.

What we didn't want was poor reproduction and layout, and at the time Mark was working for a reprographics company, which also 'bought print' for a variety of clients. This meant they liaised with printers and got the best printing deals for whatever they were dealing with. This seemed ideal to me, as it meant we could get litho printing for the 'zine at hopefully the best cost! Mark's designs and ideas were also sharp and effective, and through his company he also had access to half-tone scanning[97] of black-and-white

96 Stephen and I first met at the 1977 DWAS convention, and he later came along to some of the local meetings I held at my parents' house, and he was also at my and Rosemary's wedding on 29 September 1984.

97 In order to print a photograph in litho (and this worked for photocopying as well) you had to convert the image into a series of small dots, and this is what half-tone scanning did.

photographs for the insides and cover, as well as layout sheets to set the whole thing out on.[98]

For the content we wanted it to be a mixture of fact and fiction and art... pulling on all our various strengths and contacts. For the factual content, we wanted interviews with behind-the-scenes people and others connected with Doctor Who, but positive and interesting. Also, some news and information which people might not have heard about. For the fiction, we wanted material which was well written and effective. For the art, we wanted great artwork which looked professional and not half-baked. Overall, we wanted a fanzine which presented and felt like a professional magazine all about Doctor Who.

At that time, Doctor Who Magazine, which had started in 1979, was still going strong, but it was light in its approach and didn't really cover anything in depth. It also, understandably, tended to focus on the current series of Doctor Who rather than delving into the past, so again this was an area we felt we could add value to.

For the title, we initially came up with The Net, thinking of a fisherman's net which pulled all sorts of things together in one place, but finalised on The Frame. This was suggested by Stephen, partly because of the magazine was a 'frame' into which anything could be displayed, but also because it could refer to a frame of film or videotape (obviously relevant to Doctor Who) and also to framing an argument or point of view, as in some of the analytical features we were intended to run, so it was a 'multi-meaning' term. To sell the idea further, Mark designed the cover as a simple full-page black-and-white photograph with a printed colour frame around it, with the title in blocky letter boxes at the top. It looked very classy!

98   These were larger-than-A3 sheets which were marked up with grid lines printed in a pale blue – the litho process would not 'see' any blue and render it as plain white, so it didn't matter if they were visible on the finished artwork.

And so, in February 1987, we launched our new fanzine on the world! The first issue featured an interview with the director Christopher Barry, plus photographs from *Doctor Who* from his private collection which had never been seen before. The interview was conducted by myself and Rosemary at Barry's home near Oxford. I remember the day was really nice, sunny and warm. We sat outside and chatted! Chris was a lovely man, very friendly and more than willing to reminisce over his career. The interview concluded the following issue. Other elements included a short story and some more great photo spreads for which we dug out pictures which hadn't been seen before, and the first part of a series called 'Dalek Design', written and researched by Stephen and another friend called Tony Clark, which aspired to detail all the different variations of Daleks that there had been over the years.

Each of the first four issues did really well, with each issue doubling the print run and sales of the one before. We published it quarterly, along the same lines as I always had: it had its own bank account, we never borrowed any money, and the cost of the issues was basically the printing, plus shipping, plus a little more to cover unexpected overheads. When we came to issue five in February 1988, we had enough money from advance subscriptions to afford colour printing on the cover, so that's what we did! We also had a wonderful long interview with loads of photographs looking at the visual effects for the whole of the 1987 season of the show, courtesy of the main effects designers for that period, Mike Tucker (who worked for the BBC at the Visual Effects Department, and was assistant on pretty much everything), Susan Moore and Stephen Mansfield (who were both freelancers, but who had been around in fandom for years! Susan had produced fanzines and released small resin badges and models which were simply superb, and Stephen was a talented sculptor who has since gone on to work his magic on some of the likenesses at Madame Tussauds!). The cover featured a magnificent photograph of a 'melting head' effect used at the climax of the final story of the season, 'Dragonfire', and was very much inspired by a similar effect in the film *Raiders of the Lost Ark*. We dedicated a two-page spread in the magazine to exactly how this had been achieved in *Doctor Who*.

For the November 1988 issue – number eight – I wanted to celebrate 25 years of *Doctor Who*, and so decided to commission a cover painting from a friend and fan called Trevor Baxendale, whose artwork I had seen in various fanzines.

I was inspired in part by a book published in August 1979 called *Masquerade*, which contained images painted by an artist called Kit Williams. Each image contained a variety of items crammed into it, and each picture contained clues, which when joined up with other clues from each of the images in the book, to give the location of a jewelled golden hare which had been hidden somewhere in the UK.[99] It was a very complex puzzle to try to solve!

The main inspiration was from a 1986 book called *The Ultimate Alphabet* by Mike Wilkes, who took each letter of the alphabet and then illustrated as many items beginning with that letter as he could. For example, 'X' had just 30 items, but 'S' had an amazing 1,229 items! Again, the book had a competition associated with it for readers to correctly identify all the items![100]

I came up with the idea of having a painting of a storeroom in the TARDIS, in which are items from every one of the *Doctor Who* stories up to and including 'Dragonfire'. Mark, Stephen and I came up with a draft list, then Trevor took it away and came up with an amazing image for the cover. He suggested some alterations and variations, and also added some extra pieces which didn't relate to any specific TV story, and the end result was incredible. We also

99 The full story of this amazing book can be found here: en.wikipedia.org/wiki/Masquerade_(book)

100 Details of *The Ultimate Alphabet* can be found here: en.wikipedia.org/wiki/The_Ultimate_Alphabet

ran a competition to see if anyone could correctly identify all the items. It was harder than it seemed.

This issue also had a colour centrespread, and a brilliant article by Stephen looking at the origins of *Doctor Who*: the first time that this history had ever been documented to this level. We also featured some reviews and a piece on the first Dalek stage play from 1965, *The Curse of the Daleks*.

As the fanzine progressed it became more and more slick and professional-looking. We could afford more colour printing, so we used it. We interviewed writers and effects people about the stories they worked on, we uncovered hitherto unknown photographs and items from the show's history and presented them… all while positively celebrating all that was *Doctor Who*. It was a great time!

It was through this activity that we came to meet and interview as many people as we could who had been involved in the making of *Doctor Who* throughout its history. Among them were the amazing scenic designers Barry Newbery and Raymond P Cusick.

Barry and Ray had been with the show when it first started back in 1963. Barry had designed the very first story, while Ray had designed the second story, and with it, the Daleks themselves! They were both total *Doctor Who* royalty, as both had worked extensively on the series for so long! Barry's final credit on the show was actually 'The Awakening' in 1984!

Steve and I visited Barry and Ray so many times. We did extensive interviews with both of them, digging into and trying to understand and further appreciate the work that went into the scenic design of a show that was so diverse, challenging and complex, with different locations from spaceships to the wild west, from alien planets to futuristic cities. Moreover, in the early days they also had to design and oversee the monsters and effects as well, building them into their plans as the show required.

What was particularly helpful was that both designers had kept extensive photographic archives of their time spent on *Doctor Who*, as it was a show that they were both incredibly proud of their work on. So, there were photographs of sets and actors and effects and everything they had done. They took these outside of their day job, so to speak, just as they wandered around the studios and the sets, and we were so thankful they had kept this amazing record of their work.

Both men were incredibly modest too, happy to discuss the minutiae of cutting polystyrene into the right shapes, or getting the light on a backdrop just right to create the effect they wanted. There was also talk of pointing the camera at a mirror to increase the distance from the subject, or of how to make it look like you had hundreds of Daleks when you had just four (the answer: cardboard cut-out Daleks!)

We featured their work many times in *The Frame*, and it was an honour to know both of them. In later years, I helped the people making the extra material for the BBC DVD releases to arrange interviews with them, and to try to make sure they got appropriate recognition for their work on the show.

For the 50th anniversary in 2013, I had arranged for Barry to be a Guest of Honour at the big BBC celebration event in London, and to have a stage interview where he could receive the applause and accolades that I felt he deserved. Unfortunately, he had a fall and hurt his leg, so was unable, ultimately, to attend.

Barry died in 2015, and Ray passed away in 2013. I was proud to have known them and to have called them friends.

* * *

Returning to *The Frame*, and in 1989, we wanted to get more coverage of the series in production, so we reached out to John Nathan-Turner and asked if we could perhaps attend some location filming to see and report on what was happening.

This was because we had seen other great fanzines from the time being allowed on location – and some just turning up anyway, as they had found out where the show was being made – and felt that we should get some of that as well!

John came back with an affirmative, which did surprise me a little, as in 1983 he had been dead against me doing the DWAS magazine on 'The Five Doctors', and so Mark, Steve and I headed to Perivale for the location shooting for the story 'Survival', which, as it happened, turned out to be the last *Doctor Who* story for a fair few years.

The recording was taking place at a Martial Arts Centre which was representing the youth club in the story. It is invaded by the Master with an animatronic cat hanging around, and also one of the youths (played by Will Barton) who has been partly turned into a cheetah person.

We got to meet the main cast that day: Anthony Ainley, who played the Master, was good to speak to, but very concerned about any close-up photographs being taken. It turned out that he wore a hairpiece as the Master and was worried that it might show on any pictures. We spoke with Sylvester McCoy playing the Doctor, and Sophie Aldred playing his companion Ace. We saw the director and designer and chatted to them. We spoke with the effects guys who were on hand to wrangle the animatronic cat (which didn't seem to work properly!), and generally had a fun, productive, if very hot day with the cast and crew, recording the material for the show.

We took copious photographs and I wrote it all up for a couple of articles in *The Frame*: one published before transmission, and one, which gave away more of the plot details, after transmission. We were always trying to be responsible about what we printed, and had the utmost respect for the production team and what they were trying to achieve, and, of course, for the show itself, which remained a large part of our lives, and which we loved dearly!

This was the last time that I saw *Doctor Who* being made, although

I did have some near misses! Working at Lloyds, we had offices on the South Bank of the Thames, at a building called Red Lion Court.[101] Just along the Thames from there was the Globe Theatre, and I came into work one day in August or September 2006 to people asking me if I had been down at the Globe the previous night. I replied that I hadn't, and asked what had been happening. They told me that *Doctor Who* had been recorded there!

I couldn't believe it. Right on my doorstep, and I had missed it as I didn't know!

I mentioned before that despite all my *Doctor Who* friends and contacts, I was usually the last person to know what was going on, and this had been the case here. It was for a story called 'The Shakespeare Code', and David Tennant and everyone had been there for a couple of nights recording everything they needed!

And I had missed it all, despite working just 500 yards or so away, as no one had told me!

Just my luck!

Earlier, in April 1988, my walk to work took me from Waterloo station, across Waterloo Road and along Roupell Street towards Blackfriars, across Hatfields, at a slight angle, along Columbo Street, across the A201, to hit Southwark Street (the A3200) and to cross then to Hopton Street where the offices were in Sampson House.[102]

Little did I know that later that day, *Doctor Who* would be recording a massive Dalek battle for the story 'Remembrance of the Daleks' down Roupell Street and under the arches by the King's Arms pub. The explosions from it would be so loud that residents called out the fire brigade as they thought there were bombs going off!

In the evening, I walked home down the same route and saw

101 Which was next to the Anchor Pub, between Blackfriars Bridge and London Bridge.
102 This was just beside Blackfriars Bridge.

nothing. I had no idea that the recording was taking place, as no one had told me!

Just my luck!

I did have some luck, though. Rosemary worked for the BBC! She was in a department called Radio Programme Index, and their job seemed to be transcribing information from old issues of the *Radio Times* onto a nascent computer recording system that the BBC had, which made it easier to look up and find things in the records. Before this, all the information had been held on file cards in massive card library systems.[103] This work seems to have developed into the BBC Genome website: a superb archive of the history of BBC television and radio.[104]

More importantly from a *Doctor Who* perspective, she had a staff ID card, and this could get her and a visitor (me!) into BBC Television Centre so we could visit the public gallery and watch *Doctor Who* being made!

I can't remember the first time we did this, nor how I found out that it was possible, but certainly interviewing Douglas Adams in one of the viewing galleries must have put ideas in my head about it all.

There was a group of fans at the time who all worked at the BBC in varying capacities, and they would congregate in the viewing gallery whenever *Doctor Who* was being made. As mentioned, there were often no chairs, or just one chair, so we had to stand or sit on the floor or whatever. Cameras were, of course, present, and we would keep an eye out for what was happening on the studio floor and take photos of anything which seemed interesting. We couldn't use a flash for obvious reasons, and the studios were usually quite dark (we were above and behind the lights), and often the sets in

---

103 I have a fair few photocopies from these cards and systems in my files: all appearances and mentions of *Doctor Who* in other television and radio shows through the years!

104 genome.ch.bbc.co.uk/

use were quite distant from us, so having slowed the shutter speed to try to get pictures it was then hard to stay still as you took them (resulting in blurred images if you moved). No one thought to bring a tripod, as that would perhaps be too obvious to anyone checking the room!

We spent many happy evenings at TV Centre watching *Doctor Who* being recorded. The process they used was that they spent the day setting up and rehearsing with the cast and crew, getting the lighting right and so on, and then, after an evening meal, they would start recording, and go through until ten o'clock sharp. The union rules said they couldn't extend past ten o'clock without permission, so most often, bang on the dot, the main lights came on and they were finished for the day.

Some memories from watching the recordings stand out for me.

In a story called 'The Awakening', there's an old church at the centre of a small village which is experiencing psychic attacks and happenings, and a war game re-enactment taking place there is becoming too real for comfort.

In the church there is this massive alien head buried in a wall, and this is the Malus, an alien probe which is the cause of all the disturbances.

At one point, the Doctor and friends are trapped in the church, and the Malus manifests three soldiers from the past, who draw their swords and face them. A trooper races in and is immediately surrounded by the soldiers. They lock swords around his neck, and in one movement decapitate the luckless man!

The recording of this in August 1983 was electric... it went without a hitch, but you could tell that this was a special scene as a strange hush fell over the studio while they were doing it. It brought goosebumps to our arms, and we just knew that this would be an amazing story! As it happened, the sequence was edited for transmission as it was considered to be too scary, and all we hear in the finished show is the soldier's scream of terror after he has been surrounded.

Another story I remember was the final one for Peter Davison as the Doctor. 'The Caves of Androzani' was a dark adventure in which Peri (played by Nicola Bryant) was infected by some poisonous bats' nests, and had to seek help from the insane Sharaz Jek, a masked lunatic who had hidden himself in the caves and surrounded himself with robot helpers. Jek was played by Christopher Gable, originally a well-known ballet dancer, who left the Royal Ballet in 1967 to follow a career in acting, cast because they knew that Jek was masked, and they needed someone who could move and act well, even under a mask.

There's one scene in the story which, when it was recorded, saw the studio descend into the same sort of hush. It's where Peri and Jek are doing the whole *Phantom of the Opera* thing. Peri is in his clutches, and he's ranting away, and she pulls off his mask! She screams at what she (but not the audience at this point) sees, and he also cries out, collapses to the floor, and scuttles off to hide under a table, and Peri immediately feels sorry for him.

It's an incredibly powerful scene, excellently played by the two leads, and you really feel for both Peri and Jek at this moment. Both people broken by their respective circumstances.

What got those of us in the viewing gallery howling with laughter, though, came right at the end. After 'Cut!' was called, Gable stood up and dusted himself down, and said, in the most effeminate voice, 'Was that okay, dears?'

I also remember seeing the anti-matter monster, the Ergon, from the story 'Arc of Infinity', entering the studio and staggering across to where the set was. I thought it looked okay, but hoped it would look better on screen!

Another moment was in 1984's 'Resurrection of the Daleks', when the Daleks are invading a spaceship where Davros is held captive. There's a scene where all the crew are defending the ship, all lined up in front of a bulkhead door, through which the Daleks are going to come. There's a pause, and then an almighty explosion as the bulkhead is ripped apart and the Daleks come through, guns blazing.

Just a brilliant sequence to watch being set up in studio and to see being recorded.

Some people asked me at the time whether watching the show being made spoiled the magic for me? Whether it was better to not know anything at all?

For me, I found that knowing the plot details in advance, and having seen some of it being recorded, just made me more eager to see the finished item. It didn't spoil it at all, it enhanced the viewing experience, as sometimes you knew that you had seen that scene being made. It made it all the more special! Likewise with scripts. As time went on, so I managed to get hold of rehearsal and camera scripts before transmission, and reading these tended not to spoil a thing for me. In my mind I compartmentalised them, and when watching the story for the first time, I tended not to really remember the scripts anyway.

But all these occasions were from the public viewing gallery at TV Centre. There was one other time when I had the opportunity to go down on the studio floor to see the recording close-up and personal, and this was for a story called 'Terminus'.

David Saunders, who was co-ordinator for the DWAS at the time (this was before all the politics and fallings out), asked me if I'd like to go with him, as he'd been invited by John Nathan-Turner to come along and watch proceedings. Maybe it was my 'turn' on the DWAS committee to go along, I have no idea. Anyway, I wasn't going to turn down the chance to go on set and watch a story being made!

So, David and I headed down to TV Centre to see it all happen. This was made in October 1982, so I was 21 years old at this point.

The story was about a vast space station called Terminus, which

Top: This is me aged around 5 years old in 1966. Butter wouldn't melt …
Bottom: The Foraging Five: Jacqueline, Alan, Susan, Jennifer and myself in July 1975.

Top: Sunday 24 September 1978 and a group of friends head to Longleat House in Wiltshire to visit the *Doctor Who* Exhibition there. I'm taking the picture. L to R: Michael McManus; David Auger; Paul Tams; Gavin French; Chris Dunk; Vaughn Hancock; Kevin Jon Davies; Owen Tudor; Christina Staines (nee Sparkes).

Bottom: At the Surbiton Eye Hospital Fete on Saturday 26 May 1979, we had two real BBC Daleks to mess about with! Owen Tudor (right) and I are here enjoying Dalek/Davros races!

Top: Over the summer of 1974, my friend David Butterworth (left) and I built our own Dalek from the plans in a *Radio Times* special magazine and elements scavenged from skips and my dad's shed!

Bottom: A visit to the *Doctor Who* Exhibition at Blackpool in May 1980.

Top: I'm here on the right directing author Ian Marter being interviewed by Nicholas Briggs for Marter's *Myth Makers* release from Reeltime Pictures in September 1986. Ian sadly died some five weeks after we finished making the programme.

Bottom: Playing one of the Yeti monsters in the film *Downtime* in March 1995. The three Yeti are Richard Landen, me, and Tony Clark. Pictures © Robin Prichard/Reeltime Pictures.

Top Left: Me with actress Mary Tamm and interviewer Nicholas Briggs during recording for the Mary Tamm *Myth Makers* production on 31 October 1987. Picture © Robin Prichard/Reeltime Pictures. Top Right: My photograph of Patrick Troughton at his only UK convention appearance in July 1985. Bottom Left: David B Wake and myself with Colin Baker, celebrating the release of our book *Drabble Who* in September 1993. Bottom Right: Dressed as a Time Lord for an appearance on *Saturday Superstore* on 29 November 1986. I also provided the voice of Tony the Cyberman who was taking part in the Pop Panel!

Top: Actors Carole Ann Ford and Frazer Hines, along with myself, signing copies of my first co-written book *Doctor Who: The Sixties* on Saturday 24 October 1992. Picture © Kate Green. Bottom: Myself with Jon Pertwee, co-authors Mark Stammers and Stephen James Walker and a Dalek, celebrating publication of *Doctor Who: The Seventies* on 5 November 1994.

Top: A 'friend' studying a copy of my book co-written with Jon Pertwee, *I Am The Doctor*. Jon sadly died in May 1996, before the book was published.

Bottom: A memorable appearance with the space aliens Zig (right) and Zag (left) on *The Big Breakfast* in January 1996, promoting the book *Doctor Who: Companions*.

Top: A typical convention picture. This was at Long Island Who 3 in November 2015 and I'm on the left with my wife Sam, alongside Ian McNeice, Ken Deep (event organiser), Daphne Ashbrook, Frazer Hines, Chase Masterson, and film director/producer Joshua Lou Friedman. Bottom: At my wedding to Sam in October 2015, Frazer Hines was Best Man, and here we are pre-service, clowning as Stan and Ollie.

is where a supposed treatment centre for a virulent illness called Lazar's Disease was offered. The plot followed a spaceship delivering a cargo of patients to the centre, which is invaded by space pirates who don't know that they are on a plague ship!

The sets which were erected on the day we visited were for the spaceship, and so I prowled around them, taking in all the brilliant elements. Television sets are an amazing thing. They are solid and very real-looking, so you (and the cameras and actors) can believe that you really are on an alien spaceship! I also had my camera with me this time, having learned from the experience of 'The Creature from the Pit', and while flash was not permitted, as it could be picked up by the studio cameras elsewhere, I was taking pictures of the sets and what I found as I explored.

In a corner around the back were a couple of smashing robot things. They were all arms and claws. I took some pictures, of course, not having a clue that this was one of the robots which is sent to 'sanitise' the spaceship once the diseased cargo has been unloaded.

One of the sets was Adric's bedroom set on board the TARDIS, and there was the flight deck of the spaceship. There was also a larger area which was where the infected passengers were kept, the doors to these areas were painted with a brilliant neon skull motif. It looked fantastic!

One of the scenes was of Tegan (Janet Fielding) and Turlough (Mark Strickson), two of the Doctor's companions, who have become trapped on the ship. They are wandering the corridors and find this area.

For reasons best known to the costume designer, Tegan is wearing a tight boob tube and a pair of culottes, and when she gets close to one of the skull-doors, it starts to slide open. Grubby and grimy bandaged hands and arms emerge from beyond and grab hold of her. She screams and struggles, and eventually pulls free with Turlough's help, and the door closes again.

That was the intention, anyway.

On the first take, however, Tegan is grabbed by the hands, and in her struggles to escape, Janet lifted her arms too high and her breasts popped out of the boob tube!

'Cut!'

With much laughter from the assembled crew, the costume was rearranged, Janet's modesty returned, and the studio reset for another take. This time Janet knew not to raise her arms too high and all was fine.

To me, watching from the back, it was a very amusing moment. Who would have thought!

Being able to watch Doctor Who being made was certainly one of the highlights of the eighties for me. A show that I had grown up with, followed and loved for as long as I could remember.

I had failed in being able to actually work on it. I had applied to join the BBC's Visual Effects Department at the end of the seventies, but had been turned down as I needed an art degree, and for my A levels (and, indeed, O levels) I had gone for sciences instead as I couldn't draw or paint for toffee. It never occurred to me that the ability to create visual effects rather depended on being able to draw pictures and diagrams of what I wanted and how they would work. Never mind. Being able to just watch it being made was perhaps the pinnacle of writing and editing a fanzine at the time!

Me with a copy of my book for *Doctor Who's* 30th Anniversary in 1983, *Timeframe*. This was taken during the promotion for the paperback edition in 1984.

9

Books!

Producing *The Frame* every quarter was a lot of fun, and certainly preparing and mailing every issue kept me busy. Alongside all this activity, I had remained in touch with W H Allen, the publishers of the *Doctor Who* books, as I was interested in collecting them, and also getting as many of the cover proofs as I could.

At the publishers, editors change as people move on, and in 1987 a new editor took over the *Doctor Who* range of books. This was Nigel Robinson, and one day he reached out and sent me a letter asking if I might be interested in proofreading a new book that had come in. This turned out to be Peter Haining's *25 Glorious Years*, a large format book designed to celebrate the show's 25th anniversary in 1988. I was happy to help, so I received a pile of page proofs of the book and dutifully went through and corrected all the bits that were obviously wrong.

Peter Haining was something of a legend, and he had compiled a great many titles over the years on a variety of subjects, but I think, because he relied too much on secondary sources and reportage, his books tended to be riddled with hearsay and items for which the origin was lost in the mists of time. However, taken at face value, they were a popular and great resource.

After completing that one, I was also asked to go over updated reprints of Jean-Marc L'Officier's *Doctor Who Programme Guide* and associated titles, again trying to weed out various issues and errors. Again, I was happy to help.

The best of these titles was, I feel, *25 Glorious Years*, as the book seemed slightly better written to start with, and I was able to catch all the worst errors before publication.

At the end of 1986, W H Allen was sold, including the *Doctor Who* range, to Virgin Publishing. So, there was a new publisher in town!

As usual, I reached out to the new editor, Jo Thurm, and introduced myself, explained about my fanzine and what I did, and offered any help she might need in regard to the *Doctor Who* titles. She was somewhat distant and I didn't have much further contact with her, although I did get myself on the advance PR lists for the *Doctor Who* titles. In February 1989, Thurm left and the range was taken over by Peter Darvill-Evans.

Again, I reached out offering help and support, and Peter was far more receptive. We arranged to meet and got together in a London pub! I think it must have been at this first meeting that I asked Peter whether there was any possibility of being commissioned for a book about *Doctor Who*, and his reply was that I had to offer him one first! 'Ah,' I thought. 'That's how it's done!'

So, I headed back from the meeting and the next day got in touch with Steve and Mark (my co-editors on *The Frame*) and explained what Peter had told me. We brought another friend, Tony Clark, into the discussion, as he had been co-writing the 'Dalek Design' chapters for *The Frame*, and we put together a proposal for a book looking at the Daleks, and the many variants thereof, through the ages. We called it simply *Daleks*, as that summed up everything that the book was intended to cover.

Mark put together a beautifully designed folder for it, with page spreads, some sample contents list, pictures, cover ideas, everything… and we sent it off to Peter.

Peter loved the idea, and he knew that, certainly, we could deliver the goods, as The Frame was proving a great calling card for our collective writing, editing and design talents. So, we discussed it a little more, and Peter went away to get some contracts drawn up so that we would be officially commissioned to write a licensed book all about the Daleks! To say we were excited was an understatement!

Time ticked by and we didn't hear anything... and then Peter came back to us and said that they were waiting for a response from Terry Nation, the writer who had created the Daleks and who co-owned them with the BBC. As soon as we got a response from Terry, then we'd be all set.

So we waited some more.

And waited.

Peter was, I think, getting as fed up as we were with the delay, and so he eventually instructed Virgin to draw up the draft contracts anyway.

I think it was the day they arrived to us in the post that we heard from Peter that he had finally heard back from Terry Nation, and that Terry would not agree to this book going ahead, as he was doing his own book on the Daleks with St Martin's Press in America and didn't want another book being published as well.

We were devastated. All that work, and then all that waiting, only to be told that we couldn't do it!

When we finally saw a copy of Nation's own book, which was published in the USA in November 1988,[105] it was co-written with John Peel, another friend I knew from the early DWAS days who had gone out to live in America. Indeed, myself, Rosemary and the kids had even been to stay with him and his wife for a holiday in Long Island on one occasion! But while the book was great, it was nothing whatsoever like the one we had proposed. This was a more

105 The Official Doctor Who and the Daleks Book (John Peel & Terry Nation, St Martin's Press, 1988).

generic overview of the Dalek stories on television, with information about Nation's proposed and never-done American pilot for a Dalek series. It was completely different. And Nation must have known that when he saw our pitch, as his book had been published by the time we were discussing ours with Virgin.

I went back to Peter and asked if there was anything else he felt we could do, and between us we came up with the idea of doing a series of books looking at the entirety of Doctor Who to that point.

Mark, Steve and I kicked some ideas about, and latched onto the idea of doing a book per decade, covering all the Doctor Who in that decade. We fleshed out the ideas, and went back to Peter with a proper pitch, slightly simpler than that which we had prepared for Daleks, for the first book, which we called simply The Sixties, as that was what it covered.

Peter liked it, and by February 1991 we were discussing contracts and getting our first book finally agreed!

* * *

There was still, of course, the slight issue of writing it to think about!

The three of us mapped it out and decided who would write which chapters. We knew how many pages we had, and so we had a rough idea from doing The Frame how many words that would be. Mark was doing all the layout and design on it, so Steve and I took the lead on the words.

I did the chapter on the sixties Doctor Who merchandise, as that was something of a specialist subject, and for the rest either Steve or I, or occasionally Mark, did the writing, and then passed it to the other two to edit and tweak and try to make it the best we could.

There were interesting discussions about the chapters which dealt with the stories. The obvious approach would have been to have covered them in transmission order, but Peter felt this was perhaps not going to give the best 'read' to the book, so he suggested breaking each season up and covering the stories by theme: for example, for the first season, we'd cover all the historical stories first, and then the science fiction ones. I can't say that we weren't unsure about this, but Peter was the editor and publisher, so we did that. It came out okay, I feel, but I think it might have been better to have just stuck to the transmission order.

Our plan when doing the book was to try, wherever possible, to use first-hand sources. We were aware that much of the research and fan publishing related to the show to this point was reliant on third-hand reportage, from newspapers, or from half-remembered elements from the show. And some of this material was not correct at all. So, we wanted to try to correct that.

When writing the book, we tried hard to make it accessible to a general reader.[106] We felt we needed to explain, for example, that Patrick Troughton was the second Doctor, or that the Ice Warriors came from Mars, things which perhaps a fan of the show would know but someone who wasn't might not. We also didn't want to assume anything. To put two and two together and make five. The rule was, if we didn't know something, it wasn't included, or we worded the text carefully to make it clear what was and was not wholly factual. In this way, we hoped that the book wouldn't date. Certainly, more information might come to light, but if we said something was so, then we knew it to be so.

This drew on all the original interviews and discussions we had done with all the creators over the last ten years or so for our own fanzines and other projects, and we also went and spoke to more people while researching the book.

What we didn't have was access to the BBC's own Written Archives Centre in Caversham. At that point, awareness and access to the

106 Just as I am doing with this book!

Archives was not known about or used, so we were limited in what we could obtain and verify.[107]

To illustrate the book, we got together all the best and rarest and least seen photographs from the sixties that we could. This was a BBC licensed book, so we were okay to use any and all BBC images, but many of them had been seen in *Doctor Who Magazine* by that point, as well as in fanzines and so on, and we wanted to present something new and hopefully unseen. We raided the private collections of everyone we knew, writing letters to get permission to use the stills. Virgin had given us a very small clearance budget and we couldn't pay much at all for anything, but thankfully everyone we dealt with was kind and understanding and gave us the okay to use their stills.

Mark's layout was a *tour de force*! He had decided to make use of a three-column arrangement, with two large columns and one smaller one on the outside edge of each page. We referred to this smaller column as a 'sidebar' and we endeavoured to fill it with all sorts of facts and figures and small pieces of information and photographs that we couldn't 'fit' into the main text. It was a perfect way of getting as much information into the book as we could. I felt it worked magnificently!

Because full colour printing was still quite expensive, and as most of the photographs from the sixties era of *Doctor Who* were in black and white, Peter decided to only have limited colour pages in the book, so Mark designed it so the colour pictures appeared on those pages.

The book was eventually published in hardback on 15 October

107 Caversham is where all the BBC's production paperwork ends up. All the letters and memos and notes and scripts. All the production paperwork related to costings and contractors and studios and design and costume fittings... everything was sent there when a production had completed use of it. The material had a retention period, and also an 'embargo' period, and I think when we were doing *The Sixties*, that embargo on sixties material had not quite yet expired.

1992, and received amazing reviews! We were so pleased! All that hard work – as well as the false start – had paid off and we were now properly published authors of a *Doctor Who* book!

While we had been figuring out how to break *The Sixties* down, and who was going to write what, Peter had got in touch with me again, and asked if we might be also interested in tackling a second book, and another series. Of course, I will say 'Yes!' to pretty much anything *Doctor Who*-related, so Peter said they had been chatting in the office at Virgin and felt that a series of books looking at each of the Doctors would be good. Paperback only. And starting with a book focussing on Tom Baker, as he was perceived to be the most popular of the Doctors. It seemed that my luck was changing!

I had a quick chat with Steve and Mark, and we all felt that we had the scope and time to tackle something else as well, so we agreed, and before long had contracts for the first in this new series of books which we called *The Handbook*. Each title looking at the Doctor in question, the man who played him, and the stories and production and anything else which seemed appropriate.

Again, we three mapped out what the content should be, and allocated the writing chores. On these, Mark was not doing the design and layout, so he took a third of the writing, while Steve and I shared the rest.

I really enjoyed doing the *Handbooks*. We did one for each of the first seven Doctors, and the final book also took in the 1996 *Doctor Who* TV movie, as that had just come out while we were preparing it.

We decided to open each book with a little novelisation from the very start of each Doctor's era, and I penned these. I also took charge of the 'Script to Screen' chapters as this was an area that interested me. In a way these were DVD commentaries before such things existed. I would pick a suitable story, and then reach out to the writer, the director, the designer and the visual effects designer, and try to get them together in a room. If that wasn't possible, I would go and interview them separately.

We would watch the story (by this time I had videos of most of the existing stories), and I would record all the conversation. Then I would write it all up, adding some description to say what was happening on screen as we went through, and then pepper that with the makers talking about how they did it, the casting, the effects, problems they had and so on. As I say, it was exactly like a transcript of a non-existent DVD commentary track!

After *The Sixties*, we tackled *The Seventies* and finally *The Eighties*. For the second and third books, we were able to gain access to the Written Archive Centre and found a wealth of information and material waiting for us. The problem with the books (and, indeed, *The Handbooks*) was that it became a question of what to leave out, rather than putting in everything we had.

The Seventies and *The Eighties* books ended up being longer than the first volume, and we were granted full colour throughout as Virgin realised the sales were good, and there was a huge demand for these titles out there.

There were some smashing signings for these books as well, all organised by Virgin's amazing PR department. For *The Sixties*, on Saturday, 24 October 1992, we were joined by Carole Ann Ford, who played Susan, the very first companion in the show alongside William Hartnell, and also Frazer Hines, who had played Jamie when Patrick Troughton was the Doctor. This would have been one of my first proper meetings with Frazer! Also present was Ray Cusick, designer of the Daleks, and, as there was also a *Doctor Who Magazine* signing taking place at the same time, comics author Dan Abnett and artist Colin Andrew were there. It was quite a team-up, all hosted by London's Forbidden Planet shop! When *The Seventies* was published, there was another London signing to which Jon Pertwee turned up, resplendent as ever. Other regional events included signings with the actor Michael Craze and Terrance

Dicks too... we did a lot of travelling around and promoting the books.

But as time went on, it became obvious that the show was not returning to the BBC anytime soon.

The final season of the 1980s, the 26th, was the last that the BBC made. The show was finally cancelled as a regular series, and the production office was closed. The Doctor and Ace walked away at the end of 'Survival', never to be seen again.[108] *Doctor Who* closed its doors on 6 December 1989, when the final episode of 'Survival' was transmitted.

A sad day indeed.

* * *

Another title which I pitched to Peter at Virgin was a book all about the companions. This was at one of the irregular meet-ups which Peter arranged for all the *Doctor Who* writers at a wine bar called the Conservatory in Central London.[109] We would rock up there and talk ideas and see what everyone else was doing... it was a great social event.

I suggested a book on the companions simply because it hadn't been done yet, and Peter was a little wary at first. His rationale was that books about the whole of *Doctor Who* worked. The Decades series, as we called them, worked, as they were looking at the whole of the series. The Handbooks worked as, again, they were looking at everything.

Before Virgin had launched our books, however, they had done titles looking at the Time Lords and the Monsters from the show, and the impression I got was that these had not done quite so well,

108 Well... almost. This is *Doctor Who*, after all. McCoy made an appearance at the start of the TV movie, and has made brief guest appearances in stories later on. Similarly, Aldred has also returned to the role of Ace in the modern series of the show.
109 This place no longer exists. It was at 15 St Giles' High Street, just opposite and down a little from The Angel pub.

and Peter put this down to the fact that they only covered part of the show.

And he felt that something on the companions was again only covering part of the whole pie.

I argued that those earlier books were predominantly fiction and artwork, whereas what Steve, Mark and I were doing was proper non-fiction with photographs, and they were completely different and more in line with what the fans wanted and, indeed, what was selling well!

Peter could see my point, and so I went away and wrote up a proposal, which was accepted.

Doctor Who: Companions was, as the title suggests, all about the companions of Doctor Who, but as usual I wanted to try to push the envelope, so I decided I wanted to show the actors and actresses in the book as they were at the time they were in Doctor Who, and as they were 'now', or at least very different from their Doctor Who appearances.

I reached out to as many of the companion actors as I could to get little contributions and interviews from them. I scoured my own archives for photographs and information, and located as many of the BBC's written outlines and early descriptions of what the companion characters would be like, and finally I started looking through photographic archives for other images of the actors which I could use. I managed to find a great and diverse selection of pictures, and the book started to come together.

It turned out great! I managed to find a good selection of images, and all the additional information told a factual and hopefully interesting story of the companions of Doctor Who, but also their development and casting, and the actors who played them.

The book also helped me to achieve a long-standing ambition, and this was to meet Zig and Zag, two puppet aliens who caused havoc on the Channel 4 breakfast programme, The Big Breakfast. I loved their antics, and the people who operated them were fast, funny and quick witted. It made for brilliant television, and I tried to catch some of it each morning before I left for work!

For all the books that Virgin published they had a great PR department, and they would send out press releases and covers and review copies, and contact radio and TV for coverage. I did pretty well with all the titles I was involved with. There would usually be a day or two approaching publication when I would head up to BBC Broadcasting House in London, and do four or five interviews on different radio shows on the trot. So, you'd be in for someone's breakfast show first, then do a mid-morning chat with someone else, a lunchtime slot with another host, then the afternoon slot, and then possibly even an evening show as well! The pace was insane, and Virgin used to send me these itineraries of who I was talking to and when and which studio, and I had to try to find everything to be there on time!

When *Companions* was coming out, I asked Angela, the PR lady, if she could approach *The Big Breakfast* and see if she could get me on there. To my amazement she managed it!

And so it was that, on Tuesday, 16 January 1996, a car was sent early in the morning to take me to Lock Keepers Cottages near Stratford in London, which was where they made and pre-recorded the show!

The hosts at that time were Mark Little and Zoe Ball, and of course the irrepressible Zig and Zag. I had been lined up to appear on a feature called 'The Crunch' during the show, in which Zig and Zag took over the airwaves. The particular game we were playing was 'What's Your Hobby, Nobby', and I was provided with a 'Nobby' badge as Zig, Zag and Mark had to guess what my hobby was!

It all went well, in one take as I recall. I was enthralled by the chaos and madness around me, and with that sort of thing, you just have to go with the flow... so I did!

What impressed me most was Zig and Zag. Not only did the

two men[110] who performed the puppets operate them, but they did the voices as well. Thinking about it, that makes more sense as they could then make the mouths move correctly, and, of course, know what they were going to say and do, and this really brought the creatures to life.

When I was in front of them, though, Ciaran and Mick were lying on their backs with their feet towards me, holding and operating the puppets with their upstretched arms. After a minute or so, you completely forgot that the operators were there, and started interacting with the puppets as if they were real. It was the most surreal and extraordinary experience!

They failed to guess what my hobby was, but then I had brought a few items with me and so they showed a Tetrap model,[111] a pair of *Doctor Who* underpants from Marks and Spencers,[112] a Cyberman head,[113] and finally, a copy of the *Companions* book, which I explained was full of girls! This seemed to unsettle them, and then we were over!

It was an amazing experience, and I managed to get a photograph of me with Zig and Zag to top it off! After the show had gone out, I also got a letter through the post from the puppets thanking me for taking part, which I thought was a nice touch!

The segment with me in it was then transmitted on the morning of Wednesday, 17 January.[114]

* * *

110 Ciaran Morrison and Mick O'Hara. There is more about Zig and Zag here: en.wikipedia.org/wiki/Zig_and_Zag_(puppets)

111 A copy of one of the cave-hanging models from 'Time and the Rani', made by Susan Moore.

112 The first-ever *Doctor Who* underpants that were released. Since then, there have been literally hundreds available from virtually every clothes shop in the UK!

113 This is a genuine prop head from 'The Five Doctors', used when a squad of Cybermen are ripped apart by a deadly fighting robot.

114 If anyone fancies seeing the appearance, it can be found here: youtu.be/y5iEx6BlLQA

As we were penning official books for Virgin, I knew that 1993 was the 30th anniversary of the show, and so wanted to do an anniversary book for them. I knew that the Peter Haining titles for the 20th and 25th anniversaries had been okay, but they had been riddled with niggling errors, and were perhaps a little too text-heavy. I wanted to do something visual!

Virgin had offices in St John's Wood in London, and around 1990 they were moving to new premises up at Ladbroke Grove. As part of the move, Peter Darvill-Evans had to pack up all his stuff and to clear the St John's Wood offices. In doing so, he came across some map cabinets which were full of old cover artwork. Seeing that some of these were *Doctor Who*, he immediately grabbed them all. Anything old was headed for some large waste skips around the back of the building, but Peter's actions saved this artwork from the furnaces.

I was up at Virgin's new offices one day, and having a meeting with Peter. There was something of a kerfuffle going on, and people seemed to be dressed smarter than usual. I wondered why, and Peter explained that Sir Richard Branson, the owner of Virgin, was visiting that day to look around the new place. I was impressed!

There was a commotion over by the door, and Peter and I went out to see what was going on. Sir Richard was heading down the corridor towards us, his smile, bigger than his face as usual, was in place, and he was nodding and shaking hands with everyone. He got to us, nodded and shook our hands, and then he was off and heading for the exit.

'I think he thinks you're one of the staff,' said Peter. 'Don't worry about it!'

So, I didn't!

Shortly after that memorable visit, I was there again talking about something or other, and Peter took me over to a great stack of original artwork that he had over by one wall. This was all the art that he had rescued from the old offices. I was amazed. There were pieces here from my beloved Target covers, as well as covers for some of the larger format books, and basically material from most of the *Doctor Who* titles that W H Allen had published!

Did they never return anything to the artists, I wondered?

But this got me thinking. If Virgin now had all this artwork…

I asked Peter if he had the transparencies for the covers which had been used to create the books through the years. He nodded, and he pulled out a small box of 5x4 transparencies of most of the cover artwork.

If we had access to the cover artwork, then I could do a Target cover artbook!

I helped Peter to sort out the artwork and made a note of what was there. Then I asked Peter if he might be interested in a 30th anniversary book for 1993? He was, and so I went away and started thinking about that.

I talked with Mark Stammers, and I think it was Mark who came up with the idea of doing a scrapbook. Mark knew that I was magpie-like in my collecting, and that I had a large collection of *Doctor Who* merchandise, and also paperwork, newspaper cuttings, reviews, images, beermats… if it had a *Doctor Who* connection then I had grabbed, kept and filed a copy away.

So, the idea of a *Doctor Who* scrapbook came about and I started to think about what might be on each page. I created a page breakdown and pencilled in what we might use. I realised that I could combine the scrapbook idea with the Target cover art idea, and move through the series chronologically, presenting some art from some of the stories, while also covering the years through assorted ephemera and photographs. I added in the idea of 'classic moments' as, with access to most of *Doctor Who* now available on video, I could take five or six stills off the TV and capture some well-remembered and impactful moments from the show's history.[115]

---

115 To help me do this, I reached out, I think through the DWAS, and asked for people to send in their favourite moments. This helped to identify and refine what would be good to use.

I sorted all the materials out and sent it all on to Mark, as he had got the contract to lay the book out.

The title was something of a problem. Titles often are! Many of the obvious ones were already taken by other books and magazines, but I decided on *Timeframe*. *Time* because, well, this was a book that covered a period of time. Plus, you have the whole 'time' thing in *Doctor Who* anyway… and *Frame* because, just like our fanzine, *The Frame*, this was a 'frame' in which we were showcasing artwork and photos and so on.

The book came out in 1993 and was an amazing success. Thankfully Virgin was a proper publishing company, and were offering royalties, and the money from this one book was enough for us to build an extension on our house!

I look back on *Timeframe* with great fondness, and one of the brilliant things about it is that we managed to capture, in a book, memories. The book means something different to everyone who sees it, because everyone has different memories about the show and the eras and the Doctors and the monsters. What one person finds disappointing, is another's favourite memory! I love it when people flick through the book. I just listen to their journey and their memories coming out as they do so.

I remember watching John Nathan-Turner and his partner Gary Downie looking through it, and John, of course, had been involved on the show from the Troughton era! Their memories were different as they were from being involved and making the show, but nevertheless, they still loved seeing all the imagery, and having those memories kicked off for them.

I have tried on a few occasions in more recent years to get BBC Books to do a *Timeframe 2* for future anniversaries, but they've just not been interested. Which is, I feel, a great shame.

Another tangential benefit of doing *Timeframe* was that I located and reached out to as many of the *Doctor Who* artists as I could, and explained that we had located much of their original art. I said I was happy to send it back to them, but I was also equally happy to negotiate a price and to buy it off them. To my pleasure, many of the artists were happy to sell me the originals, and so I picked up a lot of the original Target art at this time. Where the artists wanted the art back, Peter then arranged to ship it over. After that, Peter's large pile of artwork was soon no more!

I was also in touch with other collecting friends, like Gary Russell,[116] and he also bought several of the pieces. Gary, like me, is a massive fan of the art and has an impressive collection of original pieces.

As usual, when *Timeframe* came out, there were a load of radio appearances for me to do, talking about the show and the book and the 30th anniversary of *Doctor Who*.

One of my favourites was on a special festive edition of a BBC Radio 5 show on Thursday, 16 December, called *Formula 5*, hosted by Sue Nelson. I was invited on, as usual, to promote the book, but I decided that as this was Christmas, and this was a festive show, that it might be nice to do something a little different, so I built a Dalek live on air!

Now, you might think this a strange thing to do on radio, but it really worked well! Especially as the idea was that I was building a Dalek as a last-minute Christmas present!

My segments in the show comprised sound effects of sawing and hammering in nails, while I got Sue to 'help' me by holding the pieces together, and generally describing what we were doing to build the Dalek. I 'painted' it towards the end, and overall, I think we had a lot of fun for Christmas!

* * *

116 I had first met Gary when he came in to edit CT for the DWAS. He was an actor and had appeared in several BBC Classic Children's series like *The Famous Five* and *The Phoenix and the Carpet*. Later on, he wrote many books for Virgin, HarperCollins and the BBC, edited *Doctor Who Magazine* for a time, helped start the audio company Big Finish, worked on *Doctor Who* itself as script editor, and also worked on the BBC animated stories. He, like me, has a long history with the show!

The following year, 1994, the paperback of *Timeframe* was published, and to my pleasure, Virgin managed to arrange for me to sign copies on Sunday, 14 August, down at Longleat house, as part of a big *Doctor Who* event that had been arranged there.[117]

I had been down to Longleat House many times, and the first time we went was specifically because there was a *Doctor Who* exhibition there. As I mentioned, we often holidayed in Newquay, and so from South London, Longleat was only a short diversion on the way there.

The *Doctor Who* Exhibition first opened there in 1973, and I suspect it was in 1974 that I first visited and was enthralled by the place. You entered through the TARDIS doors and then down steps into a dark corridor lined with displays of monsters and Daleks and all the things from the show that I loved! I could – and did – spend hours in there: reaching the end and then retracing my steps to the start, so I could walk through again and again! There was also a shop, and I would always buy some bits and pieces as well.

In 1994, however, I was sitting in the Orangery, variously with Nicholas Courtney,[118] Colin Baker, Sylvester McCoy, Peter Davison, and others, and over two or more sessions we were all signing postcards or books or whatever people brought, and I had a stack of the *Timeframe* paperback which Peter Darvill-Evans was there selling. It all went really well, and I was very chuffed to be actually present with some of my heroes signing copies!

We finished signing over lunchtime, and then the afternoon was my own, so I wandered about, taking in the atmosphere. I saw Jon Pertwee again, and he was working so hard, sitting in the old yellow roadster car, Bessie, that he had used in the show, and having photos taken with everyone. It was a hot day as well, and Jon was wearing his *Doctor Who* costume as he always did.

---

117 There were often events at Longleat. Because there was the official *Doctor Who* Exhibition there, it was considered a great place to organise a get-together!

118 Courtney played Brigadier Lethbridge-Stewart in the show.

I headed back to the green room for a drink, and while I was there, Jon came in. He was sweltering and had needed a break.

A slight tangent from the story here. I had known Jon for some time. We had been at a great many DWAS and other conventions together over the years, and I had interviewed him on stage as well as seen him in the green room and elsewhere.

Back in 1984, Jon had written and published an autobiographical volume called Moon Boots and Dinner Suits,[119] and it had done very well. However, it only covered his life to the end of the Second World War, and many fans had been asking when Jon was going to write a second volume which covered his radio and TV careers, including Doctor Who. Jon, being a very busy and in-demand actor, never got around to it, and so always answered politely that there were no plans.

I had been thinking for some time that it would be great if Jon did get this done, as there really was no time like the present.

When we were writing the text for The Seventies, I took charge of Jon's biographical chapter, and was so impressed with the sheer amount and breadth of what he had done. This made me feel even stronger that this second autobiography should happen, and, as I had just done all the research, maybe I should offer to help with it. I had wanted to ask him about it, but the circumstances were never quite right... he was always dashing off somewhere, or in the middle of signing autographs or whatever, and I didn't want to come over like just another fan who was asking him a question that he had heard a million times before.

Now, here I was, alone in the green room at Longleat House, with Jon... the opportunity had never been better. To begin with, I asked Jon how he was doing. 'Hot!' he replied, so he divested his cloak and jacket and got some water. I then plucked up courage – Jon was a nice man, but he had this charisma, or aura, about

119 Moon Boots and Dinner Suits (Jon Pertwee, Elm Tree Books/Hamish Hamilton Ltd, 1984).

him which made him seem much larger than life, and this just tended to make people around him act differently to how you might normally act; it was the strangest thing − and asked Jon about his autobiography. 'Yes,' he said. 'I keep being asked that.'

'Well,' I said, 'I'd like to write it with you.'

Jon fixed me with his gaze, as if assessing and summing me up, and then said, 'Well, let's talk about it. You have my number?' I said that I didn't, so Jon scribbled it down and asked me to call him next week.

With a smile and another cup of water, Jon was up and back off outside again, where a small crowd had gathered as they had seen him go in.

The life of a superstar, I thought.

The cover for *I Am The Doctor*, the autobiography that I wrote in 1996 with Jon
Pertwee.

10

I Am the Doctor!

Having set up the call with Jon Pertwee, I was understandably nervous, but I called him and we spoke. He was very receptive to the idea of working with someone on this book, and was happy to talk to me further, so he gave me his address in Putney, and we arranged to meet at his home.

On the day, I arrived promptly – I pride myself on trying always to be on time for meetings or whatever – and I think it was a Wednesday.

I say that as it was around this time, with the book writing and publishing going well, that I decided to see if I could cut down the time I was at Lloyds. I had been working five days a week, and that was fine, but all the extracurricular activities were starting to pile up.

I had, since 1984, been writing and editing the book review column for *Starburst* magazine (my friend Steven Payne had bought the magazine rights from Marvel around that time, and, knowing that I loved reading science fiction and horror, asked if I would take on the reviews for him). I did this, and ended up contributing a monthly author interview to the magazine, as well as organising events with the likes of horror authors James Herbert and Clive Barker, and sorting out monthly forthcoming books lists and whatever else I was offered by the publishers. Also, since 1986, I had been writing for Doctor Who Magazine (I compiled their 'Matrix Data Bank', which was basically answering reader's questions, as well as the occasional article and interview). The eighties and early nineties were a very busy time for me, and I was running out of time to do the things I wanted to do!

The other issue for me was one of pay and promotions at Lloyds. Because I had been there a fair time, I was no longer getting the pay rises or promotions that I felt I should have been – I was good at my job, there were no issues, nothing went wrong, and I always delivered on time, but it's the way with all larger companies. As someone once explained to me, companies are run by managers, not by the people who do the work, and so there's a limit to how far they can promote the people who actually do the work! Which is very true. So, given this apparent stagnancy in my job, I wanted to see if I could drop to four days a week, which would give me another day to work on all this other stuff!

They agreed, and strangely and completely coincidentally (and unknown to me in advance), a couple of months later I got a promotion and a pay rise, so the drop in days actually meant no financial loss to me. Which was nice. The day I chose to have off was Wednesday. I figured I'd rather have lots of short weeks than work four days in a row and then have a long weekend. I also realised that on a Wednesday, I could call around the publishers to see what was happening and what was new, and then have those books, proofs and covers with me by the weekend, so I could then start writing it all up for Starburst.

So that is why I suspect it was a Wednesday that I went to see Jon. We had a very interesting chat, he said he'd introduce me to his PA and secretary, who had all the information about what he had done and so on. I said I'd pull together a proposal for a second volume of the autobiography, and then, when we had agreed that, I'd set about trying to sell it to a publisher.

And that is what I did. I created the proposal and outline for the book, which would cover all of Jon's radio and TV credits, basically picking up where *Moon Boots and Dinner Suits* left off, and also include photos and whatever else we had.

My first port of call was, of course, Virgin, but Peter turned it down! He said he didn't really want a book that wasn't a *Doctor Who* book... and this was covering all of Jon's career. I was a little surprised but, undaunted, I then took it on a round of publishers which took months and months.

Publisher after publisher turned it down, and I was struggling to understand why. This was Jon Pertwee, one of the greatest entertainers and actors currently working. Surely there had to be some interest somewhere!

Because I was in touch with many of the publishers anyway for the material for *Starburst*, I called up one of the editors, I think it might have been at Simon and Schuster, somewhere like that, and asked why they weren't interested. Most of the rejections I got back gave no information, just that it wasn't for them, or it wasn't what they were looking for, not very helpful comments like that.

So, I spoke to the editor about it, and they said to me, 'Well, it's like this. This is a book about Jon Pertwee, yes?'

Of course it was.

'Well, does Jon or any of his family have cancer or some incurable disease?'

Not that I knew of.

'Was Jon going to talk about any of his affairs, or women he has dated, or anything like that?'

Not very likely. And not that I knew that he had even done anything like that anyway!

'Are any of his children dying, or has he lost a child?'

No. Again, not as far as I know.

'Well, there you go then. That's why no one is interested. What the publishers want are stories of overcoming cancer or the pain of death… they want a whiff of scandal, and the thought that we're hearing things which should not be heard. A book about the life of an entertainer, no matter how good or popular they are, does not automatically make for a book that a publisher wants to buy!'

Well, that told me! Seriously, I was very grateful for this editor giving it to me straight. In a nutshell I was wasting my time, and it was unlikely that any publisher would want to buy this book.

I then had the job of relaying this message, somewhat sanitised, back to Jon.

Jon was very disappointed, and I wasn't sure if he blamed me for this somehow… after all, it was his life story here!

I decided to have another talk with Peter at Virgin, as I was sure there was a book here. Peter was sympathetic, but again said that they could only publish *Doctor Who* books. So, I said, 'Well, what it if *was* a *Doctor Who* book? What if we focussed on Jon's *Doctor Who* stories and appearances and made it all about that, rather than about everything that he had done?'

This seemed to interest Peter, and so he went away and eventually came back with the answer that this would be something they would publish. I explained the situation again to Jon, and while we were both disappointed that no one was interested in something on his whole career, at least we could get a *Doctor Who* book out of it!

I reworked the pitch – the book was titled *I Am the Doctor!* – and I sent it off to Peter. He gave it the green light, and so Jon and I started work on the book.

I decided that the best way to do it was to watch the *Doctor Who* stories with Jon, and to record all the conversation, chat and stories which emerged. So, I arranged, every week, on a Wednesday afternoon, to head over to Jon's to watch a story and to talk.

This seemed to work very well, and we went through all the stories with me asking questions and prompting Jon, explaining where the locations were and so on, and this prompted more stories. As did the actors appearing in them, and the directors, and so on. I recorded the whole lot, and then, when we had completed each story, I wrote it all up.

As this was an autobiography, I felt it needed to be in Jon's own words, as otherwise it would be a biography! So, I wrote the book as though it was Jon speaking, and I got pretty good at writing how Jon spoke. The reasoning being that if people, when they read the book, could hear Jon, then I had done my job well. The idea was that they shouldn't be able to hear me at all, and if they could, then in some way I had failed!

There were a couple of amusing times with Jon. One time I turned up and he had forgotten I was coming, and was still in his dressing gown! He invited me in and got me set up with a cup of tea while he went and got dressed.

Another time he had just come back from an event or a holiday or something, and had got hold of this idea to promote chocolate-covered locusts in the UK. He had a bag full of them in the kitchen and was trying to get me to eat some, saying they were delicious! I declined, as the thought of eating locusts just turned my stomach. Jon, though, was happily munching away on them and extolling their virtues as good protein and so on... He could be a real character.

Overall, though, the Jon that I saw and got to know was fairly quiet and thoughtful. He was very driven to always do his best and to give his best, and he certainly didn't suffer fools gladly. He wanted to ensure that the people he was working with had his best interests at heart, but once he was happy about that, and that you weren't out to try to double cross him, or rip him off, then he would do anything for you.

It took over a year to work through the book with Jon. In between the sessions at his house, I was also researching and looking up everything I could that related to him. Newspaper cuttings, interviews on radio and television which he had on cassette and video, anything I could lay my hands on which contained his stories and anecdotes, because Jon was a great storyteller. Once he started, he had the audience in the palm of his hands, and his anecdotes became wilder and wilder! However, I never found one I couldn't verify! There was a truth in every one of them, no matter how incredible they sounded.

Jon would talk of being the ringmaster at Billy Smart's Circus, and of wrangling elephants, and then there was a photo of him doing just that! He would talk of riding a camel down the King's Road in London, and another photo. He was friends with everyone, knew everyone – that's what a lifetime in show business will do for you! Jon started as an entertainer on stage and on radio, and then moved to television and film and everything in between. He was an all-rounder. He could sing, dance, act, and the voices! Jon was once called 'The Man of One Thousand Voices' and this was certainly true. He could put on an accent or a voice and just become a new character. This was, of course, invaluable on the radio, where he honed these talents.

As we put the book together, I decided that it would be such a shame if none of his non-*Doctor Who* career was covered at all, so I added a short piece at the start, and then page spreads on *The Navy Lark* and *Worzel Gummidge* to try to add a little balance to the proceedings.

There was one chapter which Jon and I never got to talk about, looking at the *Doctor Who* stage play *The Ultimate Adventure*. So, I wrote that in Jon's words and using elements from other interviews that he had given, and I don't think he even noticed that we hadn't discussed it.

When I had written a chapter, Jon got a printed copy and went through it, making comments and notes as he went. I was able to then make any corrections to my files. To my pleasure, there wasn't really anything he objected to, just a few queries as to whether a given story was in the right place or not. This was something that was quite hard to do. Often Jon would tell a story about being at some stately home or large house, filming something for Doctor Who, but the people he mentioned were not in the Doctor Who story he thought it was. Or he thought the year was wrong for the location. My job was to try to fact-check as best I could and to get all this straightened out and correct, so that the right stories about the right people and places were in the correct places in the book!

Finally, we had all the text sorted out and agreed, so the next job was to sort out the images. I again raided my own photo collection, and those of friends, for anything I could find which was new and different from Jon's era. I also made a trip to the BBC's photographic archive, a place I had been before when researching the other books, and went through the files, looking for strange and unusual shots and for things that hadn't been seen.

The archive had both black-and-white images and colour. The black-and-white came from negatives, while the colour pictures were on transparency, and the interesting thing was that, for the black-and-white, they had only printed up maybe one image from each 'set' of pictures.

A photographer might take ten or fifteen photographs of each thing they were covering, but only one of those images would be selected and then used. Thus, by searching through the negatives, I could find many more images, slightly different from the one everyone knew, and ask for copies of those. Also, on those negatives, were other shots and pictures which no one had seen, and nothing similar had ever been printed. These were amazing when you stumbled upon them.

On occasion, too, the photographer might have finished his day on set, and then use up the rest of his film taking random shots of the sets or the cast or the crew. Again, these candid shots were incredibly interesting when you found them. These tended to be blurry, though, as the photographer was just using up his film, but nevertheless there were some gems to be found there!

What to use on the cover was something of a nightmare as well! I had found some nice, larger transparencies from 'Day of the Daleks' of Jon with one of the Daleks, which I felt could work, but the positioning was not quite right for a cover. Jon said he had seen some recent photographs from a chap in Australia, who Jon had sat for on a recent visit, so he put me in touch and I got hold of the pictures and they were perfect, showing Jon posed with a toy Dalek and with a very *Doctor Who*-like mirror-reflection background. So, we made the arrangements and that became the cover of the book.

We were now in 1996, and the final element that we needed was some pictures from Jon's own collection, so, on Saturday, 4 May, I arranged to go over to his house to go through the images, and record details for the captioning of them. I rocked up there and Jon had this large box of material which he then went through, each one of the pictures sparking a different memory in him as he went.

I selected the images which I liked and which I thought would work, and recorded the details for each. Jon approved the image for the cover, and then I headed off. Jon was going on holiday to America the next day, and we said we'd catch up when he got back.

Twelve days later I was at work at Lloyds, and I got a call from Virgin. It was Andy Bodle, the assistant there, and he told me that they had heard the most awful news: Jon Pertwee had passed away. It was Monday, 20 May 1996, and Jon had been only 76 years old.

I was in shock. I found it hard to believe. I had seen him just before he left England, and he had seemed okay. I went to my manager and explained, and then went home. I just couldn't function that day. Working so closely with Jon, who had been open and honest and so transparent about his life and career, I had felt we'd become friends as well.

It appeared that Jon had suffered a heart attack in his sleep and had passed away while on holiday. Terrible news!

Thinking back over all the time I spent with Jon, he had talked about and gone to various appointments with doctors and hospitals. He had always been plagued with a bad back, the result of too much water skiing and being something of an action man and daredevil in his younger days, but he was also suffering from an irregular beating of his heart, and was having electro-therapy to try to get his heart beating back in step again. Maybe it was this ailment which finally took him, I don't know.

About a week later, I wrote a piece which I called 'Going Through the Photographs' for a fanzine, which was an edited and written-up transcript of my last visit where we went through all his pictures and talked about them. It was very sad, and I'm not ashamed to say that I cried as I wrote it.

I also penned his obituary for *The Guardian* newspaper, which is reproduced here:

> To have known Jon Pertwee is to have known one of the true characters in the entertainment industry. He was a charismatic showman and everything he did was touched by a sense of style and wit. His distinctive voice could effortlessly be twisted into accents and characters ranging from his acclaimed Worzel Gummidge to *The Navy Lark's* stammering and stuttering Commander Wetherby via incredible imitations of Oscar Wilde, Lord Haw Haw, Charles Laughton and just about anyone else you'd care to mention.
>
> He was also a mine of stories and anecdotes. Jon had been everywhere, had met everyone and had done everything. Mention a theatrical name and he was off... tales of pranks, motorbikes, mistaken identities, aborted theatre performances, friends and relations across the globe, travel to far flung places... nothing was too obscure for Jon to have some valid, and often screamingly funny story about it.

As the Doctor, with his shock of white hair and impressively craggy features, he entertained and thrilled a generation of children and dressed in rags with a carrot for a nose as Worzel Gummidge he captured the hearts of yet another.

Off the screen, Jon was a charismatic and friendly man, always willing to offer honest advice and judgement and yet always supportive and loyal to his fellow artistes.

A history of his life and career is somewhat astonishing in itself.

Jon Pertwee was born John (after the apostle and disciple) Devon (after the county) Roland (after his father) Pertwee (an Anglicised version of the true family name, Perthuis de Laillevault) on 7 July 1919 in the Chelsea area of London. He was the second son of famous playwright, painter and actor Roland Pertwee, and his actress wife Avice, his writer brother Michael being three years his senior.

After leaving school in 1936, he failed the audition for the Central School of Dramatic Arts, Central's principal predicting that he had no future in the theatre. Undaunted he auditioned for, and was accepted by, the Royal Academy of Dramatic Art but was expelled and subsequently secured a place in the final tour of the Arts League of Service Travelling Theatre, directed by Donald Wolfit. In 1937 he joined J Baxter-Somerville's Repertory Players at the Springfield Theatre in Jersey, from where he was also expelled.

Jon then joined the Rex Lesley-Smith repertory company for a year before returning to London. During 1938 and 1939 he obtained several small parts including in To Kill a Cat at the Aldwych Theatre. Also in the cast of To Kill a Cat was a popular radio actor called John Salew.

On one occasion Salew was unable to fulfil his radio commitments as he was filming, and so he sent Jon along in his place.

This was Jon's break into commercial radio where he stayed for the next two years. To supplement his income, he also worked as an extra at Denham Film Studios, appearing in numerous productions including *Dinner at the Ritz* (1936), *A Yank at Oxford* (1938), *Young Man's Fancy* (1939) and *The Four Just Men* (1939).

When the Second World War broke out Jon joined the Navy as a wireless operator. On 29 November 1940, he was drafted onto HMS *Hood* and stationed at Scapa Flow in the Orkney Islands. He was then transferred to the ship *Dunluce Castle* to train as an Officer Cadet. Shortly afterwards, on 24 May 1941, HMS *Hood* had its fateful battle with the *Bismark*.

Following an incendiary bomb attack on the barracks at Portsmouth, Jon suffered a severe blow to the head and was dropped from the Officer Cadet course to be posted to the Isle of Man as a Divisional Officer. There, Jon formed a small company of local amateurs and servicemen which came to be known as the Service Players.

In 1946, Pertwee joined the cast of Eric Barker's forces radio show *Mediterranean Merry-Go-Round*. It was in this series that he was first able to indulge his flair for accents, and played numerous memorable characters. In 1948 the fictional HMS *Waterlogged* became the subject of a spin-off show entitled *Waterlogged Spa* and it was here that Jon created perhaps his most memorable radio character, the Postman, with the catchphrase: 'What does it matter what you do as long as you tear 'em up?'.

Although Jon had been appearing in films since 1936,

he received star billing for the first time in 1953 with George Cole in *Will Any Gentleman...?* in which he met his first wife Jean Marsh. They were married in 1955 but the marriage quickly broke down. It was on a skiing holiday to Kitzbühel in February 1958 that Jon met Ingeborg Rhoesha, a young German dress designer, and immediately fell in love. Jon was divorced from Marsh in 1960 and married Ingeborg on 13 August the same year.

In 1958 Jon was asked by the BBC's Head of Light Entertainment if he had any ideas for a new radio comedy series in which he might be interested in starring. Out of these discussions came *The Navy Lark*. This series was an enormous success and went on to run for almost 20 years.

During the sixties, Jon continued his career in film and appeared in several productions, including three of the popular *Carry On* films: *Carry On Cleo* (1964), *Carry On Cowboy* (1965) and *Carry On Screaming* (1966). Jon also enjoyed successful stage tours in *A Funny Thing Happened on the Way to the Forum* (1963–1966) and *There's a Girl in My Soup* (1966–1967).

In 1969, Jon was working on an episode of *The Navy Lark* when one of his co-stars, Tenniel Evans, mentioned that Patrick Troughton was leaving *Doctor Who* and that Jon would make an excellent Doctor. Jon was sufficiently intrigued to talk to his agent and it transpired that Jon's name had been on the list of potential candidates for months. Jon eventually played the Doctor from 1970 until 1974, battling Daleks, Ice Warriors, Sea Devils and many other alien life forms alongside his companions Liz Shaw (played by Caroline John), Jo Grant (Katy Manning) and Sarah Jane Smith (Elisabeth Sladen).

Shortly after leaving *Doctor Who*, Jon hosted a quiz show called *Whodunnit?* for Thames TV. This went on to become one of the most successful quiz shows of the period, running for five years. Jon also appeared in the film *One of our Dinosaurs is Missing* (1975) and an episode of *The Goodies* on television before returning to the theatre in the hit musical *Irene* (1976–1977).

Worzel Gummidge came about in 1979 after writers Willis Hall and Keith Waterhouse asked Jon if he would like to play the eponymous living scarecrow in a film they had written based on Barbara Euphan-Todd's books. The film did not go ahead but Jon persuaded Hall and Waterhouse to prepare a pilot script for a television series. This was eventually picked up by Southern Television and became a massive international hit. Worzel was even named as TV personality of the year by the Variety Club in 1981.

The series came to an untimely end when Southern Television lost its franchise and its successor, Television South (TVS) declined to take up the series. A co-production deal was eventually secured in 1987 for further episodes to be made in New Zealand. In the nineties, Jon continued to work on stage with numerous roles including in 1992 and 1993 as Jacob Marley in *Scrooge – The Musical*. Jon also provided character voices for a game based on Terry Pratchett's Discworld in 1995.

Jon returned several times to *Doctor Who*. He appeared in the 20th anniversary story *The Five Doctors* (1983), starred in the stage play *Doctor Who: The Ultimate Adventure* (1989) and starred on radio in the plays *The Paradise of Death* (1993) and *The Ghosts of N-Space* (1996).

Jon was also in almost constant demand for science fiction conventions, cabaret appearances, after-dinner speaking and guest slots on a great number of TV, radio and video productions. In the early part of 1996 he was touring in two different productions, one an evening of

171

music and comedy and the other, his popular and successful one-man-show 'Who is Jon Pertwee?'.

Throughout much of his career, which spanned over five decades on stage, radio, film, television – and even a time spent working with Billy Smart's Circus – Jon was a staunch supporter of and fund raiser for the Grand Order of Water Rats, a charity which cares for elderly and retired members of the acting profession. Membership of the Water Rats is by invitation only, and Jon was always proud to be associated with the organization. Above all else, Jon Pertwee maintained a deep respect for others in his profession, and remained a showman and a gentleman to the end.

Despite all this distraction, I still had several books to deliver,[120] so it was onwards with the photos and the captions, finalising the text and cover, and delivering it all to Virgin.

Because of Jon's death, I decided it would be nice to include some tributes in the book, so I reached out to several people he had worked with on Doctor Who and assembled some great pieces. Barry Letts wrote a lovely introduction as well. I then thought it would be nice to include a facsimile signature at the back to sign off with, and also signatures from the various people who had contributed, so I sorted all that out. At the last minute, Virgin decided to add the tagline Jon Pertwee's Final Memoir under the main title.

They published the book on 21 November 1996, and we had a little launch party on the day where Ingeborg, Jon's widow, and Dariel, his daughter, came along, together with Terrance Dicks, Christopher Barry, Barry Newbery and Richard Franklin.[121] Even the actor Leslie Phillips was there, although he had never appeared

120 As well as I Am the Doctor!, there was the next of the Handbooks due as well.
121 Richard played Captain Mike Yates of UNIT in the show.

in Doctor Who, he had appeared in The Navy Lark with Jon. It was very sad that Jon couldn't have been there to see the results of all our efforts.

In typical publisher fashion, with Jon no longer around to provide publicity for the book, Virgin cut the print-run to just 6,000 copies, and didn't reprint when all the copies sold out before publication. They also never did a paperback edition of it. I think they felt that they should just try to kill it, as they thought it wasn't going to do well, and in any case, their time publishing Doctor Who books was coming to an end. I am still asked today about copies of that book, as it is so hard to find and costly as a result of the limited number printed.

The problem with reprinting it is that the photographs are mostly BBC copyright and the text is jointly owned by myself and by Jon's estate, and the last time I tried to find out if they were interested in any further reprints, there was no interest. Unfortunately, for the moment, the book remains out of print. Which is a great shame as I was pleased with it, and people told me how they could really hear Jon coming loud and strong from all the pages and stories within it.

I hope I did him proud!

Me on the set of *Daemos Rising*. This was for a sequence recorded in Kents Cavern in Torquay, used for the climax of the film.

11

More Doctor Who...

While all these books for Virgin were being written and published, the wheels of Doctor Who were still turning, albeit slowly, and in 1996, some six and a half years after it had last been shown on BBC television, it was back!

This was a new TV movie that had been made in America and Canada by an American producer named Philip Segal.

I was very excited for the production, and couldn't wait to see it.

The production of the TV movie was meant to herald a whole new era of Doctor Who, and the lead actor, Paul McGann, had reportedly been engaged for a series if the movie did well enough... there was a lot happening!

Part of what was happening was also impacting on Virgin Publishing. Although they had been very successfully publishing the books under Peter Darvill-Evans's editorship for some years now, including a highly successful range of original novels for the Seventh Doctor, and a series of original novels featuring past Doctors, the BBC decided that they wanted to take all the licenses back in-house. This was a purely business decision, and no reflection on the quality of what Virgin had been doing.

This made for a somewhat stressful time at Virgin, as the BBC gave them just six months to close down and stop sales of all their *Doctor Who* lines – something that was somewhat tricky as, of course, Virgin had commissioned ahead in expectation that the license would renew as it always did.

For Steve, Mark and myself, it meant that the final book in the Handbook series was in doubt, as any publication date was outside of this license period. The Decades books were complete, as were *Timeframe*, *Companions* and Jon Pertwee's *I Am the Doctor!*, but the final Handbook, for the era of the Seventh Doctor, was not. In the end, Peter managed to plead and negotiate and got permission to finish the range off with that final book. Meanwhile, the fiction ranges were ended with a single novel which featured the Eighth Doctor direct from the TV movie.

The BBC were now powering ahead with projects, and, of course, I contacted them to see what they might want from me. Initially there seemed to be a lot of confusion, but the editor, Nuala Buffini, came back and asked if I might be interested in writing a very short book as part of a kids Filofax/personal organiser range. Of course I was, and I think I did the text for that in a couple of days – we joked it was the quickest turnaround from commission to delivery they had ever had. It was very simple indeed, aimed very young and without any real research needed. The book was published in October 1996.

I then realised that I probably needed to pitch them something. One of my great loves about *Doctor Who* has always been the monsters, and the book that W H Allen/Virgin published was disappointing as it was mainly made-up fiction for the text, and artwork for the illustration. I had always wanted to see a chapter-and-verse proper behind-the-scenes book all about the monsters, so that is what I pitched.

Nuala liked the idea for the book, which I called, simply, *A Book of Monsters*, and so, to my pleasure, it was greenlit.

In January 1997, however, the editor in charge changed. Incoming was a chap called Steve Cole, who had taken over from Nuala as the project editor for *Doctor Who*, looking after the BBC's *Doctor Who* ranges. I think they had realised that they needed someone over all of it, so Steve had oversight over not only all the books they were producing (they had decided to ape Virgin's successful formula of a new Eighth Doctor novel and a new past Doctor novel being published every month, as well as considering other books), but also to oversee the BBC VHS video releases of *Doctor Who*, which were also now coming out monthly.

It was a delight to create that book. I looked at all the monsters from the show, but for each era I picked out a handful to delve deeply into: mainly the ones which later recurred, but also a few notable one-offs. For each I adopted a script-to-screen approach, taking what the original script said as my starting point, and then interviewing the designer/costume designer, visual effects, make-up, the actor(s) who played the creatures and anyone else who seemed appropriate. This was then compiled to create the text, and illustrated with design pictures and photographs and anything else I could pull together.

For the back of the book, I set myself something of a challenge by including a complete A–Z of every monster that had appeared in the series to date. And I wanted a small photograph of each as well! Most were fine, but for some there appeared to be no pictures whatsoever, so I had to search and ask, and finally managed to find every one thanks to a few friends with very exclusive photographic collections which contain items that are not often seen.

One item I wanted to get for the book required some work from the BBC's office. I had remembered that when Steve and I went to the BBC's Written Archives, I had seen in a file for 'The Dominators' a colour design drawing by designer Martin Baugh for a Quark. This didn't look quite as it had ended up on television, and I really wanted that in the book. However, when you visited the Archives, at the time you weren't allowed to take copies of anything, you had to formally request and pay for them, so we were unable to get hold of it. As we had already done *The Sixties*, there was no actual use we had for the image, so we didn't follow the process to request a copy at the time.

I had to ask Steve Cole if they could put in the request to get hold of the design and include it in the book. Luckily they were able to do so, and I was so pleased to include it in there!

The book was published in October 1997, and like all the others I'd done by then, I was incredibly proud of it, and really pleased with how it turned out.

* * *

The final book that I worked on for the BBC was one which was well overdue for publication. In 1997, Steve Walker and I pitched an idea for a proper *Doctor Who* programme guide to Steve Cole, on the basis that the show had now finished, or at least was paused for however long that ended up being, and there was no official BBC programme guide for the series available.

We called our book *Doctor Who: The Television Companion*, and pitched it as containing all you needed to know about *Doctor Who*, including commentary and contemporary critical feedback.

Steve Cole liked the idea and again we were greenlit.

For the writing of the book, Steve Walker and I decided that the simplest way to do it was to just do alternate stories, so that's what we did. We worked through every one, collating the information and writing the critical appraisal pieces, pulling in whatever we could find from contemporary reports, newspaper reviews, comments and so on to provide a look at how the stories were received when they were first transmitted.

Then we both went over the completed book and edited and revised it to bring the whole thing together. It was a simple idea, but quite challenging to do as there was so much to cover. We added, right at the end, a section on the Paul McGann TV movie to bring it completely up to date.

It was published in October 1998, and again was well received. A piece of work we are both very proud of to this day.

After this, there were no more commissions. Steve Cole seemed to have his hands full, and even a book looking behind the scenes of the TV movie by Gary Russell,[122] originally to have been published by Virgin (they ultimately declined it), was also declined by BBC Books. It was finally published by HarperCollins.

I suspect that after the TV movie, and with the ratings for it not being as good as Universal, who were behind it, had wanted,[123] the expected series never happened, and the BBC were left with the book ranges for something that they had expected to be a massive world-wide hit, but which was ultimately cancelled after just one film.

From my point of view, because I was working on something for the BBC at the time,[124] I was invited to a press screening of the film. This was very exciting as, of course, this was the first *Doctor Who* that had been made in six or seven years! *Doctor Who Magazine* had been covering its production, and excitement was high as to what to expect!

The launch was on Monday, 13 May 1996, at BAFTA in London, and I arrived there and met up with the editor from the *Doctor Who* books range, Nuala. We sat together in the audience, and just down from me I could see Terrance Dicks and Barry Letts, who had also been invited. The auditorium was full!

The film played, and, at the end, I was crying my eyes out. I am

---

122 *Doctor Who – Regeneration* (Philip Segal with Gary Russell, HarperCollins, 2000).

123 Part of the reason for the slightly lowered ratings in the USA was that the schedulers put the TV movie's debut against an episode of the highly popular sitcom *Roseanne* in which Roseanne's long-suffering husband Dan had a heart attack... this was heavily promoted and, of course, pulled viewers away from *Doctor Who*. In the UK, the film managed very respectably in the ratings, with nine million viewers.

124 This was that tiny little Filofax insert!

such a softie! It was the combination of the screenplay and how the Doctor wins out at the end over the Master, and the sadness that he didn't take Daphne Ashbrook's Grace with him when he left – he really should have done, but I guess they hadn't signed her for any potential series – added to a relief that it was actually good and entertaining. I had really enjoyed it!

It seemed that I might have been in the minority, though, as there were rumblings about it being too American (whatever that means), that the Doctor wouldn't ride a motorbike (had they forgotten Pertwee!), and that he wasn't half-human (the show constantly evolves and reinvents its own mythology, so why not?!). There were also complaints about the Doctor kissing Grace, but this was more of a spur-of-the-moment in jubilation thing rather than passion, and why not anyway? The Doctor has always shown emotion where his friends and companions are concerned. Like when his granddaughter Susan left, or Jo Grant, or Sarah Jane Smith... there's a common thread of the Doctor wearing his heart(s) a little too much on his sleeve when it came to his friends.

Others who were there remember Terrance and Barry leaving early, as they really hadn't enjoyed it and felt it wasn't *Doctor Who* any more. I think this is a shame, but understandable, as both men had been instrumental in refining and defining *Doctor Who* for a new generation at the start of the seventies, and to see a fairly different interpretation to theirs must have been hard.

One thing that was nice was that as the BBC's premiere of the TV movie was on 27 May, they added a small caption to the end, dedicating it to the memory of Jon Pertwee, who had died on 20 May. That also brought a tear to my eye, as you can imagine.

* * *

A further piece of *Doctor Who* fun that I was involved in came about when Keith Barnfather approached me about writing a drama for Reeltime Pictures.

To be fair, I had been nagging him since the previous dramas he had made that I wanted to write the next one, but nevertheless I was very pleased to be asked!

This was around 2003, and Keith came to me with something of a shopping list.

He wanted to use two characters who he had introduced in a previous drama, called *Downtime*. These were the Brigadier's daughter, Kate Lethbridge-Stewart, and a UNIT officer called Captain Cavendish. The actors who played them were married in real life (Beverley Cressman and Miles Richardson), and they were keen to do something else. He also wanted to record it all in a cottage down near the south coast. In fact, this was a place owned by Miles's father, the actor Ian Richardson, and it would be ideal as a base, as well as being a great location.

There was also the possibility of filming down in a place called Kents Cavern in Torquay, so there were cliffs and sea and so on too, if we so wanted, as well as the caves.

My initial thought was to do something with the Sea Devils, as they were from the sea, so the location would make sense for that. I had a vague idea that UNIT, or someone else, was playing with genetics and trying to splice humans with Sea Devils... something like that. However, when Keith checked with the estate of Malcolm Hulke, who had created the Sea Devils, the rights were not available, so we had to rethink.

At the time I was also running Telos Publishing, and Steve and I had successfully got the rights to use the Daemons from *Doctor Who*, and they were central to a *Doctor Who* spin-off series that we were publishing called *Time Hunter*, so I suggested to Keith that this might be a good alternative. He agreed, and was able to secure the okay from the various estates to use the characters.

So, my script came into focus. To keep it simple, we had just three main characters. There was Kate and Cavendish, but in order to provide some conflict and interest, I added in a third, an apparent ghost, but in reality a time traveller who has become trapped in time as an echo, due to what an evil bunch of cultist people in the far future, the Sodality, are up to. All of this tied into the overall *Time Hunter* theme: that the Sodality are trying to bring the Daemons back to Earth so they can take their power.

Further to this, we knew from the television story 'The Daemons' that the creatures visited three times… so my story, now called *Daemos Rising*, was the second time that they came to Earth. The third time was chronicled in the final *Time Hunter* book!

I wrote the script, and it ended up being a little like all sorts of things. There were homages to the film *Suspiria* in there, bits of horror movies where you see strange dry ice creeping along the corridors of a house, and bits of *Doctor Who* with the Daemon and their mental games in trying to understand humanity, plus time travel elements as in 'The Day of the Daleks'.

We shot it at the end of 2003, and all went well. There were a few disruptions, like unexpected torrential rain and Beverley twisting her ankle. Not to mention filling Kents Cavern with smoke to the extent that no one could see, let along record anything, until the smoke had cleared! Not funny at the time, but it is now when I look back on it.

We had an amazing director of photography on the production called Neil Oseman,[125] and he was incredible. He had an eye for the best shot and the best lighting, and the atmosphere that the finished production has is a testament to his skills.

As usual with anything film or TV related, I loved being on set and being a part of the production. Sometimes it's rare for an author to get to see their work being performed first hand, but this was a real treat. Keith did a sterling job of directing, and the cast made my words make sense, which is all you can ask, really.

Even some of the fiddly elements, like making the ghost transparent

125 Neil has gone on to have an amazing career in television and film! *Daemos Rising* was just his second credit and we all knew he would go far!

in some scenes, or reflections doing something different to the main action – little nuances which help to sell the idea that there's something creepy going on – all worked wonderfully.

The film was released in 2004, and it's very pleasing that it still stands up today. The direction, visuals and sound design are all superb, and the only thing that lets it down is the CGI on the Daemon. But this was the start of the 2000s and CGI was very much in its infancy unless you had loads of money to throw at it, which Keith didn't! So, we had to use what we could get.

And anyway, in the spirit of classic *Doctor Who*, it's hard to do these things without a dodgy special effect from time to time![126]

---

126 If you want to watch *Daemos Rising*, it's available from www.timetraveltv.com.

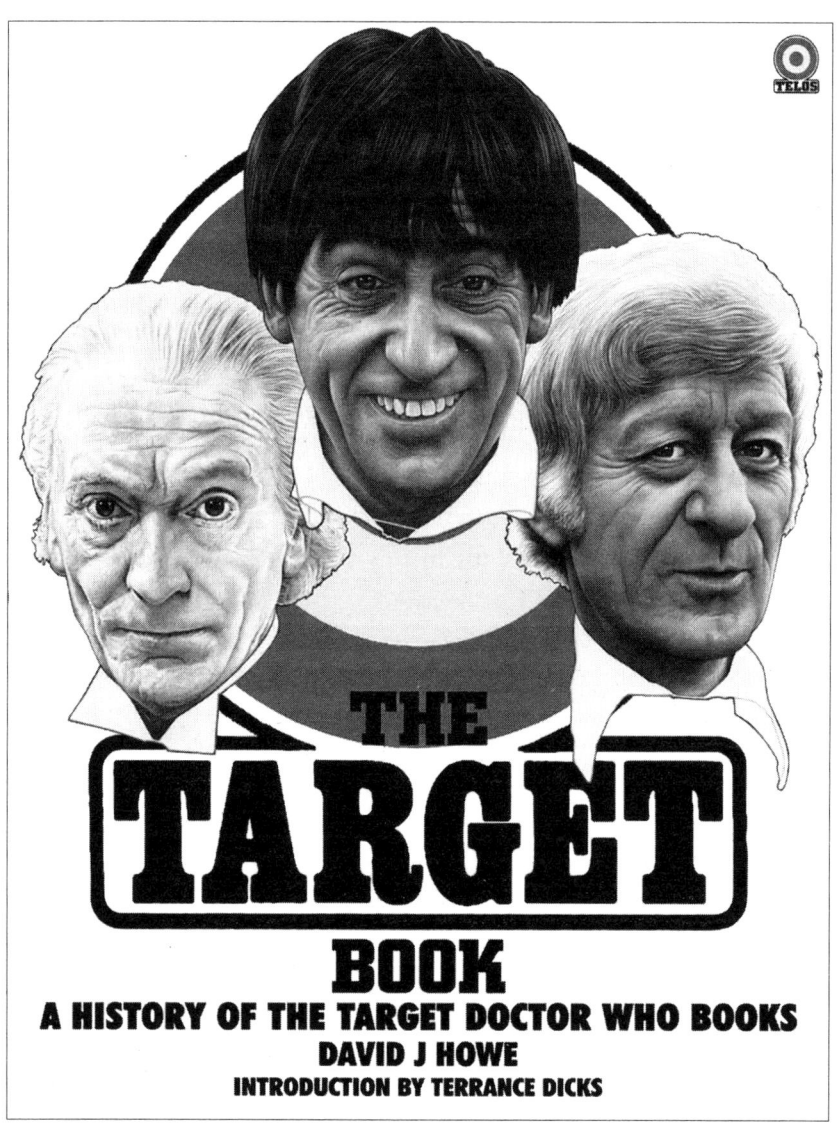

TELOS

THE

TARGET

BOOK

A HISTORY OF THE TARGET DOCTOR WHO BOOKS

DAVID J HOWE

INTRODUCTION BY TERRANCE DICKS

Cover of *The Target Book* which I wrote in 2007 for Telos Publishing. The cover art is by Alister Pearson.

12

The Birth of Telos

Throughout the nineties, as well as following my interests in *Doctor Who*, and writing and publishing books and magazine articles professionally, I was continuing with my love of horror. From those early BBC Horror double-bills in the seventies, I had loved horror films, and also through the *Doctor Who* Target novelisations, I grew to love reading as well, as I've said earlier. My first horror books were all novelisations of films. And mainly they were films I hadn't seen, just read about in the film books I loved to collect, and also from posters seen on the Underground and on buses, and also in the pages at the back of the newspaper. Films like *Rabid* and *Blue Sunshine*, and *Squirm*... I loved the novelisations of them all! My first 'proper' horror novel was Stephen King's *Salem's Lot*, and after that I read *The Shining*, and then there was no stopping me! I devoured as much horror fiction as I could get my hands on.

In the early days, my love of the films had led me to join the Gothique Film Society, as I briefly mentioned earlier, and I got to see many rare films through their meetings.[127] I went to see *Suspiria*

---

127 I can't remember what any of them are now, but I have a feeling they included Tod Browning's masterpiece *Freaks*!

in London and that was an experience and a half![128] *Phantasm* was another imaginative and clever film that I saw at the cinema. And *Alien* blew me away when that came out. And *Halloween*. I can still remember the audience screaming when Michael Myers sits up behind Laurie Strode who thinks she has just killed him during the climax of the film. Superb stuff!

In the late eighties, my work for *Starburst* led me to cover some films and directors for them, and I went to the occasional film preview. I remember among them were *Strange Days* and *Evil Dead 2*. *The Thing* was another which had a great impact on me... all superb films! I think this was where I first met Steve Jones and Kim Newman, great film critics and collectors, and it was they who invited and encouraged me to come to a meeting of the British Fantasy Society in a pub one evening in London in 1992. I went along, enjoyed myself. There were lots of writers I knew there, and it was great fun.

I discovered that the BFS was, basically, moribund at the time, with no newsletter being produced and nothing really happening except an annual convention, FantasyCon. So, me being me, I offered to help produce the newsletter... which meant that I ended up doing that myself for a few years, before I got some much-needed help from other people. Between us over the next 15 years or so, we revitalised the BFS, got the newsletter back on schedule, drew in more members, and generally had a good time mixing with writers and artists and so on.

While it was called the British *Fantasy* Society, it was far more interested in the horror side of the genre, and that suited me fine, as that was where my preferences lay, but I always tried to ensure that we covered the whole gamut as far as possible through the

128 *Suspiria* is still one of my favourite horror films. A masterclass in direction and camera work, in lighting and saturation, in terror and horror, and of course in its soundtrack, a masterful concerto of horror from the group, Goblin.

publications, and tried to find willing people to write about the different areas.

Eventually, I handed the editing and production of the newsletter over to someone else, and I moved into producing occasional special publications for them. The first one was called *Clive Barker: Mythmaker for the Millennium*,[129] and this was well received. Following this, I produced a variety of chapbooks (basic A5 folded publications, more like fanzines than books) but also a few more books, including *Manitou Man: The Worlds of Graham Masterton*,[130] which was a fully-fledged paperback and hardback book.

All this activity was a good grounding for what then happened around 1999.

But we need to step back slightly to around 1996/97 and when the internet truly started to take over. Up until then, I had not had any internet at all. There were no emails, and the only way to organise and talk to people was to either pick up the phone, or to write and send them a letter (or possibly a fax if they, and you, had that ability).

It was when Jon Pertwee died that I think I felt it most. I was getting letters from people and talking to people who were on some of the early newsgroups then, and having comments relayed to me about Jon and their memories. People knew I was doing the book, and were wondering if these things might be of use to me. As it happened, the book was all but finished by the time Jon died, and so I couldn't incorporate any of this material, but I appreciated everyone's thoughts.

So, sometime later in 1996, we finally got 'connected' and had email and internet. Though it was dial-up, and painfully slow, we could still use it.

My memory tells me that it might have been 1997 when things started to explode, and domain names became a 'thing'. A domain

129 *Clive Barker: Mythmaker for the Millennium* (Suzanne J Barbieri, BFS, 1994).
130 *Manitou Man: The Worlds of Graham Masterton* (Ray Clark & Matt Williams, BFS, 1998).

name is the bit after 'www' and before the '.co.uk' or '.com' part of a web address, and everyone seemed to be snapping them up because, of course, there were only a finite number to be had.

I had been writing a column for Doctor Who Magazine called 'Howe's Who' which was a humorous piece about collecting Doctor Who merchandise and the supposed trials and perils from my past. All of this was invented, but I suspect some people think I really was bullied in the playground by Crusher Budd over Doctor Who toys or whatever: it was just fun to write. So, I looked for the availability of the domain 'howeswho' and there it was! I bought it there and then.

I then expanded my search, just out of interest, to see what other Doctor Who-related names might be available. 'Skaro' had been taken, as had 'Dalek'. 'DoctorWho' was of course gone, as was 'Gallifrey'. 'Cyberman' was not available... but 'Telos' was available! At that time, I didn't really have any use for the name, but I reasoned that it might come in handy at some point, and I did love the Cybermen, so I bought the telos.co.uk domain as well.

Also, over the course of the late eighties and early nineties, I had been trying to sell a book on Doctor Who merchandise. I had been collecting new things the whole time, and now had a large converted attic bedroom in another house stuffed to the rafters with items.[131] I had created a proposal for a book looking at the history of the items, with photos and details of everything. I had, on an early home computer, a listing of everything which I was maintaining... but there was no interest from anyone in publishing it. I tried every publisher who had released a Doctor Who book, including W H Allen and Virgin, and the BBC, but there was simply no interest. They had done cookbooks, knitting pattern books, quiz and crossword books, travel books, kids' books... but I could not sell a book looking at the merchandise!

This was, in part, why I wanted to include extensive merchandise

---

131 We had moved from our first house in New Malden, to live in a house which actually backed onto my parents' house.

chapters in *The Sixties*, *The Seventies* and *The Eighties*: to be able to use the research I had done and the information and images that I had collected over the years. By the time of the TV movie, I had more or less given up hope of there being a proper merchandise book, but help was on hand.

Out of the blue, I got a letter from someone in America called Arnold T Blumberg. Arnold worked for Overstreet, one of the top comic guide companies, and he wanted to do a guide to *Doctor Who* merchandise. I got back to him, and we talked... we both had the same ideas and so we worked up a pitch for the book... and then his own company didn't want to do it. We were somewhat crushed by this... was this a cursed project or something?

After that, and having both put a lot of work into it, we basically decided to publish the book ourselves! I had been doing books for the BFS and knew how to present them and had printers lined up and so on, and Arnold knew how to do layout and design and to make it all look amazing on the page... so that is what we did!

I finished my listing off, and took photos of as much as I could, sourcing others from whatever I could find. Arnold laid it all out brilliantly, in the format of a proper catalogue, with unique IDs for every item and so on, and we produced the book ourselves.

When it came to thinking about how we might sell it, I realised that it would be very helpful to have a webpage to give information on it and to let people know how to buy it and so on... and, of course, I had a ready-made domain name – Telos – that we could use for that. So, we put 'Telos' on the spine, and used the domain name to host the details of the book.

And so, in 2000, the book came out and sold very well. In fact, we sold out of that first edition, so decided to do an updated edition which came out in 2003.

This was not all that was happening, though.

Two other things took place which meant that I needed to change my thinking about publishing.

In May 2000, a new TV series appeared on Channel 5. This was *Urban Gothic*, a 13-part series of individual horror tales which was right up my street. It was on late at night, and they were a great mix of vampires and zombies and voodoo and all sorts of other horror ideas and treatments. I was hooked![132]

I reached out and made contact with the producer, Steve Matthews, and the writer, Tom deVille, and discovered that they were also fans of *Doctor Who*. And indeed, *Doctor Who* was very much the low-budget 'template' they were using for the show. We got talking, and I expressed an interest both in releasing a book tying into the show, and also of writing for it! I was nothing if not ambitious, and if you don't ask, you don't get! Both ideas were taken forward, to my immense pleasure.

For the book, I discovered that they were happy to license something to me and the BFS (I was pitching the book as a BFS publication at the time), but, because of insurance concerns and so on should anything untoward happen,[133] it would be better if it was a limited company producing the book rather than a fan organisation.

The other thing that happened was that another friend in the BFS, Pete Crowther,[134] had started his own small press, PS Publishing, and was kicking off with a series of horror/fantasy novellas from well-known authors in the field. I liked the look of them, and the format, and that the writers could tell a story in a shorter form (a novella was usually 20–40,000 words), and that it could be as, or more, impactful than a longer book.

So, I wondered if I could get permission from the BBC to produce a series of *Doctor Who* novellas.

I had previously had a BBC license in 1998, when Mark, Steve and I produced an official *Doctor Who* calendar for the 35th anniversary of the show. We called it *Visions*, and for that we used some

132 There's a website all about the show here: urbangothic.atwebpages.com/
133 I had no idea what this might be!
134 A fantastic writer in his own right.

artwork which we had commissioned and used for The Frame, and also commissioned several other pieces. The idea was 'Doctor Who as if it had no budgetary constraints' and the resultant art was expansive and fascinating, showing the potential of the ideas within the show as well as the talent of the artists we used. There were no issues with dealing with the BBC over this. They pretty much just let us get on with it. Mark did all the design and layout and made it look amazing, and for this project Steve handled the distribution. I knew the people in charge at BBC Worldwide, and, through my ongoing interest with the merchandise, had been helping them from time to time with licensees, providing text, checking product, giving advice on what had been produced in the past, and things like that, and so I felt I had a chance.

I reached out to them, and they were interested in the idea of Doctor Who novellas, but wouldn't license me as an individual to do them. It had to be a limited company.

This meant that I needed to set up a proper publishing company.

I reached out to Steve Walker, as he had been working for the government as a civil servant, partly looking after small business legislation, so I reasoned that he would be a good person to help me run this company, as despite all the financial handling and work I had done on pretty much every project I worked on, I really didn't enjoy the financial, contractual and legal side of it all. Luckily, Steve loved all that side of things,[135] and so I brought him on board to help run the company. I registered Telos Publishing Ltd, and we had a limited company! Steve has been an amazing friend to me over the years, and I am always in awe at his editing acumen and his memory for details. We work together so well, and often think the same as well, which is very useful when it comes to running a company together!

Thus, Telos Publishing could now co-publish the Urban Gothic book with the BFS and protect the BFS from any fall-out, and we

---

135 Maybe not 'loved', but he certainly understood it and was good at doing it.

could also progress with the license to publish the *Doctor Who* novellas and do those as well. Happy days!

Things are never quite that simple, though.

Regarding *Urban Gothic*, we did produce the book. It was a wonderful anthology of short stories, where half were novelised by other writers from Tom deVille's original scripts, and half were original short stories which were in the *Urban Gothic* vein. I was very pleased with it. We did a limited signed and numbered hardback, and a paperback edition, and both sold well.

In terms of writing for the series, I created an outline, and when that was approved, I wrote a script. All was going well. They liked my idea; it fitted with what they were doing...

But then Channel 5 cut their funding, and rather than having 13 episodes, as with the first series, they could only produce nine for the second... so four stories had to go. And mine was one of them.

I was so disappointed. All that work and then the rug was pulled out from under our feet.

Later on, I wrote up my story as a short piece of fiction called 'Blackfriars' which I included in my own collection from Telos, *talespinning*, but it was also selected for another anthology Telos published, *Shrouded by Darkness*, which was edited by Alison Davies.[136] It's a piece I am proud of as I think it's a great story, and one which would have worked really well on television. For the part of the lead male character in it, I wanted them to try to get Colin Baker (the Sixth Doctor) as I felt he would be perfect for it. It was never to be.

* * *

136 When Telos publishes anthologies, we have a 'rule' that we don't interfere with the editors or their selections. Of course, we oversee the editing and have final say. But if the editor wants Steve, or me, to contribute, we have to do so in the same way as anyone else who is approached: pitch an idea, write the piece, and there's no guarantees that it will be used.

I actually appeared in an episode of *Urban Gothic*! It was an episode called 'The End', written by Andrew Cull, which was a neat little survival scenario where a small group of people are holed up in a house during a typical everyday zombie apocalypse. I was there all day on Friday, 29 June 2001, on location with them at the house in London, and I was made-up and dressed to be one of the zombies.

Steve Matthews asked me if I fancied playing a zombie in one of the season two episodes, and of course my response was instantaneous. With opportunities like this you have to grasp them with both hands and run with them!

Anticipation is a wonderful thing, and I was counting the days before my chance to star approached. Finally, the call came through, it was to be the next day – not much notice – and they wanted me on location at seven o'clock sharp for make-up and costume. Superb! But seven in the morning? And the location was the other side of London from me, up at a children's school in Kilburn. Undaunted, I took notes of where to go, and said that I'd be there.

So, 5.30 the next morning saw me dragged bleary-eyed out of bed and across London. Luckily at that time of the day the roads are all but deserted and I arrived at about 6.45. So far, so good. Although the crew was based at the school, the actual recording was taking place a couple of streets away in an empty house – and I was warned there was not much room.

As people arrived for the filming, it quickly became apparent that this was going to be interesting. Among those standing and sitting around munching on traditional breakfast bacon sandwiches were a couple of amputees: a chap with only one arm, the other missing from just below his elbow, and another fellow with no legs. Other people had, like me, been roped in from friends of crew members. There were two people who worked in the reception area at the film company's offices, another couple of girls turned up who were friends of someone else – it was a meeting of the enthusiastic, all prepared to spend a day being a zombie.

And so, to make-up. This is one of the strangest experiences. Watching yourself being transformed from a relatively normal human being into a wild-haired and blood-matted creature. The people waiting around were taken one-by-one into the costume trailer to change into some of the most horrendous clothes I'd seen – I ended up in a pair of jeans caked in some unidentifiable substance, battered trainers and a black jumper which was sticky with blood and other materials. I didn't like to touch myself! For the make-up, I was first made to look really pale and ill, and then blood and other gunk was added to give the impression of having been smacked around the head a couple of times with a hefty plank of wood. I got off lightly! One girl was given a slit throat, another had a massive pustular burn on the side of her face, while the one-armed man was fitted with a bloody prosthetic to give the impression of his arm having been ripped off, and an impressive gaping knife wound in his cheek. We all looked incredible. I suggested that we should all get in a car and drive it off the road somewhere, and then hang out of it to suggest the most awful accident...

I mentioned that this was a children's school, and, incredibly, the children were there, peering at us from within the classrooms. I have no idea what they thought of all these blood-caked and injured people milling around in their playground. I suspect a few nightmares ensued, as it all did look incredibly realistic. The blood is made from various ingredients, including golden syrup, which makes it sticky and very clotted, and it also got everywhere. We all ended up with tacky hands, and everywhere I sat was left with a patina of blood on it.

With everyone made-up, we then had to wait for the call to the actual location. This came at about 10.30. The crew had been recording some other scenes first thing, using some zombies from the previous day, but before long we were all bundled into cars and driven to the house – there was no way they were going to let us walk there looking as we did.

Once there, we waited outside until they were ready for us, passersby in cars, buses and on foot giving us the strangest looks. Then it was inside for our big scene.

They weren't joking when they said it was small. We were in an end-of-terrace house, and recording was taking place pretty much in the entire place. It was dirty, grimy and run down. One of the crew mentioned to me that apparently it had belonged to an old lady who had died fairly recently, and it certainly looked as though no work had been done on this house in many, many years.

The episode being recorded was called 'The End', as I mentioned, and was an homage to *The Blair Witch Project* and that type of *cinéma vérité* style. The idea was that a 'normal' episode of *Urban Gothic* starts, but it is then interrupted by live news footage from a group of policemen who are investigating a viral outbreak which makes humans go crazy in seconds, filling them with the urge to kill anything and everything, including themselves. All this footage was recorded using a single camera nominally in use by the police, and the narrative cuts back to static, to the Channel Test Card pattern, to news reports while the police try to avoid being killed or turning into crazy zombies themselves.

The scene being recorded was the one which concludes the episode, an ambitious single shot, where the police camera is taken by one of the crazies and carried down through the house. At every landing and every turn there are people moving and milling about: and guess who those people are? The only problem was that the scene had to be recorded in one take, choreographing all the movements as it went. We were initially all given roles: the girls were set to running about, one chap had to drag the dead body of one of the heroes along the passage, slit-throat-girl was to be lying in one of the rooms, one-arm-man had to emerge suddenly from a room and attack the camera, no-legs-man came on at the end and dragged himself, leaving a trail of blood, across the floor. As for me, the director decided he wanted the tallest of us to slump over the banister rail, dead to the world: thus was my fate sealed, as immobile corpse number one.

With us all in our positions, we started the camera walkthroughs, making sure that everyone moved in the right areas and that the scene all worked as a continuous pass. Then we started actual recordings, and the problems began.

First, it was very hard to cue everyone as we couldn't see the camera, and when it turned suddenly to come down the stairs, the girl running down was caught looking for her cue, then there were problems with the crazy dragging the hero along the corridor, the floor was becoming increasingly sticky and tacky with blood and his shirt was riding up, and his back adhering to the floor. Padding was added but this also stuck. The floor was washed and cleaned and more takes were tried. Finally, after about ten or fifteen takes – or so it seemed – we had something which everyone was happy with. But then we had to go again as there had been a digital fault on the tape. At about quarter to two, we completed a successful take and the scene was in the can. Everyone breathed a sigh of relief. The heat upstairs in the house was becoming unbearable, and with camera and sound crews, director, make-up, costume, special effects, sparks, chippies, continuity, assistant directors and cast, there were upwards of 30 people crammed into cluttered rooms keeping out of the way of the camera as it made its way down the stairwell to the ground floor.

Add to this the fact that slit-throat-girl had to lie with her head back and down, and I was hanging over banisters, both with our real blood rushing to our heads – it wasn't easy. At least I could stand up between takes, poor slit-throat-girl had to stay in position to prevent the prosthetic from splitting away and the blood running in the wrong direction. We suffered for our art!

With the scene in the can, it was back to the unit base for lunch, and to clean off the gunk, blood and matted grime, and to return to some semblance of normality once more. We returned to the house later in the afternoon to record just a soundtrack of movement and running, just in case there were unneeded sounds on the original takes.

All in all, the experience was excellent. To see television being made first hand is always interesting and entertaining, and to take part in it as well was something of a dream come true. Our scene was the very last scene of the show, so watch out for 'dead crazy over banister' when watching (and you may need to use the freeze frame!).

It was tremendous fun to do, and I'm eternally grateful to Steve Matthews for giving me the opportunity.

The only downside was that I suspect not many people saw it on transmission, as it was shown on 26 December 2001 at 00.30 am. As of writing, Urban Gothic is not showing on any streaming channels, but you might be able to pick up the DVD box sets somewhere!

* * *

Planning out the Doctor Who novellas was lots of fun. We had authors and artists we knew we wanted to use, I was in contact with loads of creatives through the BFS, and we had a license from the BBC!

The challenges started almost from the word go.

While BBC Worldwide had agreed the license, the pitch and the details, they were not the ones who administered it. Instead, there was another licensing department who had to approve everything, and they were hard to deal with and intransigent. They would only communicate by fax, and would never explain what the problem was, just that something was 'not approved'. Which meant we were left in the dark most of the time as to what we should do to correct whatever it was that was wrong. Furthermore, we ended up with multiple approval points on the books.

We had proposed doing the titles in two hardback editions. One a deluxe hardback with a leatherette covering, a cover stamp, a ribbon, and a signature page signed by: the writer; the introduction author; and the artist who had created the artwork which was on a plate at the front of the book. The other edition was a standard hardback with a standard covering which contained just the introduction and the text, with none of the other embellishments.

For the two editions, we had to get approvals on: the text outline; the finished text; the cover material and colour for each book; the colour of the ribbon in each deluxe book; the artwork sketch; the finished artwork; the design of the signature page; the design of the stamp on the front of the deluxe edition; the foil stamp on the front of each book; and finally, the actual finished and printed copies.

Now, some of these things never changed from book to book, but we still had to get approval every time. The books didn't have cover artwork, we were using different coloured and textured special fabrics each time, and matching the colours and feel to the 'sense' of each book: so, for example, one set in a jungle might be green; another set at sea might be a blue; while a desert world might be a sandy brown. I asked if I could perhaps send all the cover material samples in, and then they tell us overall what we could/could not use, and we would then adhere to that. But no. We had to get the colours agreed by fax for every book. They also came back and told us that we could only use blues and silvers. Other colours were not allowed. When we asked why, they initially wouldn't discuss it, but eventually told us it was branding, and that *Doctor Who* was 'blues and silvers'.[137]

This was the way it went on. Discussion after discussion. All about things that, to my mind, were just not important, and certainly not in the spirit of what we had pitched for the license and what we were trying to do.

137 I recall that *Teletubbies* was 'reds and oranges', and *Walking with Dinosaurs* was 'browns and greens'.

Then the BBC insisted we use a copy editor of their choosing for no reason that we could see. The books had no problems with spelling or grammar, and we had received no complaints. The copy editor was lovely to work with, but an additional expense for us.

They refused to approve the first piece of artwork, which was by a very famous and well-known graphic novel artist, Bryan Talbot. The discussions and arguments about this rolled on and we missed our first publication date because of it. In the end, they grudgingly agreed because it was the same as the sketch, and they had approved the sketch, but they weren't happy.

Another piece of art they refused to approve as they said it was a photograph. It wasn't, it was art from photorealistic artist Chris Moore. Again, the discussion raged, and eventually they agreed after seeing examples of Chris's other work. We even offered that Chris would talk to them on the phone to prove he was real and this was real artwork.

Nevertheless, we persisted and managed to get the books out, which were well received and sold very well.

Unknown to us, there were other things rumbling, and after about a year, Steve and I were called in to see the people from BBC Licensing and told in no uncertain terms that our four-year license was not being renewed. As to why, they couldn't or wouldn't give us a reason. Sales were good, the books looked great, and despite all the challenges and hassle over the approvals, we were learning what they wanted and so the issues were reducing.

But, after one year, we were told we had to stop. And of course, that came with a load of requirements around not being able to commission anything else: we could only publish what we had agreed at that point, so if an author had to drop out, then we couldn't replace them with another writer and idea.

We later discovered that part of this abrupt close-down was because an assistant in BBC Books, who had been 'assigned' to oversee what we were doing, felt that they didn't like the range, and would prefer that the new audio company Big Finish be given the books license.[138] So, when Licensing came and asked them how we were doing, they allegedly said we were dreadful, and that the license should not be renewed.

We played out the next three years with the titles we had commissioned at that point, and the range came to an end in February 2004 with a rather lovely Dalek novella by Simon Clark called *The Dalek Factor*. This featured an 'unknown' Doctor who had lost his memory and who had been captured by the Daleks. The story played out that *everything* on Skaro had been 'infected' by the Dalek Factor and thus the vegetation, the Thals, everything was in fact 'Dalek' and were controlled by them.

I was amazed that we had even got permission to include a Dalek story, and furthermore that the BBC would handle any payments to Terry Nation's estate from it – we didn't have to do or pay anything additional. Though it did take them about a year or so to agree Simon's story outline.

The novellas had been very well received by the fandom, and some were (and still are) hailing them as the best and most consistently good range of licensed *Doctor Who* fiction there has ever been.

However, Steve and I had realised from the outset that we couldn't build our own company on a property that was owned by someone else, and so we had already started publishing other titles of our own. We continued this approach, and when the *Doctor Who* novellas stopped, we had enough other books being published and in plan that it didn't seem to matter. And so, Telos moved forward.

Since Telos started, we've used an astonishing 540 ISBNs[139] across all that we have done in various formats, and we're still going strong! Steve handles all the finance and contracts side of the company, plus editing and layout, while I handle the editing and

138 This is indeed what happened.
139 The ISBN is the code that every book is assigned to uniquely identify it.

design, all the covers, and all the distribution and despatch side. It's a great arrangement and plays to both our strengths.

* * *

Going back to the start of the 2000s again, and in 2001, my dad passed away on 3 December. This was an event that rocked my world. The death of a parent always is.

He had been taken ill overnight on 19 November, and while my dad, always underplaying it, said he was fine, my mum insisted on calling an ambulance. He was taken to hospital and kept in for observation.

He had had a small heart attack, it seemed, but was weak. I went in to see him and took him a copy of the next week's *Radio Times*, as he loved to see what was coming up and what he wanted to watch.

He never got to do that. On the night of 2 December, we got the call from my mum. The doctors had asked her and the family to go into the hospital. This was after midnight, as I recall, so we all went in. Dad had died earlier at around one in the morning on 3 December, so we were too late to see him. He had had a second heart attack and had just not been strong enough to survive it.

Mum, Alan and Robert went to see his body, but Caroline and I preferred not to. So, we sat. And stared at nothing. And pondered on the futility of it all.

Mum and my two brothers came back. They were quiet.

We then said our thanks to the doctor and nurses and went home.

It was a very sad time.

The next day was sunny, and I was driving somewhere. Don't know where. I had the week off work because of the death. But I could see all the people going about their business. Cars were driving, shops were selling things. But none of it meant anything. I couldn't understand how this could all be so normal when my dad had just died. This was the first day he would never see.

Most people have to experience this in their lives. Usually you lose your parents at some point. And for me, it was a very sobering time. He was 76 years old. Strangely, the same age as Jon Pertwee had been when he died.

Dad dying changed the way I looked at things, at the world. Whether I realised it at that time or later on, I just wasn't happy. I felt different. And, although you learn to live with the loss, you never quite get over losing a parent when they've gone.

* * *

I mentioned earlier that there were moves afoot that we didn't know about with regards to Telos's *Doctor Who* license, and in 2005, what had been going on became apparent.

There had been a lot of rumours and rumblings of various companies and individuals trying to get the rights to make *Doctor Who* once more. Once the TV movie furore died down, there was a lot of low-level 'noise' around the fandom. People claimed to know this or that, or had heard something, or seen something. But this is just fandom. Some people love to be the centre of attention and to claim they know *secrets* when in fact they know nothing of the sort. This has been the case since way back in the seventies when I first got involved.

Personally, I don't do that. If it's something I know that I'm not supposed to say, then I won't say. I much prefer to wait and see than to listen to rumours and gossip anyway.

In this case, the 'wait and see' turned out to be the return of *Doctor Who* in a brave new series on BBC1, helmed by Russell T Davies, and starring Christopher Eccleston as the Doctor, with Billie Piper as his companion, Rose.

And it was amazing!

With 2005 technology, CGI effects, modern prosthetics and recording techniques all rolled together, the revived series hit with a bang and from there just kept on getting bigger.

But for me, it was all a little like a party going on that I wasn't invited to.

There were no more book offers coming in, and when I did try to suggest ideas to BBC Books, they were all knocked back.

In 2005, just after the new series aired, I received a letter from the BBC saying they were thinking of reprinting my *A Book of Monsters* volume, which would have been amazing. I got straight back in touch and offered to update it or whatever they wanted, but the next thing I knew, they weren't going to reprint it at all, and instead they did a book by Justin Richards (who was working at BBC Books on their publishing programme) called *Monsters and Villains* in 2005. This was basically a photobook, with minimal text. I guess they thought that was what the market wanted, or that it was maybe cheaper to do that than to reprint a book they already had. I don't know.

I've never been asked to do another *Doctor Who* book for BBC Books since, although I have helped with photographs when they occasionally needed them, and even stepped in to write some small elements of a big book called *Dalek*, published in 2017, when they were running out of time and needed some text in a hurry.

I was still enjoying watching *Doctor Who*, but of course the days of recording each episode onto tape, or even taking photographs off the television screen, were long past. With the technology now available, there were DVDs, so the series could be watched whenever you wanted, and computers could now play DVDs and you could capture off-screen images directly on the computer, so there was no need for messing about with cameras and film.

We also all had our early iPhones or Android phones, with great cameras in them, so there was no need to carry a hefty SLR film camera around with you. And any pictures you took you could see instantly. No need to wait to send film off to be developed before you got to see the results.

With nothing new coming from BBC Books, I decided after some time that I would publish some of my own work through Telos.

After all, I had set the company up, and we were publishing guides to other television and film subjects to much acclaim, as well as fiction, including a series which we spun off one of the *Doctor Who* novellas, called *Time Hunter*.[140] We had not, however, set the company up to self-publish ourselves, and so were initially wary of going down that route.

Back in 1999, I had researched and written a series of articles for *Doctor Who Magazine* looking at the history of the Target novelisations, and that had been well received by the readers. I still had all the original text and illustrations and much more, so I decided to bring everything together into a book which I called, simply, *The Target Book*. I wanted to include biographies of all the authors and artists involved, and to assist with that workload, I asked a fellow fan, Tim Neal, if he could help. Tim had created and been running a brilliant website devoted to the Target Books, and had much of the material there already, so I was pleased to have him on side. I also did some more interviews and research for the book to cover areas not covered by the shorter *Doctor Who Magazine* pieces, and the result was published in November 2007!

I organised a launch event for the book in London on Saturday, 3 November. I wanted to try to get together as many of the artists who had worked on the range as possible, and I was so pleased that we managed to get so many to come along. Many of the fans who had been collecting the books had never actually seen or met the artists behind the covers before, and I don't think that many of the artists themselves had met their fellow cover creators. It was great to see the interest and enthusiasm in the book and in the artwork on the day.

It was an amazing success. I was so pleased with the end result. The book was definitive while also being visually beautiful – and

---

140 I co-wrote the last of the *Time Hunter* novellas as my co-author, George Mann, suddenly had a major deadline for something else and was unable to continue it. It was a pleasure to work on some fiction for a change!

that was all down to Arnold T Blumberg, who did an incredible job in making it look so good. We have reprinted it a few times with an updated Coda at the back, as BBC Books had started to publish the Target books again in 2011, and BBC Audio had also started releasing audiobooks of all the novelisations.[141]

Another book that I decided to do myself was called *The Who Adventures*. The origin of this was another series of articles written for *Doctor Who Magazine* in 2001, and this time they covered the history of the *Doctor Who* original novels published by Virgin in the 1990s. Again, I still had the text and all the imagery, so I edited it all together while we were all locked down with nowhere to go during the Covid 19 pandemic, and it was published in 2021. The layout this time was by Steve Walker, and again the book drew enormous praise.

It's another title that I'm very pleased with. It just goes to show that you should never throw anything out!

I continued writing reviews and pieces for my website too, keeping my hand in covering all the new *Doctor Who* episodes as they were transmitted, as well as reviewing books and films and anything else I felt like talking about.[142]

---

141 One thing that I was very happy to be working on was the sleeve notes for all the audios of the Target books. The editor, Michael Stevens, had got in touch one day to ask if I could help with that, and I was pleased to revisit all the novelisations and to write short notes about the original books, and how they differed from what was seen on television!

142 The website is at www.howeswho.co.uk and is still updated whenever I can find the time!

Me with Sam and Frazer Hines in February 2009 enjoying the sunshine in LA after the Gallifrey *Doctor Who* event that we all first met at.

13

A Complete Change

During the later 2000s, I was increasingly unhappy at home. Things weren't right and I didn't know what to do to sort them out.

In the end, I had to do the hardest thing I have ever done, and just tell Rosemary that I wasn't happy and I had to leave. This day in October 2008 was rotten!

I literally, over a couple of days, sorted myself out a local flat to stay in. Luckily, I was able to find something that I could afford, and moved my basic stuff there.

I hoped that James and Andrew might understand, or come to understand, but it seemed to be my mum who was the only one who had really realised how unhappy I was. Even I didn't realise it! But then they say that, that sometimes you really are the last to know!

So, I stayed in this flat in Surbiton, and it was okay. I could walk to the station to travel to work in London. Come home and get something to eat. It was okay.

The only light I had at this time was someone I'd met the year before in October at the annual FantasyCon convention. Sam (Samantha) was an author, and she was promoting her first novel there. She ended up on a table next to the Telos table and we got talking… we had very similar views and sense of humour, so we just enjoyed chatting.

At the end of the event, she gave me a copy of her first book[143] and asked me to read it. So I did, and I thought it was great, and the following February I arranged to meet her in London, so we did that and had a lovely meal… and then we just corresponded by email and by phone.

She revealed that she had also just left her husband, and for similar reasons as I was feeling, though I later found out that she was also being badly abused by him in the relationship. I went to visit her in Prestatyn, where she was living at the time.

When she found out that I had left Rosemary, she was incredibly sympathetic, and came down to London to see me. I went up to see her that Christmas. Realising that the lease on her house in Prestatyn was coming up, she decided to come and stay with me in the flat… and the rest, as they say, is history.

It was my mum who said that the change in me was immense. I had gone from someone who always seemed quiet and slightly upset to a lively and enthusiastic person again. My friends also commented on the change in me… it seemed that everyone had known how unhappy I had been except me! As true friends and close family can do, they welcomed my new happiness and Sam became part of their lives too.

It was in February 2009 that the next change in my life happened, as someone came into it who I hadn't expected for a moment!

*   *   *

For many years I had been travelling over to America to attend the annual *Doctor Who* convention in Los Angeles. This was organised by Shaun Lyon, and Shaun was (and is) amazing. A powerhouse of

---

143 It's a vampire novel called *Killing Kiss*, written as by Sam Stone. You should read it as it's brilliant!

organisation and planning, he was kind and efficient and treated everyone the same.

His philosophy was that if you had done something... anything... in the worlds of *Doctor Who*, then you were welcome at his event. Thus, he welcomed the stars from the show, as well as the writers, directors and backroom people, as well as the novelists and publishers and artists, and people from *Doctor Who Magazine*... as I say, if you had done something creative, then you were welcome.

The first event I attended was in 1998, and was called 'The Nine Lives of Gallifrey One', and I was made to feel so comfortable that I made a point of trying to return every year! The guests there were always astonishing, and the camaraderie and friendliness of everyone, from the guests to the organisers to the attendees, was legendary.

They also used to run a cabaret on the Saturday night – this has now stopped – and the guests would get up and do a turn of some sort. I was usually too nervous to try, and I have no natural talent for performing: I can't sing or play any instruments, and I can't dance. So, I decided one year to read a poem by the great British poet John Cooper Clarke! This I did, but I think the audience had no clue what I was talking about, so it was received... quietly.

For the 2009 event ('Gallifrey One 20 to Life') in February, I had arranged to go out there as usual, and this time Sam was coming with me. She was a teacher and had arranged time off work to attend, and we had enough money to make it work for us.

I had also arranged for us to stay on for a few days afterwards, as I thought it would be nice to show Sam some of LA – she had only been once before – and there were a fair few things I loved seeing out there! So, we got the plane from Heathrow and travelled the 13 hours or so to LAX.

As usual, when you get somewhere after a long flight, you might have been able to sleep, but even if you had, it still felt a bit like you hadn't, so we were groggy and tired... but Shaun had arranged to pick us up at the airport so we didn't have to struggle too much finding shuttles to take us to the hotel.

The bus arrived, and our luggage was dutifully loaded, and then we were off on the short trip to the hotel, the LAX Marriott.

In the bus with us were a few other guests. I can't recall everyone, but I think composer Mark Ayres might have been one of them – but sitting opposite us was a face I certainly recognised. It was Frazer Hines, who had played Jamie in sixties *Doctor Who*, and who I had literally grown up watching. Sam recognised him as well, but she knew him from his role as Joe Sugden in *Emmerdale* and she said to me, 'Is that Frazer Hines, I didn't know he was in *Doctor Who*?'

Frazer always has a twinkle in his eye, and when he saw Sam the twinkle intensified.

We got to the hotel and as usual there was then the queue for reception, to get rooms and so on. That done, we dumped our stuff then headed down to the lobby, and more importantly, the bar!

It became a tradition at Gallifrey that we would have a Long Island Iced Tea, and a bowl of cheesy chips when we arrived. I think it may even have been this event, as Sam wanted something to take the taste of the in-flight food and drink away! So, we sat with friends, I introduced everyone to Sam, and away we went for the weekend!

Over the weekend, we were busy on a table in the dealer hall selling Telos books that I had arranged to have sent over, and also socialising and chatting to all the attendees. I may have had a panel or two to talk on, or to moderate, that usually happened as well.

Sam told me that she saw Frazer again, and he had asked her if she was single. She had pointed at me and said, 'Sadly not, I'm with David.' I think the twinkle slightly dimmed, but Frazer was in his element. Each evening, when he had finished with his daily duties, he would come to the bar and make a beeline for us. We were laughing and joking, and drinking and eating. Just having the best time!

I think this must also have been the first time that I met Daphne Ashbrook, an American actress who appeared as Grace in the 1996 *Doctor Who* TV movie. Daphne was very friendly, and easy to talk to, and again she and Sam, over several different conventions, became inseparable! We have since all become good friends, always nattering on the phone and putting the world to rights!

Daphne is great fun at events. She's a straight-speaker who tends to tell things how they are, and this results in some hilarious anecdotes, and happenings during the making of the many shows that she has been involved with. And there are a lot![144]

We love Daphne a lot, and always try to get to spend time with her when she visits the UK.

Also at the event in 2009 was an agent named Emily Danyel, who was friends with some others of my pals, including a great chap called Joshua Lou Friedman, who has become the world's best first assistant director for horror films in LA, if not the world![145] I would usually meet up with Josh after the convention for an evening film show at his house, where he would show us some things he had recently worked on. This is how I came to find great films such as the hilarious *Bitch Slap*[146] and the intelligent time-travel thriller *Detention*![147] Seek them out, they're crazy brilliant!

Anyway, Emily was interested in taking Frazer on as a client for events in the USA, so she was chatting to him and to us, and we were all getting on like a house on fire. She was also interested in getting Sam and I out there as guests to events, too. Sam at this

---

144 Daphne's impressive body of work includes *Doctor Who*, of course, but also *Knight Rider*, *Fame*, *The A-Team*, *The Fall Guy*, *Falcon Crest*, *Star Trek: Deep Space Nine*, *Murder, She Wrote*, *Sleepwalkers*, *Kingpin*, *CSI*, *Cold Case*, *Ghost Whisperer*, *Law and Order*, *NCIS* and *Hollywood Heights*!

145 In 2024, Josh directed his first feature, *Marrying Mary Martindale*, and we can't wait to see it!

146 Bitch Slap: www.imdb.com/title/tt1212974/.

147 Detention: www.imdb.com/title/tt1701990/.

point had written two novels and her second was due to be published later that year.

As the convention ended on the Sunday evening, we all needed to get to where the next part of the holiday was for us. Frazer had arranged to see an old girlfriend who lived somewhere in LA, and had booked a hotel near to where she lived so as not to terrify her by turning up on her doorstep. He was thoughtful that way. He hadn't actually heard back from her before he left the UK, but decided to leave his hotel booking in place. So, he needed to get to that hotel for the night.

As for Sam and I, well, we had booked into a different hotel which was slightly nearer. I had found it online, and it had seemed okay when I booked it, and we needed to get there too.

Emily had nothing to do, and she had a large car and so offered to drive us to each of our hotels. I thought this was incredibly kind of her, so we all bundled our cases into her car, said farewells to our friends at the event and headed off.

Well. We arrived at the hotel that Sam and I had booked.

Total. Hotel. California.

It seemed to be on an Interstate crossover, on the roundabout beneath it. There was nowhere obvious to go, no shops. Nothing. Just the busy roads. And the car fumes.

We drove in, and nothing was looking hopeful.

I went into reception with the others behind me, and there was no bar, no social area, just a plain wooden room with some unadorned tables and chairs in it right by reception. The lady on the desk seemed nice, and when I asked where the bar was she said there wasn't one. There was a swimming pool which was through a door beside reception. We stood and looked around, and Sam said that she wasn't sure she could stay here. The place was a dump! There was no atmosphere and no one at all around.

I didn't know what to do, and then Frazer said, why didn't we try to get a room at the hotel he was at? That was sure to be nicer.

So, he found the details, and I apologised to the lady and explained that we were with our friends, and that it would be better if we were all in the same place, so would she let me use her phone to contact the other hotel to see if they had rooms.

To my amazement she was fine with it, and even said we could cancel the room there with no charge. So that was a bonus! The two hotels were in the same chain, which helped, and so they could transfer our booking to the other one if there was room.

I called the other hotel and they went away to check. When they came back, they had no rooms available except an executive one with a Jacuzzi… well.

I looked at the run-down hotel we were standing in. Looked at Sam's face, which was panicked bordering on hopeful, and said, 'Oh, f**k it, she's worth it,' or words to that effect, and booked the other hotel, my wallet only wincing slightly at the cost.

With profuse apologies to the lady in Hotel California, we headed back to the car and Emily drove us on to the other hotel. Even Emily was surprised at how grotty this first one was! It was the kind of motel where you would rock up if you had a fly-drive situation, and, as there was nowhere you could possibly walk to, not suitable for us.

When we got to the one that Frazer had booked, what a difference. Bright, airy, busy, on a street with loads of shops and restaurants. It was high-rise, had a pool outside. Lovely.

We checked in and made arrangements to meet with Emily the next day. She was again free and so offered to come and pick us up and to drive us around places.

The next morning, Frazer reported that he still hadn't been able to contact his friend. She just wasn't answering or replying to his messages. And I don't think she ever did! He doesn't know to this day what happened to her! So, we were basically free for three or four days until we were flying back home.

Emily arrived and we went sightseeing. I remember seeing Griffith

Park Observatory,[148] and the Hollywood Bowl. We drove all over. Probably to City Walk at Universal Studios... all the touristy things.

Frazer made plans on one day to see his friend Roy Dotrice,[149] and asked Emily, Sam and I if we'd like to come along and meet him for lunch. We headed off to a lovely restaurant on Hollywood Boulevard. Roy was such a lovely man, and a gentleman to boot. We enjoyed a great meal with good company, and at the end Roy asked what we were doing that afternoon. We had thought of visiting the La Brea Tar Pits, so Roy said he'd not done that and asked if he could come along. Of course, we were more than happy to have him join us.

We headed off to La Brea and spent the afternoon at the tar pits and the museum, looking at all the skulls and other items that they had found buried in the tar at the site.

Outside the museum was a large statue of a bear, and we had some photos taken, joking that Emily and Sam had a 'bear behind' in the picture, and look! There it was!

Finally, we hit the gift shop, and while we were looking around Roy slipped away. When we saw him again outside, he presented Emily and Sam each with a brown paper bag from the shop. Inside was a small model mammoth! He had gone and bought them without us knowing as a present. It was so kind of him!

The mammoth now sits proudly on our kitchen windowsill, and he is named 'Roy' in memory of the lovely man who bought him for us!

We made good use of the Jacuzzi bath in our hotel room, and Frazer found a cigar shop in the street outside, so we headed out there one time to browse what there was to see. Good food, good

148 Where, of course, scenes from The Terminator were shot, and many other films besides.

149 Roy was a BAFTA Award-winning actor of some renown, having appeared in many TV series and films, including the original 1987–90 TV series Beauty and the Beast, Hellboy II, and Game of Thrones among his 135 IMDB credits. He died in 2017.

drink and good company. It was a smashing and relaxing break for us after the convention, and moreover it really allowed us to bond with Frazer and he with us.

He told us later that he thought he had reached a time in his life when he didn't need any more friends, but when he met us, he thought maybe he was wrong and decided to 'let us in', which was lovely.

For Sam's first trip to LA, it was certainly memorable!

When we got back to England the next week we went to stay at Frazer's house, the week after that he came to us… and since then there's barely been a week when we've not seen each other or spoken, except when Frazer goes off on one of his 'world tours' and visits America and Australia and wherever he is off to at the time! He's very popular and much in demand.

* * *

The next few years saw Sam and I doing lots of conventions, and being asked more and more to be guests. We continued to go to Gallifrey One every year, and Sam, with many more books under her belt, was also welcomed by Shaun as a guest. During this time, we also went to an event organised by Jarrod Cooper in Florida, Hurricane Who, for a couple of years running, consolidating our relationship with Daphne, who was a guest at the event too one of the years.

In 2012, Sam and I were delighted to be invited as International Author Guests of Honour to a new convention in America called GalaxyFest. This was held in Colorado Springs, a place that neither of us had been to. Frazer was invited too because of his *Doctor Who* work, and so we all set off on the plane to Colorado, and then on to Colorado Springs.

It's a beautiful part of America. It's near the north, so it can be cold, and right at where the Rocky Mountains start with the massive Pike's Peak dominating the horizon. Pike's Peak is also close to where there is a large security establishment, called the Cheyenne Mountain Complex, buried beneath the mountains!

We were there for the convention and had a day or so to spare afterwards to do a little sightseeing.

One of the great things about the conventions is that not only do they bring diverse fans together, and you can meet people that perhaps you've only 'met' online, but they also bring diverse celebrities together, people you have only ever heard of as being on the shows you watched... and sometimes this can have very beneficial results.

The organisers of the event, the lovely David and Diann Wacks, did all they could to make us welcome. We were very jetlagged when we arrived, in part from the flights and time difference, but also because Colorado Springs has a high altitude, which makes you react strangely to alcohol and the oxygen difference in the air. They had arranged a welcome party on the night before the event, and I was so tired from the travel that I had to go to bed... but Sam and Frazer went and partied!

The next day, Sam seemed fine, and my jet lag was receding, so we had a smashing convention, meeting everyone and talking about books and writing and *Doctor Who* and everything.

At a guest mixer, Sam 'bonded' with Denise Crosby, who played Tasha Yar in *Star Trek: The Next Generation*. But when they realised that the wine at the party was not to their taste, they got more from our room and hers and carried on drinking! We've since seen Denise at a lot of conventions and we all spend time catching up when we can.

Denise went on an organised trip to the security complex under the mountains, and when she came back, she revealed that she had apparently been shown some things that the normal visitors never got to see. They had recognised her as the *Enterprise*'s security chief from *Star Trek* and reasoned that she therefore had clearance. We thought this was a lovely touch.

We also met the author Kevin J Anderson, who is local to the event, and he was so nice! Such a prolific and talented writer... and his wife too, the writer Rebecca Moesta. They have an amazing work ethic which boils down to treating writing like a real job. If you were a doctor or a dentist, you wouldn't take the day off just because you felt like it... you buckle down and do your job!

They kindly invited the three of us out to their home in the hills, and that was very special! Kevin literally lives in a little castle, and seeing all his manuscripts and awards, and book covers on the walls, was amazing.

But there were two other people at this event who became very special to us.

The first was actress Chase Masterson.

Now, I'd seen Chase before at the Gallifrey event, as she lived in LA and often dropped in there. But I'd never spoken to her – mainly because I had no real reason to, and I didn't want to come over as strange or something. I'd also never seen her in *Star Trek: Deep Space Nine*, not being an enormous *Trek* fan.

So, again, Sam and Chase got talking, and discovered that they had a lot in common. We spent a lot of our spare time with Chase in Colorado, even going Western riding, which I'd never done before. I'll admit I was a bit worried about getting on a horse for the first time, but Frazer reassured me that Western saddles were really hard to fall out of. After just a few minutes on the horse, I was really happy, holding the reins with one hand, while taking pictures with my phone in the other – so Frazer was right, as he usually is!

As a result, we all became great friends, and since then Chase has stayed with us whenever she visits the UK. She has a penchant for the English afternoon tea – a scone with clotted cream and strawberry jam – so we try to make sure she gets that at least once when she's here.

In my life with Sam, we have bought and sold two houses and

now own our forever home. But the first house we bought was in North Wales. This was where Chase first visited us, and we showed her the gorgeous scenery on road trips through Snowdonia National Park. Chase, like many other friends from America, loved seeing the mountains and the valleys, and the sheep! People always seem taken aback that there are so many sheep roaming about there.

We've also taken steps to help Chase with her charity work, supporting what she does for the Pop Culture Hero Coalition,[150] an anti-bullying charity which helps those who are bullied for whatever reason. She works tirelessly for this cause and, like Kevin, her energy and commitment are astonishing!

The other new friend we made at this event was Dean Haglund. Dean came to fame playing Langley, one of the Lone Gunmen in The X-Files, and was also guesting at the event. I liked Dean immediately. He was funny and personable and friendly, and we hit it off. So normal and down to earth.

On the Sunday night after the event, David Wacks had arranged for Dean to perform his improvisational comedy show at a local comedy club, so we all headed off to that when everything was finished.

This was the funniest show I think I have ever seen! Dean was on form, picking up elements from his audience and twisting them into funny scenarios... and he was so quick-witted! My sides were splitting, and I don't think I could have laughed more! If you get a chance to see him doing comedy, then grab it! You won't regret it!

Dean was living at the time in downtown LA, and the next year we were at the Gallifrey event, we arranged to meet up. His apartment was in an amazing art deco block in the Downtown area. It's the one with the large clock on the top which has appeared in

150 You can find out more here: www.popculturehero.org/.

several TV series and films,[151] the Eastern Columbia Lofts. There is a large swimming pool at the top which we went and sat around, and the whole building is just amazing.

We found out later that Johnny Depp acquired five penthouses there in 2007! We didn't bump into him, though.

Dean took us on a guided tour of Downtown and we saw cinema frontages used in a whole load of films and TV, as well as the Bradbury Building,[152] which at the time we visited was home to the LAPD, but was memorably used as a key location in *Blade Runner* and in the 'Demon with a Glass Hand' episode of the series *The Outer Limits*, as well as a vast list of other productions. That was incredible!

While we were in LA, we also took part in Dean's podcast, *The ChillPak Hollywood Hour*,[153] which was co-hosted by himself and Phil Learness, a film producer and director. By a strange coincidence, we knew Phil anyway as he was a regular contributor to a local radio show that we were often asked on when we were in Lincoln! So, we spent a happy hour or so chewing the fat with Dean and Phil!

Dean came over to stay with us in Wales, and we again enjoyed a lovely day taking him out and about. What we didn't realise was that he was also an artist, and he had a little sketch pad into which he was creating watercolour images of the places we went. We would see him sitting on the bank of a river, serenely painting the scene, or roughly sketching in something he would paint later. He's a very talented man. When we asked him about this, Dean told us that he felt he captured the places he visited better in his memory for having drawn and painted them as opposed to taking photographs. We thought this was genius.

Dean has since moved to live in Australia, so we don't see him as often as we would like.

151 Including *Moonlighting*, *Lucifer* and *Predator II*.
152 At 304 S. Broadway.
153 chillpakhollywood.com/.

Other people we met at this event included Tony Todd, the tall actor who was impressive as the Candyman in the film of the same name, and Noah Hathaway, star of the film *The Neverending Story*... both sweet guys!

We all had a great time, and while the Colorado atmosphere made us all cheap dates – one drink of alcohol and we were drunk! – we managed to come out of it mostly unscathed!

We went again the next year and had an equally fun time. Then David Wacks died suddenly in 2014, and we didn't get to go again. The annual convention eventually stopped in 2020. It was a great legacy to him, and we still miss going!

*　*　*

'Do you fancy coming to the races?' asked Frazer one day.

Well, I had no idea. Racing has never been my 'thing', and I'd never been. Sam had, however, and she was certainly up for it, and so we headed off with Frazer down to Newmarket.

A fascinating place, full of people and money, and we arrived and got ourselves settled with some Pimm's and watched all the activity taking place around us.

It transpired that Frazer had a stake in one of the horses that was running that day, called 'Simply Perfect' as her formal name, but they called her 'Pretty Polly' as her regular name, and while we were drinking our Pimm's, he went off to make some calls.

When he came back, he encouraged us to drink up.

'We're going to see the horses,' he said, so we quaffed the remainder and headed off with him.

It turned out that the destination was the paddock, which is where only the owners and jockeys can go. So, we went and stood with everyone else and watched as the horses, led by their jockeys, paraded out and around us. Frazer's horse seemed a little skittish and didn't seem to want the jockey to get on, but eventually he did, and it started parading around with the others.

Interesting to get that close-up view of what was happening!

The race was due to start in ten minutes or so, and Sam wanted to put a small bet on 'Pretty Polly'. I needed a quick toilet break too after the Pimm's, so we headed back into the main area where we could do both.

I left Frazer standing by a patch of greenery surrounded by a small foot-high fence, and when I came back, he gestured me over to him. There was another chap standing there too, on the green area, and I smiled at him.

Frazer said, 'David, this is my old friend Tommo!'

Tommo smiled at me and I shook his hand. 'Can you step over,' he said, and so I stepped over the low fence and onto the grass.

Tommo looked at me, and then off to one side. 'Three. Two. One. Hello, and welcome back to *Channel 4 Racing* from Newmarket! I have with me now, one of the owners of one of the running horses, and also a *Doctor Who* writer, David Howe. Hello David.'

And there was a microphone shoved under my nose, and a camera looking at me from the other end of the green patch.

I had no idea what was going on, but knew that Frazer had set me up!

'Hello,' I said with a smile.

'So this horse you have, you're one of the owners?'

'It's a syndicate,' I said. 'There's a few of us, yes.'

'What do you think her chances are today?'

Goodness me. I know nothing about horses, or horseracing… what am I supposed to say!

'Well,' I started, 'she was a bit skittish out at the paddocks, but she got over it. She looked good, and I think she's got a good chance.'

Good job I'm a fast thinker.

'Well, the race is about to start… so thank you David, and good luck! This is Tommo for *Channel 4 Racing*, and it's back to the studio!'

Tommo turned to me and said, 'Thanks David, that was great!' and then was off to discuss something with the cameraman.

I looked at Frazer, who was innocently smiling all over his face. 'You knew that would happen!' I said.

'Yes,' he replied, 'but you did well! I knew you would!'

Typical Frazer!

Tommo was, of course, the top racing commentator Derek Thompson.

As it happened, 'Pretty Polly' didn't win, but she did come second! And Sam had put a bet on each way, which meant she did win a little money – not much, though, as she only put a few pounds on for the fun of it. We aren't big gamblers. We didn't have any luck with any other races that day, though! Even so, it was a fun day out, and I got to appear on *Channel 4 Racing*!

After the races, we headed to see Jinks James, one of Frazer's old friends, with whom he has a share in the Brookside Stud farm that Jinks runs. Jinks was beaming when we drew up in the car.

'I saw you on Channel 4,' he said! And we laughed, as we all knew it was just so funny because I really didn't have a clue about horses!

I had hoped that it hadn't been transmitted or something, but it was!

Unfortunately, I don't have a copy, and searches online have not turned it up either. Maybe one day I'll see my starring role as a racing pundit!

* * *

Another friend who Frazer introduced us to was the amazingly talented and strong Ayshea Brough.

Like many people of my age, I had a small crush on Ayshea back in the day! She was the first Asian presenter on British television, and hosted a pop music show called *Lift Off* (later *Lift Off with Ayshea*) on at around five o'clock on Wednesday afternoons in the early seventies. There would be all the latest pop bands on, from Slade and The Sweet and The Bay City Rollers, to David Bowie and

Wizzard… and Ayshea would usually sing a song, too, all interspersed with puppets[154] and links and comedy. It was great fun!

Ayshea also played one of the SHADO operatives on UFO, the show my dad wanted to watch, and she also appeared in several other films and TV over the years. She is also iconic for appearing in the UFO opening credits, and also that she is the very first person seen on screen in the series proper, walking into SHADO HQ.

Ayshea and us just bonded. She was so funny to talk to, with stories of her life in LA – she was best friends with Kris Jenner when she lived there, and knew all the gossip about everything! She worked as a home designer to the stars, and was married to the president of CBS.

We have stayed in touch with her and try to meet up whenever we can. She's an amazing lady and we're very proud to know her!

* * *

Frazer had published an autobiography, a book called *Films, Farms and Fillies*,[155] after his three favourite things, but the publishers, Boxtree, had gone into liquidation shortly before it came out, and so there was not much publicity for it at all. As a result, it pretty much sank without a trace. So, soon after we became firm friends, he mentioned that he had always been upset that there had been no hardback edition of the book. We decided to rectify that.

I had a copy of the original book in the collection, and so Sam retyped it all, correcting a lot of the typos and spelling mistakes that she found, and also talking with Frazer to add extra content and stories so that it offered more than the original book. Then I went through it and checked every name, spelling, profession and everything else. There were a fair few errors, though all the actual facts were present and correct as Frazer has an amazing memory

---

154 One of the puppets was called Fred Barker, a cheeky dog, voiced and operated by Ivan Owen, who had also created and voiced Basil Brush!
155 *Films, Farms and Fillies* (Frazer Hines, Boxtree, 1996).

for that sort of thing. The only major gaffe was that he had confused Ice Warriors with Daleks at one point in the *Doctor Who* stories, and had a description of how the 'death' effect from an Ice Warrior's sonic weapon was achieved, placed as though it was a Dalek weapon. I corrected it, of course!

The other thing that Sam did was to go over the text with Frazer and ensure that the emotion was correctly there for each of the life events. When writing factual events, it's easy to forget about the emotions you felt at each point, and so she was trying to make sure that these were present in the book too.

When all this was done, we prepared a lovely new hardback edition of the book, now renamed *Hines Sight*, and released it to the world!

The book sold really well, and the hardback was soon out of print, so we prepped a paperback edition, which is still available today![156]

To celebrate the release of the hardback, we planned out a little tour for Frazer, and combined it with a signing for Sam as well, as she also had a new book out!

Thus, on Friday, 12 November 2010, we set off on a road trip down south to Yeovil as Frazer had arranged to meet up with an old girlfriend there. We stayed overnight in a lovely and quirky place called Thorne Coffin, and Sam and I explored a little, discovering an amazing old manor house! We then headed down to Truro, where we had another signing, and after that went to Newquay as I wanted to drop in on my Nana who was now feeling the signs of age, and who was 96 years old!

We all went in to see her, and she was so happy to see us, if confused as to who Frazer was and why he was there as well! I loved my Nana greatly, and I remember her being so sparky. It made me very happy to be able to introduce Sam and Frazer to her as I wasn't sure when I might see her again.

---

156 Check out www.frazerhines.co.uk for signed copies.

That Christmas, though, my uncle Brian brought Nana down to my mum's house to celebrate with us all. Me, Sam and Sam's daughter Linzi were spending Christmas with my mum that year, and Christmas dinner was made for about 12 or more of us by Mum with help from my brother Robert. Nana was frailer, but still such a strong personality and told Sam off for fussing over her because 'she wasn't an invalid'. That was just the sort of person she was, tough until the end!

This was the last time I saw Nana, though, as, following Christmas, she took a downward turn and died a few months later on 23 March 2011, aged 97. A sad day indeed. She had been so vital and vibrant for her whole life, battling everything that came her way with gusto and determination.

We have great memories of her that gave me so much comfort. One year in Newquay, realising that some seagulls had nested on the chimney of her house, she went up a ladder with a bucket on her head and a broom in her hand, to bat and sweep them away. She needed the bucket as the gulls are very aggressive if their nests are approached and will dive bomb you and peck at you. She was an old lady at that time, and the thought of her up a ladder was terrifying for us, but the event was funny nonetheless. But this was Nana! She was a true force of nature!

I was very pleased that we had managed to get to see her, and that she met Sam a couple of times before she passed. Sad, too, that she didn't make the round 100! But I guess not many people do!

In Newquay we stayed the night in the gorgeous Atlantic Hotel,[157] which is out on one of the headlands there with incredible views back over Newquay beaches, cliffs and town, and then at three in the morning we got up for the long drive ahead.

Frazer had suggested that we go to Loch Lomond, up in Scotland,

---

157 Used as a location for the Beatles' film *Magical Mystery Tour* in 1967!

as he had part-ownership in a lodge there by the loch. He had checked and it was free, so he could go and stay if he wished.

So we set off, and drove from Newquay to Loch Lomond, a distance of 555 miles, which would take around nine hours if driven non-stop!

To be fair, we did stop every three hours for a coffee and a break. We went past Gretna Green,[158] where we stopped, and there was a Scots piper outside – all the touristy things! – and then on past Glasgow and up to Loch Lomond!

It was an amazing journey and we arrived in the evening. Once we'd located the lodge, and stowed our cases, we drove out to find a restaurant that had been recommended. But after driving around for a while, we struggled to locate it. We stopped and asked this chap who had a broad and incomprehensible Scots accent. Giving us directions at great speed ('Ye goo roond ta roond, tek eh reet, than eh left, roond agin, oop ta hill, doon ta te tree, roond, an bak oop...')[159] we eventually found the place.

The next day we did a little touring and saw the loch, and stopped for lunch at an amazing pub called the Drover's Inn,[160] which is again on Loch Lomond, and which is allegedly haunted. The proprietor showed us the bedrooms, which were all differently decorated, and the lobby had an unsettling number of stuffed animals in it, including a large bear!

We enjoyed a haggis meal with neeps and tatties,[161] and of course a wee dram of whisky on the side. The bar there was amazing and stocked with every make and type of whisky you can imagine! This

---

158 Where Frazer tricked Sam into walking under the marriage arch with him. He now claims she is married to him!

159 We literally could not understand what the chap was saying, as he was speaking so fast and trying to give directions with his arms waving and flailing as he did so! It was very amusing.

160 www.droversinn.co.uk/.

161 Haggis is a traditional Scottish delicacy, much prized. Neeps are turnips and tatties are potatoes.

was where we discovered a single malt called Knockando, which is simply delicious!

After another day or so looking round, we drove back home again, tired after our adventurous road trip, but pleased that Frazer and Sam had sold a few books, and that I had managed to see Nana again.

With regards to Frazer, we have become so close that I almost think of him as my replacement dad! As my father died back in 2001, I have missed him terribly over the years, and I wish he could have met Sam as, among her many talents, she is a singer with a great love for musical theatre, and my dad loved these productions too. In his inherited record collection, we have discs of things like *South Pacific* and *West Side Story*, and I know that she and him would have got on well.

But Frazer seems to fill that hole in my life. He's fun and crazy and personable and kind and generous and just about everything that you could want in a friend... or a father. As you can tell, I love him to bits!

Enjoying a glass of red wine before the special screening of the 50th Anniversary *Doctor Who* story 'The Day of the Doctor' at the BFI in London, November 2013.

14

Fifty Years of Who

On 23 November 2013... I, like many others, was at the Excel venue in London enjoying a day of *Doctor Who* immersion at the BBC's celebratory 50-year celebration of the show. It was a marvellous affair... guests from the show all signing and doing panels and talks, areas looking at the different aspects of making the show, merchandise tables, and a great atmosphere. I was there because I had arranged for Barry Newbery (BBC Designer) to appear, to receive applause and ovation for all his many years working on the show, but as luck (or not) would have it, he had hurt his leg and could not walk... so was unable to go. Thus, I took his ticket and was there on my own. Sam had to go to a different event in Birmingham that weekend, and so she couldn't join me either.

Thankfully m'pal Frazer Hines was on hand to look after me, and it so happened that the daughter of one of Frazer's chums, Steve, who lived in Australia, was working for BBC Worldwide on *Doctor Who* branding and merchandise, and Frazer knew that this was something I was interested in, and so arranged for us to meet. Julie Holmes and I hit it off instantly (and we are still great friends, even though she also now lives in Australia), and while Frazer was off doing his signing and interview duties, we hung out and watched what was going on.

At one point, I was listening to the announcer in the halls, and realised that, as it was a Saturday, they could actually announce the exact time of the anniversary: at 5.16 in the afternoon. So, I headed for the green room and had a word, and they got the message to whoever was on the microphone (I think it might have been actor and Dalek operator Nick Pegg). At 5:15 they started the announcement, did a little countdown and the whole place erupted in applause when it came to the exact time.

It was a very special and moving moment to see everyone pausing in what they were doing to mark the anniversary of the show. I'm glad I was there to suggest that this little moment happened.

Because she was with BBC Worldwide, and also in and out of the press room, Julie had found out that there was to be a special screening of that night's episode of *Doctor Who*, 'The Day of the Doctor', at the BFI after the public show at the Excel closed, and that there was some sort of after-party happening there also… and so, of course, I was intrigued and wanted to be there too.

When Frazer had finished, he was quietly told about the activities as well, and Julie and I made sure we stuck to him like glue as all the guests were assembled to get taxis over to the BFI for the event. We arrived there and there was a small gaggle of photographers outside, snapping away as the stars from *Doctor Who* went through and into the BFI.

We were shown into a small-ish room with a normal-sized television on a stand at one end, with various seats and sofas set up facing it. It looked like someone had hastily cobbled together a way for additional people to watch the episode. All the actors were taken off into a proper screening room for them to see it… it was just us 'others' who had to watch on the small telly.

Thus, we settled down on a sofa and watched 'The Day of the Doctor' with all the other friends and families of the actors who were there. Jules had somehow managed to snag a couple of glasses of wine for us as well.[162] I remember talking to one girl who was the girlfriend of the presenter of the after-party show, Rick Edwards. Anyway, the episode was great, and there was even a cheer when the eyes – just the eyes – of the Twelfth Doctor, Peter Capaldi, were shown... I thought that was a very cool idea, to preview an unseen Doctor (he had been cast, just not seen in the show as yet). And of course, the sequence at the end with Tom Baker as the mysterious Curator[163] was just sublime.

The episode finished, and everyone was ushered downstairs to a main studio for the after-party. Julie and I still had little idea what was going on, what it was, or what was supposed to happen, but Jules had obviously done this sort of thing before, as she dragged me along with her, making sure we were among the first to hit the studio. We took up a position by a large bar which had been set up behind a sort of floor area with sofas – obviously to interview people.

Then, when all the assembled masses, friends and family people (including some fans who had been allowed in as they were from abroad or something) were in place around the bar and so on, they brought the guests out, and they were directed to sit at various tables upon which were table decorations relevant to their eras of Doctor Who. I don't recall all of them, but Frazer's had a rather nice gold thing made from recorders stuck at angles in a base. At the end of the evening, Frazer asked what was going to happen to these things, and might he take 'his' one with him. He was allowed to do that. He still has it on one of his hallway tables!

So, they sat everyone down, and I remember Frazer chatting to Zoe Ball, who he knew – Frazer tends to know *everyone* in *every*

162 She was very good at doing things like that.
163 Obviously they wanted to get Tom Baker into the show, but the idea that past Doctors somehow become eternal 'curators' for the 'Under-Gallery' on Earth was rather interesting!

situation. With the career and work he's done, I'm never surprised. After some faffing about, the show started, and Zoe Ball and Rick Edwards started the presentation. They had some cards on which questions were written for the guests – after it was all over, Zoe (I think) just dumped hers on the bar right by me, so into the inner pocket of my jacket they went! No one seemed to have a clue what was going on, least of all the presenters and the guests. They careered from one set of interviews to another, bringing people in to sit on the sofas. Matt Smith and John Hurt walked right past us at the bar on their way to be talked to, which is the closest I ever got to Matt Smith.[164]

While all this was going on, there were people dressed as Ood[165] working at the bar, serving drinks, but I don't think we got any.

The guests from Doctor Who, meanwhile, had no idea why they were there. There were a few questions aimed at them from Zoe and Rick, but nothing focussed or organised. Then, out of the blue, they decided to play some sort of game and wanted all the guests to stand up. None of them had a clue what was happening, and so they stood, there were questions and they sat down again if they got them wrong. It was all so chaotic, and Jules and I just watched it all unfold.

They had Jean Marsh and Maureen O'Brien there, and both rarely do PR or appearances for Doctor Who, but neither were spoken to. And the other guests were barged out of the way and generally treated disrespectfully.

We had no idea whatsoever why there was a live link to talk to the lads from popular singing group One Direction (I actually had no idea who they even were), and then the link wouldn't work, and the sound all got out of synchronisation – obviously someone

---

164 I was able to meet John Hurt briefly at one of the Gallifrey conventions. He was very sweet and warm and shook my hand. A gentleman and a legend of television and film!

165 A Doctor Who monster with tentacles coming out of its mouth.

hadn't realised that there might be a sound lag between London and LA, and this caused more chaos as One Direction were trying to answer a question as Zoe (or Rick) was asking another, desperately trying to fill the dead air! What a nightmare!

Then it was all over, and they wheeled out a large celebratory cake which was duly cut up and shared out to everyone. Frazer got his table decoration and we were all bundled into taxis to return us to our respective hotels.

It was memorable for all the wrong reasons. For the lack of organisation or apparent planning, the lack of any rehearsal with anyone at all, the non-briefing (or poor briefing) of the presenters. At least they both coped with what they had been faced with, and Zoe at least had a good track record on The Big Breakfast and other live presenting gigs not to be too fazed when it all went wrong. I had no idea who Rick Edwards was, though. This must have been something of a baptism of fire for him!

Given the array of talent that they had in the studio that day, this could and should have been a fantastic 30 minutes of chat and interest, going through the eras perhaps, memories from those who were there, and properly celebrating the 50-year heritage and history of Doctor Who. Instead, it was a chaotic scramble of jokey poke-funs, silly interludes, and fluff which was just embarrassing for everyone involved. A somewhat interesting way to end what had been a fantastic weekend celebration of the show!

Visiting the TARDIS set in Cardiff in 2016.

15

Attack Stops Show

It was 2015, and I was planning to visit the *Doctor Who* Experience in Cardiff for the first time. Our friend, Andrew Beech, was working at the time for BBC Worldwide, in part curating the exhibits, and he'd arranged for us to get in.

We were also with our joint friend from America, Steve Sigel, and his friend Jess.

The morning started like any other. We were staying with Andrew in his house in Gloucestershire, and the plan was to drive to Cardiff to the exhibition and to spend the day there. We had a hearty breakfast as Andrew loves to cook – sausages as I recall – and headed off. I was sitting in the front of the car as Andrew drove, with Sam, Jess and Steve in the back.

As we went along, I started to feel ill.

I get motion sickness from time to time. There was a time when I couldn't read in a car at all or I would be sick, but this seems to have tailed off in recent years. Nevertheless, it felt like I had a bout of motion sickness coming on. My arms were a bit tingly and I was just not feeling good.

Partway over the Severn Bridge into Wales, I started to feel really ill, like I was going to throw up. Was it those darn sausages?

So, Andrew pulled into a service station just past the bridge and I all but fell out of the car, intending to head to the toilets before I was physically sick.

I never got there.

At some point, I collapsed and ended up lying against a wall as my arms cramped in intense pain. I'd not felt anything like this ever! It was so painful and I could barely grab a breath.

The others realised this was a serious situation and so Andrew called for an ambulance to come as soon as possible. This was an emergency!

I don't recall much of the sequence of events from here on in, but I do remember the paramedics arriving and checking me. They asked me if I wanted to know what was happening, and I said to tell Sam. She tells me that they told her I was having a heart attack!

They asked me to try to relax, and I replied through gritted teeth that it was hard to relax when you were in so much pain!

I was placed on a cot and put in the back of the ambulance, which then sat there for forever. I overheard them saying that the ambulance I was in had developed a fuel leak and could not be moved, so they had called for another ambulance!

I switched ambulances and was blue-lighted at speed to Cardiff University Hospital. I was, I think, shifting in and out of consciousness by now, but I do remember them taking me to one ward, where the nurse said they were in the wrong place, and I needed to be in surgery in the basement, or something like that! So, it was off on the gurney again.

They wheeled me in somewhere else, and then it all went black.

I think they must have hooked me up to something, maybe morphine, as when I next opened my eyes (an instant for me), there was a doctor looking at me. I promptly turned my head and threw up all over his shoes!

I was very apologetic, but there was nothing I could do.

They wheeled me into a quiet room where I was left for a while. I assume to recover.

I was feeling a little better, but exhausted and groggy and not quite knowing what had happened.

Sam, Andrew, Steve and Jess came in to see me. Sam had been crying, and Andrew was trying to keep her together.

It seemed that the doctors had been able to emergency stent me, and this had saved my life. It had been a blockage in the left aorta, a blockage of a type referred to as a 'widowmaker'. I had been incredibly lucky to survive.

So, my friends went off, and I stayed in the hospital for about a week while I recovered. I was in an isolation ward (maybe it was ICU, I'm not sure) for a day or so, and then they moved me to another ward where there were a number of other patients, including one poor chap who was convinced that someone was there to kill him... he kept saying he would do away with anyone who tried. In the end, they separated him to a room on his own and put him on 24-hour watch. Very worrying to be helpless in a hospital ward with someone who might attack you in his delusions.

It was all rather surreal in the beginning. At first, Sam told me, they said I'd had a 'mild heart attack' and she was communicating this to my mum and sons and to Frazer, but every day they gave us more news, and so by the end of the week they admitted that my heart had been significantly damaged.

Sam got accommodation for the week nearby with a friend of Frazer's, who runs a bed and breakfast just for actors who are on the road, Kathryn Dimery. Thanks to Kathryn's kindness, Sam was therefore able to spend every day at the hospital with me until I was able to go home.

After about a week I was discharged, and Sam came and got me. I was pleased to be heading home as hospitals are no places for ill people.

I had managed to survive an incredibly near-fatal occurrence, and it's all thanks to my friends, and the brilliant doctors and nurses at the hospital. They knew exactly what to do!

I was told they went in through my right wrist, up and into my heart and stented the blocked artery that way. Amazing! And all I had to show for it was a tiny and rapidly fading scar on my wrist!

Of course, I am now on what Frazer and I call the 'keep you alive pills' for the foreseeable, but they just help to regulate everything and prevent any recurrence by keeping my blood pressure, cholesterol and heart function at an optimal level. I'm not completely out of the woods, though, as my heart was quite damaged by the attack, and I have yearly checks and monitoring, as well as some newer medications to try to improve my heart's health. It's a long road, as they say, but I seem to be travelling it okay!

But we try to keep a sense of humour about it all, and Sam often reminds me of my failed attempt at 'doing anything to get out of our wedding', which was in October 2015, a few months later.

Our very special day took place in Lincoln at the Assembly Rooms, with a theme of Doctor Who and Steampunk, which we were both into a lot. Several of our great Doctor Who friends came over from America, including Joshua Lou Friedman, Daphne Ashbrook, Chase Masterson, Emily Barker, Jen and Ed Comstock and Howard Hayes.[166] Other long-term friends related to Doctor Who were Jason Haigh-Ellery and Keith Barnfather, and for the first time we brought together our families with Doctor Who and the Steampunk community within which we had also made many new friends, including Karen and John Naylor, who run the Victorian Steampunk Society.

---

166 Emily, Jen, Ed and Howard are all great friends who we met through fandom and who we spent a lot of time with, both at conventions and at our own homes. It was with great sadness that Ed died suddenly in August 2024 after years and years of serious ill health, all of which he faced with stoic humour and pragmatism. We all miss him terribly.

Frazer, being my absolute best mate, was of course my best man, and I can't think of anyone better equipped for the role. This was an amazing day, full of love, fun and laughter, and Daphne was last woman standing on the dance floor, long after Sam and I hit the road to start our married life together.

* * *

It seemed that Fate was trying to stop me visiting the *Doctor Who* Experience for a while, so when I had another opportunity in July 2016, I was taking no chances! I had a Doctor with me!

We had decided to visit when a few friends from America were over, and so Sam, Frazer and I headed down to Cardiff to meet up with them all.

We joined up with everyone in the Millennium Centre, where many *Doctor Whos* and *Torchwoods*[167] had been recorded, and then walked over to the Exhibition area. But joining us was actor Paul McGann,[168] who was free that day, and had been invited along by one of our friends, convention organiser Ken Deep, who runs the superb Long Island Who event each year – and who just decided to come and hang!

I've met Paul several times, and he's such a nice chap. So normal and down to earth, and a hardworking actor!

We all trudged over to the Exhibition building, and, if you went to it, you'll remember that at the start of the Exhibition, there's an interactive part where you have to control the TARDIS to get it to the right place. There is a guide/actor there to help choreograph the moves and so on, but I don't think that he was expecting to see a Doctor and his companion in the ship on that day! Paul and Frazer threw themselves into it, and helped navigate the ship (with

---

167 *Torchwood* was a popular *Doctor Who* spinoff which starred John Barrowman as Captain Jack Harkness. 'Torchwood' is actually an anagram of 'Doctor Who'!

168 Paul played the Eighth Doctor in the 1996 TV movie.

a pre-recorded Eleventh – and current – Doctor, Matt Smith, on the monitor) to arrive at the next port of call, which was a haunted forest full of Weeping Angel statues!

From there it was through the junkyard doors at 76 Totter's Lane,[169] and into the exhibition proper.

We all had a fun time browsing through the astonishing array of items that were on display. So many costumes and props and monsters from the whole 50-odd years of the Doctor's travels in time and space. There was also some material from the 50th anniversary docudrama *An Adventure in Space and Time*, which helped make up for the slight lack of sixties material.

Paul and Frazer had a good time, and enjoyed seeing some of the items from their eras. I remember there was a display of all the costumes of the Doctors there, and Frazer went up to the one of the Second Doctor, Patrick Troughton, and slightly misaligned his bow tie. The Doctor never had a perfectly straight bow tie, explained Frazer. It was always askew!

After we had visited the Exhibition, Paul had to leave, so we said our farewells, and went on to the next port of call, the TARDIS itself!

We had been in touch with Edward Russell, who was the brand manager on *Doctor Who* at the time, and he had very kindly offered to give us a tour of the actual TARDIS set from the show! This was incredible. As I have mentioned before, I love seeing and being on sets… so this was a very rare treat for me.

Frazer too was looking forward to it, as were the rest of our party.

We went into the BBC Television reception there and Edward came and got us. We headed for a quick glimpse of the production offices first, before we headed down loads of corridors to the set.[170]

169 Which is where the TARDIS was sited in the first ever episode of the show.
170 There's an argument that all BBC Television offices are themselves like TARDISes, bigger on the inside and full of corridors!

My first glimpse of the set was of a vast studio space, and in the middle I could see the back of the set itself. All wooden and curved, it looked a little like the outside of some vast deep sea nautilus sphere or something.

A metal staircase took us past some discarded parts of a Dalek and up to about halfway on the sphere; the lower part was all the bit below the actual control room level, while the upper part housed the spacious area above.

We entered via the actual TARDIS doors, and into the set, which was just magnificent.

This was the TARDIS set for Peter Capaldi's Doctor, all modern and sleek lines, with upper galleries containing blackboards and bookcases, and an area below with pipes and wires and storage, and, one presumes, the TARDIS's engines and so on.

We spent an hour or so just wandering about, somewhat in awe, taking photographs and studying the detail, which you never see on television. Edward got the filming lights turned on so we could see the proper effect, and it really was special. The console itself had differing switches and levers, and some of them made lights come on, all to help enhance the effect that you were controlling the ship. It was truly television magic come alive.

I did a walkthrough with my camera along one of the upper galleries, which was amazing.

It was a privilege and an honour to be allowed access, and I'll forever be grateful to Edward for the opportunity!

We also saw some incomplete sets from something else, but we weren't allowed to know what it was for. We later found out it was for an episode of *Class*,[171] but they were literally just a corridor with no defining features, so to be honest, it could have been from anything!

It was a memorable day seeing both the Experience exhibition,

171 *Class* was a short-lived *Doctor Who* spinoff series, set in the school featured in the show's very first episode, Coal Hill School.

and the actual TARDIS set! And I still can't believe how large the space was. It really felt like genuinely the real thing – and definitely bigger on the inside!

* * *

A few years later and we met Paul again, and this was at a friend's wedding!

Not really much of a surprise, as the friend was Jason Haigh-Ellery,[172] who runs the audio company Big Finish among other enterprises, and he was getting married to the lovely Cara in October 2021.

Paul had appeared in a lot of audio adventures for the company, and was continuing to explore the Eighth Doctor through them, so he knew Jason well.

It was really nice of Jason to invite us, and so we headed down to where the wedding was taking place, and found that among the guests – many of whom we didn't know – was Paul McGann. Katy Manning (who played Jo Grant in the seventies) was there too, as were top writers Steven Moffat OBE[173] and Mark Gatiss![174]

Paul seemed to make a beeline for Sam and I, recognising us from past meetings and events, and we had fun chatting with him as the party ebbed and flowed around us. Katy too was delightful, and at the meal, we found ourselves sitting opposite Steven and his wife Sue Vertue,[175] so we chatted away and had some laughs.

At one point, knowing that Russell T Davies was coming back

---

172 I've known Jason for years, and have followed his amazing career.

173 Steven is one of the greatest writers to have worked on Doctor Who! He has won more awards for his writing than I have had hot dinners!

174 Mark is a talented actor and writer. As well as contributing scripts to Doctor Who, he is part of the League of Gentlemen comedy team, and masterminds a 'Ghost Story for Christmas' for the BBC each year.

175 Sue is the CEO behind Hartswood Films, the company which brought us Sherlock, Dracula, The Devil's Hour, Douglas is Cancelled and many other top TV series.

to executive produce *Doctor Who* again, I mentioned to Steven that I hoped he was ready, as after Russell leaves, then of course it's his turn to come back, assuming they're following the same order as before! Steven laughed and said there was no way that was going to happen. 'I still remember what it was like doing it the first time!' he said with a smile. But I think he was telling the truth! We had a lot of fun with Steven and Sue that night, and chatted about a lot of different things. I'm sure we'll catch up again soon at another event!

*   *   *

Over the years, I have always collected items related to *Doctor Who*. Some of the instances are recorded in this book, but there have been loads more. My collection has been photographed for local newspapers, and has been featured on television several times. I've organised displays at conventions and have enjoyed tracking down and finding items, reaching out to the various manufacturers to find out more and to get review samples of items where available.

After a literal lifetime of collecting all these items, one of my biggest desires was to be able to share it with others, and so I long wanted to be able to display and show it to people. There's nothing worse than having a pile of lovely things, but they're all stuck in boxes where you can't see them and you can't find anything.

When we moved to our current house, one of the things I wanted was somewhere that I could set up a proper 'museum' for all of my *Doctor Who* collection. I wanted to be able to display it and to be able to find things myself, as I am often asked questions related to different aspects.

We managed to find a lovely house with large outbuildings in which I could do this, and so it was to my great pleasure in September 2023 that we were able to finally 'open' the *Doctor Who* Merchandise Museum for people to come along on designated days to see the collection and have a chat. This, of course, couldn't have happened without the massive help of our friends Tracey and Mick Herod, who we also met on the *Doctor Who* circuit and who have become our helpers at some events. I love getting together with them. They're always so positive and fun and willing to help on whatever hair-brained scheme Sam and I have cooked up.

We also decided to combine these 'open days' with a special guest, so the first guest we had was Daphne Ashbrook, who played Grace in the *Doctor Who* TV movie, to combine with a planned social visit with us.

She spent the day with us for the first open day, and chatted to the folks that came, signing pictures and, of course, drinking tea! And then we retired to the local pub, which has a large screening room, to watch some *Doctor Who* with friends, and to have a smashing pub dinner! Couldn't have been nicer!

Our second guest was the awesome Frazer Hines, and again, another lovely day was spent in his company.

We hope to have more open days and more guests in the coming years.[176] I love to share the museum with people who haven't seen it before, as every time I show it to someone new, I see it myself with fresh eyes.

* * *

At the end of 2024 I was honoured to be asked by organiser Dan Harris to be a guest on his annual Sci-Fi Sea Cruise.[177] This is an event which has been running for many years, and basically involves Dan organising cabins on one of the large cruise ships which sail to the Caribbean and other places, for a small group of *Doctor Who* fans along with several guests from the show. The idea is that the

---

176 To check on what's happening, keep an eye on the Facebook group for the museum: www.facebook.com/DoctorWhoMM.

177 Details of the cruises can be found online at www.scificruise.com/.

group travels and eats together each evening, visiting the various ports along the way and allowing the fans to really get to know the guests. It's a great premise for a very different sort of fan event, and of course there are a lot of fans who love cruising and seeing the world!

So, to be asked along by Dan for this 25th event was a real treat. He was gracious enough to extend the invitation to Sam as well, and so the two of us set off on 4 December for Miami, on a cruise which was to take in several Caribbean destinations: Puerto Plata, Dominican Republic, San Juan, Puerto Rico, St Maarten, St Lucia, St John's and St Croix.

Among the *Doctor Who* guests were several old friends. Frazer had been asked to come along as well, and of course this reunited 'the three Musketeers' for another set of adventures and shenanigans!

Actress Sophie Aldred was also attending. I first met Sophie a million years ago, before she had even appeared on screen in *Doctor Who*. She had been presenting a children's show called *Corners*, and had been cast as the new companion, Ace, opposite Sylvester McCoy's Doctor. However, at the annual DWAS convention in 1987, before her first episode was screened, she was a surprise guest. Because no one knew who she was, Gordon Roxburgh, the event organiser, decided to put on a little bit of theatre. At one point on the main stage he announced that there was a special raffle taking place, and that the winner would win a trip to the TV studios to watch *Doctor Who* being made. A winning raffle ticket had been put 'randomly' under one chair and whoever was sitting there would win!

So, everyone checked under their chairs, hoping that the ticket might be there, and a girl at the back excitedly raised her hand and squealed that she had the ticket!

The winner (who was, of course, Sophie) made her way to the stage followed by many envious glances, and then had to explain that, actually, she had already been to the TV studios as she was playing the new companion! Gordon then chatted to her about her experiences so far of the show.[178]

It was a neat and clever way of adding a little extra to the event, and, of course, Sophie went down a storm with everyone once they realised the 'trick', and she is one of the nicest and kindest of people to meet.

I've met Sophie many, many times over the years and she never fails to delight. She's a talented actress and presenter and recently has been doing more and more work with Keith Barnfather on his various *Doctor Who* spin-off productions. So, to see her on the cruise was a real treat.

Also attending was the very first companion from *Doctor Who*, the Doctor's granddaughter Carole Ann Ford! I didn't know Carole so well, but again our paths had crossed several times over the years. She was accompanied by another old friend, Rob Craine, and Rob and I have enjoyed many good times together. When Frazer was performing his one-man show across the UK, Rob helped secure a venue on the Isle of Man for him, and looked after us all, taking us on a little tour of the island while we were there, which was very much appreciated.

Some monsters from *Doctor Who* were also represented, with three of the actors to have played them. Tim Dane Reid is a lovely chap, very friendly and dapper and with many stories of playing all sorts of creatures – we first met, I think, at Long Island Who a few years previously. Joining Tim was Jon Davey, another very talented creature performer. You don't just shove the costume on and stomp about! There's clever and considered nuance to every performance, and for a show like *Doctor Who*, everything has to be convincing. Jon also has many stories of his time on the show. The third monster actor was Jonathan Watson, someone I didn't know, but who played one of the Sontarans during Jodie Whittaker's time as the Doctor.

178 Which weren't many, of course. Even if she could have talked about what was coming up, common sense said that she couldn't give away any secrets!

It was also great to see writer Robert Shearman and his actress wife Jane Goddard along. Robert has a nice line in sardonic banter, and a very quick wit, totally appropriate for the excellent writer that he is!

Sam and I had decided that, during the trip, we wanted to achieve something of a bucket list item, and this was to meet and swim with a dolphin! Living in the UK, you rarely or never see a dolphin outside of a zoo or marine centre, and so the chance to get up close and personal with one of these amazing creatures was not to be missed. So, at Puerto Plata we booked up for a trip to Ocean World to achieve it.

While Puerto Plata seemed quite poor and run down when driving through it, the people seemed happy and friendly, and Ocean World was nicely set out and the animals seemed well cared for, which was important to us. To meet the dolphins, we were split into groups of about ten, and then taken to a small pool area where the encounter would take place. We were led into the pool where there was an underwater ledge to stand on, alongside a deeper pool which actually connected to all the other pools (the main walkways were boardwalks above the water). Then, the trainer summoned a dolphin and it came up and greeted us. It was amazing. They're large animals and very intelligent. It knew (or had been trained) to come and give us each a peck on the cheek and a hug, to swim upside down in front of us so we could touch its belly, and to variously splash us and talk to us.[179] It was an amazing experience, and to see the others in the group enjoying it too was special. There was a young boy who was scared and didn't want to, and a lady as well... but that was fine. We tried to persuade them...

The dolphins generally were very sweet, and as we wandered

179 When it talked to me, of course, I had to reply: 'What's that Flipper? Timmy's down the well!' in a cod Australian accent, referencing the old TV series *Flipper* from the sixties! Well, it made me smile anyway.

around, we would see them playing and cavorting in the water, coming up to the side to say hello when we got close to the edges of the pools. It was a very special experience for us.

But then the whole cruise was full of experiences! Frazer, Sam and I would head out to explore and find a local bar, enjoying some delightful cocktails along the way.

Something that I had done during December for the previous couple of years was to get a 'wine advent calendar' and to record a little video of us trying the wine each day and giving our opinions on it. However, this year, of course, we were not at home and so couldn't continue the tradition. So, I hit on the idea instead of presenting a 'Christmas Cocktail Advent Calendar' and videoing me trying all manner of different cocktails which I then posted each day. The idea was fun, and allowed me to sample all sorts of different drinks... seemingly (but not really) getting drunker as time went on. Such fun![180]

When we got to St Maarten, there was another surprise in store for us. A visual effects designer called Nick Maley lived on the island and had set up a little museum dedicated to his work. He termed himself 'The Yoda Guy', as he had designed and built the original Yoda puppet for the Star Wars films, but he had done so much else besides, including Lifeforce, Superman, Krull, Inseminoid and The Shining. Just google him or look him up on IMDB and see. His museum was well laid out and was a trip through some of the most incredible films and effects from the late seventies and the eighties... including one of my own favourites, Michael Mann's The Keep! Those effects of the smoke monster Molasar are still awe-inspiring to this day!

So, we met with and chatted to Nick, and admired all his models and photographs and designs... it was a very special visit, and I

---

180 And I didn't have to drink every cocktail myself. Some were ones friends had ordered, and I just sipped them for the video, and where I (rarely) didn't like one, there were several folk keen to take it off my hands!

recommend it to anyone interested in film effects![181] Plus, St Maarten was such a lovely place. We took a sea ferry across from the cruise ship dock to the main strip of the town, and then just wandered about, taking in the shops and the sea front and the people. Everyone was happy and smiling and the whole place had such a lovely atmosphere. We ate in a small place called Bold Buddha, and had the most delicious food. Just delightful.

Sadly, Sam and I hadn't brought much actual cash with us, intending to rely on the good old credit cards as needed, but on the sea ferry, you needed cash to buy a bottle of beer. The day had been very hot, and while I had enjoyed a cold beer with my lunch, I'd not had anything else to drink. So, when we returned to the ferry, I was parched. They were selling bottles of cold beer for two dollars, but all we had was a 100-dollar note! We asked if they could change it, but they had no change. But then, one of the crew took pity on me and just gave me a bottle of beer! It was delicious and I drank it with relish, hoping to persuade some other passengers to buy one as well. And this just summed up to us the people of St Maarten. Kind and friendly, and if someone obviously needed a beer, you gave them a beer! Not necessarily an approach you might find anywhere else in the world!

Also on the cruise were some friends of ours, who had come along in part because they knew that Frazer, Sam and I would be there, so it was really good to hang with Taunya Gren, Howard Hayes, Andrea Mayo, Emily Barker, Abie Eke and Christina Nicholls, along with the other fans on the trip who became friends as we travelled. As always with such a diverse group, there are a lot of different backgrounds, experiences and jobs to explore with people, and learning about their lives and challenges was fascinating and educational. Some of the group went zip-lining in the rain forests, others went to the beaches… hopefully everyone had an amazing adventure!

181 Nick's museum is called 'The Yoda Guy' and can be found at 19a Front Street, Philipsburg, St Maarten.

On one trip we all took catamarans to a deserted sandy beach somewhere and swam in the warm seas, watching flocks of pelicans fly overhead as we sang along to the music on the boat, while drinking a strong rum punch and eating finger sandwiches and pineapple pieces! Elsewhere we watched turtles swimming in the sea. So many experiences.

In Miami, and Sam and I visited the Soho House complex (as Sam was a member) and enjoyed a gorgeous dinner and then relaxed by the rooftop pools with views out over the city. Miami itself was very crowded and busy. Too many cars, and trying to get anywhere by taxi was a nightmare and took forever! But nevertheless, it was an experience to visit for the first time.

Overall, this was an amazing break for us even though it was part work, but much needed at the end of 2024, and we were honoured that Dan had invited us to join everyone for it.

* * *

My involvement with *Doctor Who* continues to this day. Telos Publishing continues to produce a wide range of factual books looking at different aspects of the show, and we have always tried to expand the remit and to explore different avenues.

Shaun Lyon[182] and then Stephen James Walker have written several guidebooks focussing on each season of the show since it returned in 2005, and Stephen has also edited interview books which bring together the best of the behind-the-scenes chats from many different sources over the years. We have celebrated the book ranges, and the artistry of the show. We have updated and reprinted titles like *The Television Companion* and *The Handbook* into coherent and complementary volumes of information... as well as adding volumes looking at the Dalek films of the sixties, a history of the *Doctor Who* exhibitions, a history of *Doctor Who* in the comics, and even a definitive guide to

182 A friend who has headed the annual Gallifrey One convention in LA for many years.

how and why the BBC 'lost' the *Doctor Who* episodes, and the attempts since to recover them.[183]

For the 60th anniversary of *Doctor Who* in 2023, we decided to 'attack' the show from three different angles.

The first was in celebrating the factual basis and origins of the show itself. We have long been fans of the behind-the-scenes aspects of *Doctor Who*, and we had been pitched a book by fellow historian and researcher David Brunt, which was literally a day-by-day look at the origins and production of the William Hartnell era of the show. This was an amazing project, drawing on material from the BBC's own Written Archives, but also supplemented by newspaper articles and press information, as well as other paperwork and documentation which still exists. David pulled it all together into a coherent history of the show. Taking the reader through day by day and revealing what happened. This also has the effect of putting all the random information into context with what else was happening at that time, so you get an excellent view of what the *Doctor Who* production office was facing as they made the show. The book, which we called *The Doctor Who Production Diary*, also acts as a history of how BBC television was made in the early sixties. Many have described it as one of the very best factual books about the show!

The second line of attack for the anniversary was to celebrate the entirety of the show itself, and we had been pitched an idea from the artist Daryl Joyce, where he would create an image (or sometimes more than one) from every single *Doctor Who* story to date! This massive undertaking was called *The Illustrated Journey*, and while we simply couldn't fit paintings for literally every story into it, we made a very good attempt at it! The book was beautiful and stylish and celebrated all our favourite memories and elements from the show. In many ways it was an artwork equivalent of my own *Timeframe* book from the 30th anniversary.

---

183 All these titles and more can be found at www.telos.co.uk.

Finally, we wanted to celebrate *Doctor Who*'s rich and creative fandom, and what better way than to explore the world of fanzines. Alistair McGown, a great designer and writer for *Doctor Who Magazine* among others, was up for the challenge, and he pulled together *The Fanzine Book*, which detailed the history of *Doctor Who* fanzines in the UK from the very beginning in the sixties, right up to the end of the eighties. Many of the illustrations and details came from my own large collection of fanzines, and we also attempted to list at the back every one we knew about.

What was interesting was that the book not only covered the fanzines, but it ended up being a social history of *Doctor Who* fandom in the UK as well, celebrating all the creative people who had ever put paper in a typewriter and produced a fanzine!

Again, the book was beautifully designed by Alistair, and the final product was a fitting celebration of fan culture over the years.

I'm so proud of everything that Telos Publishing has achieved over the years. Steve and I have published some superb books, and carried forward our interest in the show – as well as many others – through the titles that we have commissioned and published. It's quite a legacy!

Me and Sam with the brilliant Paul McGann.

16

Cliffhanger Ending

As we're coming to the end of the book, I thought it was worth going through a few instances where I have met some of the other actors who played the Doctor...

I talked about Patrick Troughton and Jon Pertwee earlier, and so to Tom Baker.

I have always found Tom to be very inscrutable. A little like Jon, perhaps, in that you get the feeling that his public persona is different from his private persona. But with Tom, I think it's even more so. I've met Tom a few times, but always in a convention or a signing situation with him, so he's always been 'performing' as Tom. I don't think I've ever caught him 'off', so to speak. But he's always been pleasant and polite, happy to chat to fans and sign his autograph. But he's always been a little eccentric too, preferring to go his own way when it came to the show. There was a period when he wanted nothing to do with it... and he didn't even want to appear in the 20th anniversary story 'The Five Doctors', which led the production team to use his Madame Tussauds waxwork for the press photo call, and to use some clips from another production in the show itself.

The last time I saw him it was at an event, and he had finished signing and was literally on his way out. I wanted Sam to meet him, and nevertheless he shook her hand and said hello in his typical Tom Baker way... I like Tom. He's a true British eccentric of the sort that we don't have nearly enough of. And, of course, he is a legend to Doctor Who fans.

I have met Peter Davison many times, and I find him pleasant and disarming when in a social situation. He's talented and a good conversationalist, and has turned his hand to so much in his life. He's a musician and songwriter, an actor, a singer, a director... he's done serious roles and comedy, musical theatre... all sorts of things. I last saw him at an evening meal at an event Sam and I were co-organising.[184] It was just Sam and I, and Peter and his wife, the novelist Elizabeth Morton. It was a lovely meal, lots of chat and a few laughs.

Colin Baker it seems like I've known forever. I like Colin a lot. When he was playing the Doctor, a group of us used to try to go and see him (and, indeed, the other Doctors/Companions) in whatever play they were touring with over the summer months. I remember one in particular where Colin had his costume from the Doctor Who play The Ultimate Adventure with him, and he modelled it for us on the seafront! Colin has been at numerous conventions and events with me as well, both in the UK and the USA, and he's usually friendly and happy. I think he likes and appreciates the interest from the fans, and enjoys the interaction!

Sylvester McCoy I find a little guarded. Like Tom Baker, I don't think people see the real person, and this could be because 'Sylvester McCoy' is not his real name![185]

Sam and I did spend a crazy evening with Sylvester in New York following a convention in Long Island one year.

184 This was for the SciFiWeekender that Sam and I co-organise each year. More information is at www.scifiweekender.com.
185 His real name is Percy James Patrick Kent-Smith. But this is something common to many of the Doctors: Jon Pertwee's real name was John Pertwee; Peter Davison is Peter Moffett; David Tennant is David John McDonald; and Ncuti Gatwa is Mizero Ncuti Gatwa.

I had been contacted out of the blue by someone named Guy Wegener in New York who was interested in my books, and wanting to buy some from Telos Publishing. So, I sorted out what he wanted, and he was really pleased I had done that. At the end of the discussion, Guy said that he managed a restaurant in New York,[186] and if we were ever there, then we should look him up.

So, as we were coming to New York for this event, I did just that. I called Guy and explained we were coming, and he was so excited! He said we had to come to his restaurant, which was opposite Carnegie Hall, and he would treat us to dinner! Could we bring Frazer perhaps, I asked, as I knew he would be with us, and Guy nearly fell off his seat. As a long-time Doctor Who fan, he would love us to bring Frazer! Superb. That was settled then!

Towards the end of the event, I think Frazer mentioned to Sylvester that we were staying on a day or so, and that we had this meal date on this evening. It turned out that Sylvester was also staying on and had no plans, so he asked if he might tag along too.

Well, we knew that Guy wouldn't have a problem with this, so we said sure!

On the evening, we all rock up at Guy's restaurant and Guy dashed out to see us, and was blown away that Sylvester was there too! We got seated and Guy then treated us to basically whatever we wanted. The wine was Guy's choice, too, and was a delicious selection. We had starters and amazing mains, and then a selection of desserts. This was an Italian-based restaurant, so you can imagine the selection!

We were stuffed when we finished!

The table next to ours was empty when we arrived, and much to our amusement a family came in and sat there, and one of them had a Doctor Who shirt on! They were very amazed and pleased to see Sylvester and Frazer at the table next to them! So, they signed

186 It's the Trattoria Dell'Arte on 7th Avenue, and is wonderful. Well worth a visit!

some autographs for them and had some pictures taken. It was a truly great evening, and in fact the following night we treated Guy, as Sam, Frazer and I were meeting and eating with one of our other friends, Emily Barker, and we insisted that Guy join us for a lovely Thai meal.[187]

After the meal at Guy's, we asked if there was anywhere we could go for a drink, and Guy mentioned that there was a rooftop bar a couple of blocks down... so we thought, great, we'll head there!

Well, we walked for half an hour and found no bar! It seemed to have vanished off the face of the Earth, and even Google Maps was no help! In the end, we turned around and retraced our steps until we accidentally found the place. It had no signage, and access was via an unmarked lift! We headed up there and had a drink. Unfortunately, Sam didn't like the height (she is somewhat vertiginous) and so we took our leave of Frazer and Sylvester and made our own way back to the hotel.

I mentioned Paul McGann before, and I really like Paul, who has always been warm to us. We first properly met and started talking to him at an event in Peterborough, called The Greatest Show in the Galaxy, which we were also guesting at. This was a massive show with a stunning line-up of guests, including Eric Roberts, who we chatted to for the first time, and Christopher Lambert and Adrian Paul from the *Highlander* film and TV series. But since then, we've seen Paul at many events and he's always lovely and personable, not to mention incredibly talented.

Christopher Eccleston we met properly, or rather Sam did, at one of the LA Gallifrey conventions. In fact, we'd met him before! We were in London, shopping for Christmas presents. There were a couple we hadn't managed to grab, and we were up by Baker Street. I spotted a branch of Maplin, and thought I'd nip in and see what

187 This was at a smashing restaurant called V{IV} on 9th Avenue and W 49th St.

tech things they had which might suit someone. I left Sam outside, and who should then walk in behind me but Chris Eccleston! Sam held the door from him and sort of did a double-take and said hello. He smiled and said hello back! She quickly came in and found me, and told me what had happened. We were both too shy to go and speak to him properly at that time, so I caught a fleeting glance as he went about doing his shopping too.

That was it… a brief random hello in Maplin in London!

When Sam met him in the green room at Gallifrey, he was really pleasant and she reminded him of this fleeting earlier meeting, which of course he didn't remember, but had a giggle with her about because she confessed how stupid she'd felt saying hello to him as if they had met before. This often happens to celebs who are household names! Regrettably, I was away looking after Telos's sales table at the time and didn't get to meet him.

David Tennant I have never met, but I would really love to. All the reports I hear are that he is such a nice man!

Matt Smith, again, I have never met. But he walked past me at the 50th anniversary after-party event, as I said earlier – so near and yet so far!

Peter Capaldi… now, there's a story. I mentioned earlier that I was a great fan and collector of the Target novelisation cover art. Well, there was an exhibition of the artwork at the Cartoon Gallery in Central London, and I had loaned some of my pieces for the display. So, they organised a special opening evening for the owners and artists, and other invited guests and journalists and so on. I was there with Sam, and a lot of my friends were there also.

Chris Achilleos was attending, as were the artists and friends Jeff Cummins and Andrew Skilleter, plus many others besides.

We were standing around just chatting and drinking. Steven Moffat was there talking with Terrance Dicks. And suddenly there was a sort of hush and a mutter went around the room. What was happening?

What was happening was that Peter Capaldi, who was apparently in a play or something nearby, had come in early to see the exhibition. I don't think it's a secret that Peter is one of the biggest fans of the show around. There are photos of him visiting the set with Elisabeth Sladen and Jon Pertwee back in the day, and there are his letters in early fan club issues and in *Doctor Who Weekly*!

He was just wandering around and looking at the artwork. I got to meet him and explain who I was, and his reply was, 'I know who you are! I have your books on my shelves!' which was amazing for me! Chris Achilleos got to meet him too, and Peter was so nice and breezy and just normal! We were all taking pics. It was like a long-lost reunion.

I'd love to meet Peter again. He was lovely and I'm sure we'd get on!

Jodie Whitaker was next, and again I had the pleasure of meeting her in LA at one of the Gallifrey conventions. She was Guest of Honour, but she had time and a smile for everyone. Her queues were through the doors and around the hotel and back again! But she never complained or was anything but a delight.

Sam and I bumped into her in the green room one morning at breakfast, and she was so sweet and normal. I think it was the first day and she said she was a little nervous as she didn't know what to expect, so we put her mind at ease and explained that this event was amazing and everyone was so friendly, which it was and they are! She kept touching my arm as we spoke, and she was really nice.

An example of how nice came at the end, when she had finished her massive queue and was just chatting to people and clearing up. I'd had a photo taken with her earlier in the day, with great thanks to Jason Joiner from Showmasters[188] who had arranged for her to be there, and so I sidled up her and asked if I could cheekily

188 Showmasters organise loads of ComicCon events in the UK and have part-
nered with the Gallifrey event to help bring guests out to the USA.

get a signature. She looked around and said, of course. And signed my pic. That was really good of her, and appreciated, as she had just finished a tiring day of work.

The current Doctor, Ncuti Gatwa, I have yet to meet. Maybe one day.

* * *

And so we're almost up to date! There's still things happening, though... Doctor Who never quite lets you go!

And I must say more here about the wonderful Terrance Dicks, who was just so warm and lovely to me all those years ago when I was a teenager.

It was around 2012, I think, when I met up with Terrance at a lovely intimate event in the Wirral, run by Erica and Alan Lear. Terrance did a double-take when he saw me as our paths hadn't crossed for ages at that time. 'Oh my God! It's David!' he exclaimed, before moving in for a hug.

I introduced him to Sam, and he and her just hit it off in this really unexpected way.

We met Terrance again in LA at Gallifrey One the following year, as Shaun had managed to get him over there. Terrance hadn't done many US conventions, and he spent a lot of time with us that weekend, and Sam said to him that he should do Long Island Who as well. Terrance looked taken aback and said, 'I'd love to!' so Sam took him off to meet Ken Deep to help facilitate that, because she really liked him, in no small part because of the stories of him I'd told her.

Terrance did indeed go to Long Island Who later that year, and said afterwards that all people needed a 'Sam' in their life to help make things happen. I thought that was very sweet. We met Terrance again at the unveiling of a special memorial plaque for Jon Pertwee at the Wimbledon Theatre.

When we heard of Terrance's death on 29 August 2019, I was

very upset. It was utterly awful for me, and for Sam, who'd really grown fond of him, even when he'd been a bit curmudgeonly with her at one time. Terrance had been a large part of my growing up. He was the first *Doctor Who* celebrity that I ever met, and he had taken me at face value and been welcoming, kind, thoughtful and helpful over the many years since.

He would call me up and ask random questions about *Doctor Who* books or foreign translations, knowing that I would have the answers. And if I needed to ask him something, to come to an event, or to be interviewed for something, then he was always willing to help.

Terrance's widow, Elsa, very kindly invited me to his memorial in London, and Sam and I travelled down for the day. It was a great little gathering, with people from all walks of life there to remember and to celebrate Terrance. I met his kids there – who I had remembered as running around as children when I visited – and we all celebrated Terrance.

If anyone was my mentor through my early life, it was him. He was encouraging with advice and support, as well as just being the greatest *Doctor Who* writer on the planet. In many ways, I wouldn't be where I am now without him.

* * *

As I write this, we're progressing through 2025 and there's a blazing new season of *Doctor Who* airing.[189] Ncuti Gatwa and Russell T Davies, along with sparky new companion Belinda Chandra played by Varada Sethu, making a nonsense of it all! I'm sure it will be hugely enjoyable!

The recent interest and injection of money from Disney has given *Doctor Who* a massive boost, promoting it on the Disney+ streaming channel across the world, while in the UK it is, of course, on the

189 The second of Gatwa's seasons as the Doctor.

BBC iPlayer streaming platform. This alone has given it a potential audience far in excess of anything the BBC alone could manage, and the money that has been put into the show as a result of the deal is plain to see on screen as the effects, sets and imagination on display are all awe-inspiring.

The new series has just kicked off with 'The Robot Revolution' and I note that its BBC One screening achieved two million viewers overnight and was the fourth most watched programme of the day, and the second most watched on BBC One (*Gladiators* just pipped it with 2.9 million viewers).[190]

The previous season (Ncuti Gatwa's first), according to Disney, 'was a top 5 series on Disney+ globally every week it aired', and they also commented that it was 'one of the most watched programmes on [BBC] iPlayer, as well as being the BBC's top drama for under 35s this year' (2024). Which is not at all shabby for a 62-year-old show!

I've just submitted, too, a new venture for me: a story! And by the time this book comes out, then you might have learned what that is. But it's very exciting for me as a writer and as a *Doctor Who* fan.[191]

Sam and I have the second year of our film festival in 2025 as well, and I'm excited about that. Just seeing the quality of the films we have submitted gives me enormous pleasure. I can't wait to watch them all and to celebrate those which are judged the best![192]

My 'real work', as I call it, the IT job, has been a lot of fun of late as well.

It was interesting working over the year 2000, too. I remember all the fuss and concern in the press as we approached New Year's Eve 1999. Planes might fall out of the sky! Computers might all

190 The overnight figure does not take into account anyone who watched the episode on BBC iPlayer.
191 I can't talk about it here until it's announced officially.
192 This is the Sykehouse International Film Festival: www.slhfilmfest.com/.

stop working! Banks would have to close! You might lose all your money!

In fact, none of these things happened. And why? Because computer analysts, programmers and implementation managers had been working day and night for years beforehand to make sure that all the code which ran the systems was corrected and thus wouldn't fail!

In 2006, I decided to go freelance, mainly because of the lack of promotions and pay rises at Lloyds at the time. I needed to see more of the world! Of course, that just meant that most of my work ended up being back at Lloyds. It's like there's a piece of elastic which keeps pulling me back there.

But I really don't mind, as I know the systems and processes and − I hope − how things (should) work there. I've worked on some of the biggest migrations there, from the acquisition of TSB and MBNA to the eventual divestment (again) of TSB. From 2021 to 2024, I was engaged again there on some more fascinating implementation work with the best team of implementation managers you could ever hope to meet and work with. I said I'd give them a shout-out in this book, so this is for Anne, Wendy, Andrew, Diane, Karen, Mark, Mike, Charlie, Bryan, Kiran and Emma: as promised! The Implementation A-Team! We had a blast!

I really enjoy the implementation management work, but, as usual with contracting, who knows if there will be any more on the horizon. The job market is tough and it's hard to get to actually meet or see anyone in relation to a job, let alone actually be offered it! We shall see.

In the meantime, we have more charity work, and more conventions to attend... more people to see and to laugh and celebrate with.

Because Sam and I,[193] we're always celebrating. We celebrate the

---

193 And Frazer.

successes, and the normal days. We chink glasses in memory of those we've lost, and of those we love. All in all, we celebrate just being happy.

And that's something that's always worth celebrating.

Raise a glass with me.

Cheers.

To health, and happiness, to those we love and have lost.

And above all, to a crazy television show called *Doctor Who*!

In September 2023 I finally opened my *Doctor Who* Merchandise Museum.
Here's me toasting all those who came along on that day!

Epilogue

The global pandemic of 2020/21 was something to live through, and we lost a few good friends to the dreadful illness. But somehow, I think it changed people. There have long been keyboard warriors out there, people who love to attack and snipe and be rude from the safety of anonymity behind their computers. Really, if you would not say it to the person to their face, then don't say it. It's that easy.

It's also easy to fall into the trap of saying or thinking that such-and-such a person is wrong, or they're a fool, or whatever, without really knowing the facts of whatever it is you're calling them out for. And to get on your high horse about something for which you only have partial information and one side of the argument would seem to be foolish indeed.

But that seems to be increasingly the way of things. So many people react and complain and moan and whinge about things which either have nothing to do with them personally, or which they don't really understand what they're complaining about in the first place!

And there are those in our society who love unrest and dissent, as it allows them to promote unfair and unjust practices, and to attack rights every which way with, it seems, impunity.

It's such a shame!

Doctor Who has always shown another way.

And this is why, in my opinion, the show has endured for so long. It presents a view of a better and nicer way of dealing with real life.

Perhaps Steven Moffat said it best on stage during the 50th anniversary celebrations in London in 2013:

> It's hard to talk about the importance of an imaginary hero. But heroes *are* important: heroes tell us something about ourselves. History books tell us who we used to be, documentaries tell us who we are now; but heroes tell us who we *want* to be. And a lot of our heroes depress me. But when they made this particular hero, they didn't give him a gun – they gave him a screwdriver to fix things. They didn't give him a tank or a warship or an X-wing fighter – they gave him a call box from which you can call for help. And they didn't give him a super-power or pointy ears or a heat-ray – they gave him an extra *heart*. They gave him two hearts! And that's an extraordinary thing. There will never come a time when we don't need a hero like the Doctor.

That's a great message.

Doctor Who has also always been on the side of the underdog. The Doctor is not (or should not be) a sexual being, he doesn't fall in love. He has friends of all persuasions who he accepts at face value. Even those who, initially at least, want to do him harm, he wins over. He convinces them that immediate attack is not the best form of arbitration.

This is why, I feel, *Doctor Who* has attracted so many fans who are themselves underdogs. Minorities due to disability, race, sex, colour – so many elements, and increasingly so in today's society

– are drawn to the Doctor and his unjudging stance. He is a friend to all, and everyone can feel safe with him. Even if 'he' is sometimes a 'she' – it just doesn't matter!

Again, it's a message of sorts. That to 'win' you need to be able to see all the sides. You really need to not judge until you have walked a mile in their shoes. And you need to try not to support the true monsters.

Take a story like 'The Ark in Space', where there is an 'obvious' monster in the insect Wirrn and their larvae, and an 'obvious' friend in the humans in cryogenic storage.

Is it obvious, though? The Wirrn were just trying to survive, and were using the solar stacks as a place to lay their eggs to hatch. That there was also a 'food source' in the sleeping humans isn't the Wirrn's fault. Nor is it the humans'. It's just the pattern of life. One life form needs to destroy another in order to live. The hunter and the hunted. Is the lion 'evil' because it chases, catches and eats the gazelle? No, it's just nature. Is the fig plant 'evil' because it takes and dissolves tiny wasps to pollinate itself and to create what we know as a 'fig'? No, it's just nature. Is a Venus flytrap 'evil'?

So, one can see in 'The Ark in Space' that there is no actual 'good and evil' here… it's just nature.

Interestingly, in that story it's not the Doctor who comes up with the ultimate solution. It's one of the humans. Specifically, one which has been absorbed by the Wirrn and yet retains enough humanity to lead the Wirrn onto the rocket ship which he knows is going to take off and explode. One final, selfless act to save his fellows.

The Doctor seems to shrug it off, but I do wonder if deep down he was as upset as he was with the Brigadier when he blew up the Silurian base under Wenley Moor. The Silurians, too, were not as a race demonstrably 'evil'… they just wanted to survive. And blowing them up was not quite the solution the Doctor had in mind.

You can find this sort of theme running all the way through the show. Depictions of good and evil as being grey... and of solutions being found which tread the line of diplomacy and a shared success, rather than blasting the invader from the face of reality.

But then real life is not often that simple or as straightforward.

I know I have lived my life trying to be nice to people. Not knowingly or willingly upsetting or crossing others. And when I have, I don't like it. It's not me. It upsets me.

Unfortunately, there are some who thrive on that sort of upset and mess. But it's not me.

Hopefully my story here is of interest to others, and may even inspire others to just get out there and do it! Whatever 'it' may be for you.

David J Howe

Writer, filmmaker, editor, publisher, events organiser, screenwriter, novelist, historian, researcher, fanzine editor, cover designer, art editor, logistics manager, Dalek builder, collector, actor, photographer, implementation manager, interviewer, blogger... the list goes on and on!

Bibliography

Aside from my own collection and generic Google and Wiki searches, the following sources have been helpful when writing this book:

collection.sciencemuseumgroup.org.uk/objects/co8412068/
    hoover-constellation-vacuum-cleaner-with-attachments
cuttingsarchive.org/index.php/Malcolm_Hulke_obituary
fantasiesofpossibility.wordpress.com/tag/malcolm-hulke//nostal-
    giacentral.com/television/tv-by-decade/tv-shows-1960s/
    knock-three-times/
woorillacaught.com/roneo-machines/
www.kingstononline.co.uk/surbiton-lagoon/
www.mindat.org/loc-1184.html
BBC Genome Project (genome.ch.bbc.co.uk/)

Doctor Who and the Curse of Peladon (Terrance Dicks, Universal Tandem
    Publishing Co., 1975)
Doctor Who Exhibitions (Bedwyr Gullidge, Telos, 2020)
Doctor Who Radio Times Special, The (BBC Magazines Ltd, 1973)
Dr Who in an Exciting Adventure with the Daleks (David Whitaker, Armada

Paperbacks/Mayfair Books Ltd, 1965)

Fanzine Book, The (Alistair McGown, Telos, 2023)

Frame, The fanzine (David J Howe, Stephen James Walker, Mark Stammers (eds))

Making of Doctor Who, The (Malcolm Hulke and Terrance Dicks, Piccolo Books, 1972)

Myths and Legends: The Reeltime Pictures Story (Dylan Rees, Telos, 2025)

Oracle fanzine (David J Howe, Chris Dunk (eds))

Radio Times

Target Book, The (David J Howe, Telos, 2007)

Who Adventures, The (David J Howe, Telos, 2021)

Wiped! Doctor Who's Missing Episodes (Richard Molesworth, Telos, 2013)

Acknowledgements

I am indebted to the following people who have helped with this book.

First and foremost to Maxim Jakubowski. Without whom this book would never have happened.

Thanks to my stellar agent Camilla Shestopal, for negotiating our way through the contracts and agreements.

Thanks to my wife Samantha, for endless support and encouragement and telling me that I could, indeed, do this! She was right, as she invariably is.

Special thanks to my amazing mum, Sheila, for her incredible memory for details way, way back in the past. And, of course, for baked beans on buttered white toast. Still the food of champions.

Thanks to my lifelong pal Stephen James Walker, for reading through the manuscript and providing helpful corrections and notes along the way. He's always got my back, and I'm so grateful for it.

Thanks to Paul Simpson, for giving the manuscript another pair of eyes remembering those early days in the seventies. Another lifelong friend with an incredible memory.

Also thanks to the following for miscellaneous facts and figures and for clearing up elements of doubt, whether they knew they were helping or not:

David Brunt

Alistair McGown

Richard Molesworth

Ralph Montague

Patrick Mulkern

John Peel

Owen Tudor

Jeremy Williams

About the Author

David J Howe is among the most respected voices in *Doctor Who*'s history, with over forty years of experience as a researcher, writer, and publisher. As Editorial Director of Telos Publishing, he revolutionized *Doctor Who* literature and won multiple awards, including the World Fantasy Award. His work spans over thirty-five *Doctor Who* books, countless magazine articles, and consulting roles for BBC merchandise. Beyond *Who*, he's an accomplished horror fiction writer and former Chair of the British Fantasy Society. Currently, he contributes liner notes for BBC Audio's *Doctor Who* releases while maintaining one of the world's largest collections of *Doctor Who* merchandise.

Bedford
Square
Publishers

Bedford Square Publishers is an independent publisher of fiction and non-fiction, founded in 2022 in the historic streets of Bedford Square London and the sea mist shrouded green of Bedford Square Brighton.

Our goal is to discover irresistible stories and voices that illuminate our world.

We are passionate about connecting our authors to readers across the globe and our independence allows us to do this in original and nimble ways.

The team at Bedford Square Publishers has years of experience and we aim to use that knowledge and creative insight, alongside evolving technology, to reach the right readers for our books. From the ones who read a lot, to the ones who don't consider themselves readers, we aim to find those who will love our books and talk about them as much as we do.

We are hunting for vital new voices from all backgrounds −with books that take the reader to new places and transform perceptions of the world we live in.

Follow us on social media for the latest Bedford Square Publishers news.

🐦 @bedsqpublishers
❶ facebook.com/bedfordsq.publishers/
⦿ @bedfordsq.publishers

https://bedfordsquarepublishers.co.uk/